The Necessity of Pragmatism

The Necessity of Pragmatism

JOHN DEWEY'S CONCEPTION

OF PHILOSOPHY

R. W. Sleeper

Introduction by Tom Burke

UNIVERSITY OF ILLINOIS PRESS
URBANA AND CHICAGO

First paperback edition, 2001
© 1986 by Louise C. Sleeper
Reprinted by arrangement with the copyright holder

Introduction © 2001 by the Board of Trustees of the University of Illinois
All rights reserved
Manufactured in the United States of America
♾ This book is printed on acid-free paper.

For permission to quote from a letter by John Dewey to Sidney Hook, grateful acknowledgment is made to Sidney Hook and to The Sidney Hook Collection of John Dewey, Collection 143, Special Collections, Morris Library, Southern Illinois University at Carbondale.

Library of Congress Cataloging-in-Publication Data
Sleeper, R. W., 1925–
The necessity of pragmatism: John Dewey's conception of philosophy / R. W. Sleeper ; introduction by Tom Burke.— 1st pbk. ed.
p.   cm.
Originally published: New Haven : Yale University Press, ©1986.
Includes bibliographical references and index.
ISBN 978-0-252-06954-3 (pbk. : alk. paper)
1. Dewey, John, 1859–1952. I. Title.
B945.D44 S58   2001
191—dc21   00-061953

P 6 5 4 3 2

FOR L. C. S.

Inference is the advance into the unknown,
the use of the established to win new worlds
from the void.

—John Dewey

Diese übersichtliche Darstellung vermittelt
das Verständnis, welches eben darin besteht,
daß wir die "Zusammenhänge sehen". Daher
die Wichtigkeit des Findens von
Zwischengliedern.

—Ludwig Wittgenstein

Contents

Introduction
Tom Burke

This book is an important milestone in the study of Dewey's philosophy, particularly his logical theory. Numerous contemporary writers have interpreted and reworked various aspects of American pragmatism, but this is the book to look to once one realizes that an assiduous study of classical pragmatism is in order if one is to understand Dewey's logical theory. Sleeper is an especially careful scholar. His philosophical sophistication is plainly evident in his skillful analysis of the work of a complex philosopher who is notoriously easy to misunderstand and misinterpret. The quality of scholarship and depth of insight make the book an invaluable resource for any serious study of Dewey's thought.

Sleeper examines the full scope of Dewey's metaphysics and logical theory in its historical context and as a coherent system of thought on its own terms. The book's main theme is the distinction between Dewey's "logic of experience" and his "metaphysics of existence." Although Dewey characterized logic as the theory of inquiry, Sleeper shows how Dewey's conception of logic is more fundamentally rooted in a theory of experience, yielding not an experiential (or psychological) theory of logic but a "logic of experience." By the early 1890s, Sleeper maintains, "Dewey [had] arrived at the conception of the relation between logic and metaphysics that he was to maintain until the end. It is the conception of logic as the critical theory of experience, of experience as pedagogical, and of metaphysics as the critical theory of existence, the 'ground-map of the province of criticism,' which is sustained by logic, as inquiry" (26). This is a key issue insofar as Dewey scholars are prone to attribute to him a "metaphysics of experience." In Sleeper's view, this misinterprets Dewey's conceptions of logic and metaphysics. Sleeper's persistent assault on this confusion presents a clear challenge to any attempt (intentional or not) to collapse the distinction between experience and existence in Dewey's philosophy.

The book follows a historical trajectory. Chapters 1 and 2 provide a general orientation to Dewey's philosophy, beginning with his early turn toward pragmatism and away from his Hegelian roots. Sleeper's discussion of Dewey's 1893 "The Superstition of Necessity" at the end of chapter 2 is particularly noteworthy. In addressing the problem of the relationship between logical form and a world of real objects, Dewey "was trying to work out a conception of logical necessity that would accord with our actual experience of inquiry in the natural sciences . . . [and] he reached the conclusion that the concept of necessity arises from the practice of inquiry, that it is, in a sense, the a posteriori product of thought rather than its a priori principle" (35). This article indicates the general direction and shape that Dewey's later logical theory would take in his "lifelong effort to naturalize both logic and epistemology" (35). More interesting, one can already begin to see how Dewey's pragmatism would diverge from both Charles Sanders Peirce's and William James's, a topic that Sleeper addresses extensively in later chapters.

Chapter 3 examines Dewey's early logical theory as it developed during his years at the University of Chicago, where the basic outlines of his logic of experience began to assume a recognizable shape evidenced early in *Studies in Logical Theory* (1903) and refined over the next five decades. Sleeper's analysis of Dewey's debts to and differences from both Peirce and James at this stage in his career is particularly insightful (47–57). Sleeper's views on what the differences were and how early they emerged in Dewey's thought are clear: "Dewey's conception of logic differed from that of Peirce less in terms of how each understood the methods of experimental science than in the ontology each thought those methods to be based on. And Dewey's conception of experience differed from that of James less in terms of ontology than in terms of the relationship between psychology and logic. . . . We ought to get our logic from our ontology, Dewey maintains, not our ontology from our logic. Nor should we get our logic from psychology, for it is not the psychology of experience that matters, but its logical forms" (47). Contrary to Richard Bernstein's claim that "Peirce supplied the intellectual backbone to pragmatism" while Dewey only developed the educational, social, and political implications of Peirce's thought, Sleeper asserts that "this presents a curious notion of what comprises the intellectual backbone of pragmatism and may reflect Bernstein's opinion that

Dewey 'lacked Peirce's creative logical genius.' . . . In my view, however, it was Dewey's creative logical genius that allowed him to see the flaw in Peirce's conception of logic, the same flaw that he later saw in the Frege-Russell conception" (72). This kind of claim will not garner sympathy from Peirce enthusiasts, but it indicates the tenor of Sleeper's critique of Peirce and James from a Deweyan perspective. Of course it poses a challenge for Dewey scholars to show how his logical theory is worthy of the kind of respect that Peirce's work deserves, and to some degree receives, because of its mathematical sophistication.

Dewey's early approach to the logical foundations of mathematics is broached in chapter 3 (59–60). Sleeper writes that, in holding that mathematics has its genesis in actions undertaken as means to practical ends, "Dewey's point was to make clear that he was not attempting to undermine the structure of higher mathematics, [but] merely that he had worked out his own theory to account for the ultimate origins of abstract concepts. He was saying that if mathematics has any logical foundations, those foundations are to be found in the logic of experience" (60). This topic is revisited in later chapters (81–87, 155–59), Sleeper's aim being to show that Dewey's revolutionary views on mathematics were cogent, challenging, and anything but naive: "Even after Alonzo Church and Alan Turing had shown that one of the consequences of the work of Kurt Gödel was that elementary logic could not be completely mathematized, Russell stuck to the belief that mathematics should be considered primarily as an uninterpreted system. . . . Dewey, of course, had taken it for granted [all along] that, since all knowledge begins with synthesis, mathematics begins with measurement and counting off. We begin, in other words, with an interpreted arithmetic and arrive at uninterpreted mathematical systems only by abstraction. He still held this view in his 1938 *Logic*" (104).

Sleeper chides "two generations of critics" for failing to see the subtlety in Dewey's logical theory, having focused too much on instrumentalist and functionalist aspects of the theory and not enough on his fundamental "conviction that formal concepts originate in action, arising always in the context of some problem-solving activity" (59–60). Sleeper challenges us to take Dewey's view seriously that "what begins with interpreted systems in arithmetic and geometry, counting and measurement, moves to uninterpreted systems and abstractions as a matter of course" (156). Sleeper contends that "like Wittgenstein, Dewey is not rejecting what can be learned from [pure mathematics]. Indeed, what Wittgenstein and Dewey are after is a clearer conception of the relation between purely symbolic uninterpreted systems of reasoning and the interpreted systems of the experimental sciences" (156–57). Hence the notion of action (exemplified by but not limited to counting or measurement operations) should be fundamental in a study of the logical foundations of mathematics insofar as that study should first attempt to account, at least generically, for the interpreted systems out of which mathematics incrementally emerges.

Chapter 4 looks at the development of these ideas after Dewey's move to Columbia University in 1905, focusing on such texts as *Essays in Experimental Logic* (1916) and *Reconstruction in Philosophy* (1920). The main theme of the chapter is a definite metaphysical turn in the development of Dewey's logical theory, influenced by his Columbia colleagues and by critics who failed to see anything more than instrumentalism in his logical theory:

> . . . Dewey gradually came to see his developing theory of philosophical logic as having ontological implications that he had not directly addressed in his early work. These implications were pushed to the foreground. . . . A very considerable part of Dewey's work during this period is given over to the ontological roots of knowledge reached by means of inquiry, the existential metaphysics that supplies the background theory for these ontological roots, and the theory of language that links the subject-matter of inquiry with that metaphysical background. It is in this period that the lineaments of a system start to emerge, in which it begins to be possible to see how it all hangs together. (80–81)

A running debate with Bertrand Russell that geared up at this time (and persisted into the 1940s) was especially important in these developments insofar as Dewey found himself having to reissue criticisms that he had directed earlier at Rudolph Hermann Lotze in *Studies in Logical Theory* but were now just as relevant to Russell (83, 221n16). At this point, Dewey found himself at cross-purposes not just with Lotze, Peirce, or Russell but with a ground swell of support for a view of logic that he had been criticizing for more than a decade.

In this and later chapters, Sleeper articulates Dewey's distinction between existential inference and formal implication: "[W]hile Russell finds himself in the awkward position of trying to derive a proof of the external world from the character of the implications that obtain with respect to his logical objects, Dewey is in the happy position of working from the other end of the problem. Instead of trying to ground inference in implication, he grounds implication in inference" (86). For

Dewey, just as formal concepts originate in concrete action, so abstract relations (e.g., implications) originate in existential inference. Dewey espouses a kind of realism that, according to Sleeper, "takes inference as action, as behavior that causes changes in reality through interaction with things. It is transactional realism as the metaphysical background theory of the logic of experience" (83).

This theme is central to understanding Dewey's conception of mathematics—an issue at the heart of his disagreements with Russell. Sleeper pulls no punches in his defense of this view against Gottlob Frege's logicism and Russell's analytical realism. Most mathematicians agree that Zermelo-Frankel set theory, including refinements that handle problematic consequences of Russell's Paradox, is consistent and true of a natural domain of sets. But this does not vindicate Frege's logicist approach to the foundations of mathematics. Russell had uncovered a fatal flaw in Frege's *Grundlagen* but was undeterred by it himself. While Russell and Dewey were sniping at each other's work in the first two decades of the century, Russell was still of the opinion that this logicist flaw would eventually be eliminated. Sleeper contends that Dewey, meanwhile, was ready to argue that "Frege and Russell had been looking for the foundations of mathematics in the wrong place. . . . For it was part of Dewey's case against analytical realism that [Russell was] simply mistaken about the nature of [his] logical entities" (83). Russell's Paradox was just what it seemed: a disproof of analytical realism as a foundational enterprise.

As Sleeper points out, in Dewey's alternative "transactional realist" view, "'logical objects are things (or traits of things) which are found when inference is found and which are only found then.' . . . Inference is an event 'belonging to action, or behavior, which takes place in the world.' Inference does not merely give us a picture of things, we might say; it gives us hands-on knowledge, or a way of proceeding. It is an activity: 'It belongs in the category where plowing, assembling the parts of a machine, digging and smelting ore belong—namely, behavior, which lays hold of and handles and rearranges physical things'" (84). One might wonder what this has to do with classes, sets, or Zermelo-Frankel set theory. Physicalistic constructivist commitments would seem to undermine any prospects for taking such a view seriously. But this kind of reaction fundamentally misconstrues Dewey's point. Consider by way of contrast the move in Alfred North Whitehead and Russell's *Principia Mathematica* to eliminate sets (classes) as logical objects: "The symbols for classes, like those for descriptions, are, in our system, in-

complete symbols; their *uses* are defined, but they themselves are not assumed to mean anything at all. . . . Thus classes, so far as we introduce
them, are merely symbolic or linguistic conveniences, not genuine objects."[1] Dewey would applaud the effort to reconsider the ontological
status of sets, certainly in contrast with the Platonic realism of Russell's
earlier *Principles of Mathematics.* Perhaps (with a nod to Wittgenstein)
the emphasis here on *uses* of symbols is the key to Dewey's emphasis on
activity and behavior, but without all of the plowing and smelting.

Yet what Whitehead and Russell are referring to are uses of symbols
in relation to other symbols, where no mathematical proposition as such
can mention particular objects. Zermelo-Frankel set theory essentially
preserves this perspective. In particular, the axiom of separation per-
mits the formation of sets on the basis of specific logical formulas (so
long as the resulting sets are subsets of previously obtained sets et cetera), in which case the theory rests at bottom on first-order logical
formulas and their constituent uninterpreted terms. It is remarkable
what can be done with just a couple of primitive predicate symbols
(identity and membership), even when one pretends not to know what
they mean except as they are defined by their "uses" in Zermelo-Frankel
set theory.

Dewey argues that this is not enough if one wants to understand
mathematics in itself and in its obvious practical relation to inquiry in
general and to the world at large. The relations represented by these
primitive predicate symbols are results of abstractions from everyday
ingrained abilities to compare and contrast, collect and disperse, include
and exclude, and so forth—abilities that reside and function outside of
any symbol system as such, but not in Russell's timeless realm of Being
or in Frege's realm of propositions. The *uses* at the roots of Dewey's
philosophy of mathematics are our uses of concrete things: plows, smelt-
ers, looms, presses, levers, wheels, gears, pulleys, hammers, fences, lad-
ders, troughs, urns, pockets, scales, metersticks, clocks, pigments, horns,
drums, alphabets, numerals, hands, teeth, tongues, eyes, ears, and the
like. This is the realm where inference operates as well.

Along these lines, one can understand Sleeper's claim that in Dewey's view, unlike Peirce's,

> the "interpretant" of a "sign" is not just another "sign" but a *known ob-
> ject.* Moreover qualities are signs that lead back to the objects of which
> they are qualities. They are natural signs of a causal connection between
> sign and object and not, as Peirce would have it, indexical signs already

embedded in a linguistic and conceptual semiotic. Linguistic practice, Dewey argues, follows the existential practice that governs behavior of all organisms by means of the sign-signified relation, the causal, existential connection of the quality with the thing as qualitatively individual. What Dewey is arguing is that we get our semiotic from our semantics, not our semantics from our semiotic. He is arguing that theory derives from practice, language from action. (138–39)

There is no restriction here on one's freedom to define terms and postulate axioms. Dewey is instead making a point about the existential origins and ontological basis of the ideas with which one works. Add to this a recognition of processes and properties of recursion, computability, decidability, and the like, along with the claim that "mathematical operations [applied to conceptual or symbolic materials] are conducted on the same pattern as existential operations of experimental procedure" (157), and one obtains a robust conception of mathematics whose subject-matter may be "nonconstructive" and otherwise as abstract as one might wish even while acknowledging its genetic links to existential activities.

We would have a lot to digest if Dewey had stopped publishing in 1925 at the age of sixty-five, but the best was yet to come. In chapters 5–8, Sleeper examines Dewey's later thought as it appeared in such books as *Experience and Nature* (1925/1929), *Quest for Certainty* (1929), *Art as Experience* (1934), *Logic: The Theory of Inquiry* (1938), and *Theory of Valuation* (1939), among others. Sleeper focuses on "the reconstruction of philosophy—in metaphysics and logic—that comprises the deep structure of Dewey's philosophy of culture" (101). "I shall try," he writes, "to show how it all hangs together in a comprehensively reconstructed theory of intelligent behavior and a cultural philosophy of meliorism" (101).

In chapter 5, Sleeper discusses Dewey's enigmatic characterization of metaphysics as "'a statement of the generic traits manifested by existences of all kinds'" and thus as a kind of "'ground-map of the province of criticism'" ("'if philosophy be criticism'") (129–30). This characterization appears all the more puzzling when considering Dewey's statement in 1951 of a preference for the term *culture* over *experience* in the title and text of *Experience and Nature* had he rewritten the book.

Contrary to Richard Rorty's contention that Dewey had given up on metaphysics altogether in his later philosophy, Sleeper claims that this misses Dewey's point that "nobody needs a metaphysical system of the traditional (foundational) kind" but that he was still proposing "a new use for the term *metaphysics*" (108). It would be a background theory for his conceptions of experience, meaning, and intelligence—a background theory whose modest function is, in Sleeper's words, "to note those empirical features of existences of all kinds that make other kinds of inquiry both possible and necessary—a very limited task indeed . . ." (132). According to Sleeper, while Rorty would turn philosophy into an open-ended conversation without realist constraints, Dewey would render philosophy as "a generalized theory of criticism" against the background of a realistic metaphysics, where "it is not the leading principles of science that are the key to metaphysics but what science shows to be the generic traits of particular existents of all kinds" (131).

Also contrary to Rorty's contention that Dewey had abandoned the term *experience* in favor of *culture*, Sleeper insists that the shift was only a matter of vocabulary, reflecting what *Experience and Nature* was all about in the first place—namely, the central role of communication as a condition of human experience. *Experience and Nature* was not, Sleeper insists, an attempt to get at the real "by means of a priori categories of experience" (116) or "just another attempt to set forth the categories of existence or of 'being' in the style of traditional metaphysical systems, to set forth the basic principles of reason, or to lay the foundations of knowledge in a first philosophy" (117). Rather, the book was "an attempt to work out a [naturalistic] theory of how communication is possible, and why we need it. It is an attempt to discover the relationship of communication to nature, to disclose the traits of nature that support it as well as those that impede it" (117). Sleeper thus argues that Dewey's metaphysics is *part of* a general theory of communication and meaning insofar as the latter theory is a connecting link between his metaphysics and his logic. Hence "Dewey's account of communication as the means of intelligent behavior shows that discourse is the *condition* of [human] experience. . . . It is the sine qua non of experience in the logic of experience . . . " (118). Sleeper goes on to contend:

> If anything should be regarded as Dewey's first philosophy, it is his genetic account of communication. . . . Dewey maintains that the error in classical thought was that it derived its sense of the essences of things from the structure of its grammar. What Dewey contends, rather, is that the structures of discourse are derived from the structures, relations, and properties of *things*. . . . In arguing that it is the empirical generic traits of things that make discourse possible, Dewey wants to show how the forms of reasoning are generated from the practice of communication. (118)

Sleeper argues that "despite the evident similarities between Dewey's approach to communication, Wittgenstein's approach to meaning as use, and Austin's analysis of doing things with words," Dewey thought these latter two approaches were "still beholden to the classical habit of thinking that grammar controls our way of knowing things, as opposed to seeing that it is our way of knowing things that ought to control our grammar. Instead of deriving his ontology from the forms of discourse, Dewey derives his forms of discourse from his ontology" (119).

According to Sleeper, Dewey's theory of language "'as the instrument of social cooperation and mutual participation'" would acknowledge a genetic continuity "'between natural events (animal sound, cries, etc.) and the origin and development of meanings'"—a link "forged in action and judgment, in common action and common judgment . . . existential in character through and through" (123). This is a more general application, in the philosophy of language and mind, of principles we have already seen at work in Dewey's philosophy of mathematics. In this broader context, the existential activities to which Dewey is referring are explicitly common activities and undertakings "necessary for the making of a society or culture" (126). A contrast between culture and nature in the title of the book would thus have better represented the book's genetic account of the natural emergence of human mentality as, in Dewey's words, "'a function of social interactions'" (123). This emphasis on social cooperation, communication, and culture is, of course, a far cry from Rorty's antirealist cultural relativism.

Chapter 6 is devoted wholly to Dewey's later philosophy of logic, which extends old arguments against Lotze, Peirce, and Russell to later work in formal logic. Dewey "had distanced himself from the prevailing rigorous formal techniques, abjuring even the commonplace methods of . . . *Principia Mathematica*" (135), treating such methods as prime targets of attack not because of their formal rigor as such but because of the half-baked metaphysical commitments usually conjoined with them. As Sleeper puts it, Dewey is insistent "that an adequate system of symbolization is contingent on both a better theory of language than was then available to philosophical logicians and a better theory of the materials to be symbolized" (135). Dewey makes this point in the preface of his 1938 *Logic:*

> In the present state of logic, the absence of any attempt at symbolic formulation will doubtless cause serious objection in the minds of many readers. This absence is not due to any aversion to such formulation. On the

contrary, I am convinced that acceptance of the general principles set forth
will enable a more complete and consistent set of symbolizations than now
exists to be made. The absence of symbolization is due, first, . . . to a need
for development of a general theory of language in which form and matter are not separated; and secondly, to the fact that an adequate set of
symbols depends upon prior institution of valid ideas of the conceptions
and relations that are symbolized.[2]

Dewey's 1938 *Logic* is designed to address such needs, going so far as
to posit a proper conception of language and at least a rudimentary
survey of possible logical terms and propositional forms, but unfortunately not to the point of presenting a mathematical treatment of such
matters.

The issue of not separating "form and matter" (135–38, 186–88) is
just a generalization of a theme already encountered in Dewey's treatment of implication and inference and in his conception of abstract
mathematics and its existential roots. Nowadays, one looks back on
ancient science and marvels at how anyone could assert on the basis of
reason alone that heavier things fall faster than lighter ones (et cetera)
when properly conceived controlled observation could easily refute such
claims. Similarly, our descendants may look back and wonder how the
logical theory of present-day analytic philosophy could lack grounding
in a proper conception and analysis of actual inference. Scholastic methods and attitudes have been displaced in the physical sciences but apparently not yet in logic. One cannot deny the superb technical ingenuity involved in Aristotelian-Ptolemaic cosmology or in contemporary
mathematical logic, but Dewey is telling us that both are based on er-
roneous background assumptions and methodologies.

The key to instituting "valid ideas of the conceptions and relations
that are symbolized" in logic lies in developing a proper conception of
the ontology of natural kinds that avoids an empty nominalism or an
ontology of eternal essences (145–55, 175). The objects, properties, and
relations "symbolized" in mathematical logic should be viewed as being grounded in existential operations and their qualitative results. This
holds not just for the sparse primitive vocabulary of Zermelo-Frankel
set theory but for the terms of all such formal languages across the
board.

Likewise, a proper conception of reasoning is a prerequisite to formulating *norms* distinguishing *good* and *bad* reasoning. There is little
chance for a viable normative theory of valid reasoning if one cannot
say something about what reasoning is or at least establish that how one

reasons (and thus what one presupposes) about reasoning itself does not skew one's account of *valid* reasoning. Dewey explains what reasoning is in terms of the transformative use and function of discourse in experience—though his theory of experience moves him to focus more broadly on the nature of *intelligence* rather than mere reasoning as the more central issue for logical theory. Chapter 7 addresses Dewey's conception of intelligence as "the power to reflect on past experience and then use it to reconstruct the present and shape the future; it is the power to analyze ends and means and generic conditions in relation to intentional purposes" (180). Sleeper argues that Dewey formulates this conception of intelligence not only as a matter of cognitive psychology but also in conjunction with his *moral theory*. More than just a reasoning agent, an intelligent agent is one capable of exercising such reflection in answer to needs to orchestrate practical affairs, determining pertinent facts of the matter in conjunction with properly ascertaining what one ought to do in those circumstances (177–80). For Dewey, there is no strict separation between intellectual and moral judgments, no sharp dichotomy between facts and values (173–78, 181, 193–95). Just as moral theory would benefit from closer attention to objective methods of determining facts and proposing solutions to moral issues, there is no absence of valuation in scientific inquiry.

Would that Mars robots, star-wars weapons, autopilots, and other so-called smart machinery were actually smart in this sense. In Dewey's view, a smart Mars robot, if truly autonomous, would have to be heavily invested in doing what it *ought* to do or not do to maintain its own viability as a self-directed agent serving people who placed it in an environment that harbors unpredictable challenges. It would have to be capable of more than just recording data and following preestablished protocols, and it would certainly have to be more than just a remotely controlled, mobile sensing device. Of course, Dewey gave no thought to cybernetics or machine intelligence, but his genetic sociocultural account of the natural emergence of human minds, selves, and rational experience might well yield a basic architecture for autonomous machines with capabilities that at least begin to mimic intelligent human behaviors. As with experience and logic, motion and physics, so it has gone with intelligence and cognitive science. Much of the work in this area has been done in a scholastic mode with too little regard for clarifying in the first place what *actual* intelligence is. Dewey's theory of intelligence would certainly involve a broader range of concerns than modeling minds as computers. Unfortunately, there is a persistent temptation to look for the keys to intelligent behavior in the light of methods and metaphors with which we are already comfortable rather than deal with the issue on its own terms.

Dewey was concerned with people—their education and their social and political endeavors more generally. He was concerned with the difficult problem of clarifying what constitutes intelligence in human behavior—a matter of determining norms and principles that would distinguish better and worse methods of effectively and conclusively dealing with disturbances, challenges, disruptions, or difficulties. There is also the recurrent practical issue of a community's determining how it may foster unforced shared assent to such norms by groups and individuals who already have a natural capacity to do so but too often fall short of actualizing this capacity. Dewey's later work on such questions (from the 1930s onward) was couched in the context of efforts directed against a tide of positivist scientism that was then overtaking philosophy in the United States. Sleeper opens chapter 7 by discussing Dewey's 1939 *Theory of Valuation*—his contribution to the *International Encyclopedia of Unified Science*—as a bit of guerrilla harassment against the noncognitivist ethical emotivism of Moritz Schlick and A. J. Ayer and against the reductionism of the "unity of science" movement as a whole (169). "Science, including the social sciences and ethics, Dewey argued, needs no foundations of the type that would be envisaged in the twenty monographs that were to comprise the first two volumes of the *Encyclopedia*" (170). The dualisms this movement envisaged between science and ethics (174, 177) and between the physical and social sciences (177–81) were incompatible with Dewey's contention that theory emerges from practice, science from art, fine arts from practical arts, and so forth (171–73, 190–95). Dewey, Sleeper contends, "calls for a more effective sociology and cultural anthropology as the needed conditions for a more powerful theory of valuation as an 'effective instrumentality, for human organisms live in a cultural environment.' He argues that only such a theory of human behavior can break down the 'separation alleged to exist between the "world of facts" and the "realm of values",' the stock-in-trade of logical positivism" (194).

In this context, Sleeper pursues a discussion of Dewey's philosophy of art and makes the extraordinary claim that "there is a clear sense in which Dewey had already written the revisions of *Experience and Nature* that he was projecting in the last years of his life in *Art As Experience*" (186). "In *Art As Experience* Dewey sums up the task of criticism in words that apply equally to art and science, morals and politics, en-

gineering and education. He expresses the intent of philosophy as criticism of criticism and as the aim of inquiry. It is a text that would be at
home if inserted bodily into the central chapters of the *Logic* or the
concluding pages of the *Theory of Valuation*. It is possibly the clearest
statement we have of Dewey's version of pragmatism and of the character of its method" (188).

If one is concerned that Dewey's emphasis on sociology and cultural anthropology in his theory of intelligence entails a potential loss or
homogenization of self and individuality in deference to social and
cultural conditions, then one should consult *Art as Experience*: "Individuality itself is originally a potentiality and is realized only in interaction with surrounding conditions. In this process of intercourse, native
capacities, which contain an element of uniqueness, are transformed and
become a self. Moreover, through resistances encountered, the nature
of the self is discovered. The self is both formed and brought to consciousness through interaction with environment. The individuality of
the artist is no exception."[3] In this view, a self is essentially a work of
art cultivated through its own processes of making works of art. One
is as free as one manages to make oneself—as free as one can be in
making a work of art, answerable to environmental conditions and yet
capable of innovation; free through the power and discipline of abstraction and reflection and yet constrained by available means and methods and styles of communication. Neither spontaneity nor necessity,
neither complete autonomy nor determination by law, neither novelty
nor tradition can account for intelligent selfhood. "For art is the fusion
in one experience of the pressure upon the self of necessary conditions
and the spontaneity and novelty of individuality," Dewey asserts.[4] If it
is not already clear that Dewey's conception of intelligence presents high
standards and a formidable challenge to machine-intelligence research,
then this should give one pause. A truly smart machine, with some
capacity to cultivate its own individual identity, should on this account
be something like an artist—not that this is just some ideal goal but that
it is an essential constitutive requirement right from the start (e.g., a
minimal condition for passing the Turing test).

In the final chapter of the book, Sleeper summarizes some major
points of the preceding chapters. Several pages are devoted to reviewing how Dewey's version of pragmatism differs from those of Peirce and
James (201–4). Dewey's running battle with Russell and other propo-
nents of mainstream formal logic is also recapped, the point being that
"Dewey was not trying to block the development of formal logic, but

[that] he *was* trying to block the road to its application in the ontological reductions of logical positivism" (205).

In this effort, Dewey has been aided and abetted by philosophers as
disparate as Wittgenstein and Heidegger. But Sleeper points to one
defining feature of Dewey's philosophy that is perhaps unique—a principle or theme of *meliorism*. This stems from Dewey's "concern with
the application of philosophy once released"—a "concern regarding the
practice of philosophy in social and political criticism or the relation of
knowledge and action in social and political practice" (206–7). This
persistent theme can be traced back to his earliest work in logic and
ethics:

> In the 1932 *Ethics* the focus has shifted once again to the central position
> of judgment and to the inescapable presence of valuation in all judgments,
> whether of science or of morals, that Dewey had emphasized in his 1903
> essay on the "Logical Conditions of a Scientific Treatment of Morality."
> Far from accepting [a] reduction of James's pluralism to neutral monism
> and a theory of value that took "value as any object of any interest," the
> 1932 *Ethics* accepts that the pluralism of values is a generic condition that
> means that the *de facto* presence of value disparity—in other words, cul-
> tural relativism—is but the problem and not the solution. It recognizes
> that the theory of value does not end with the discovery of the *de facto*
> valuations that divide us, but must move to *de jure* values, or valuations
> that will serve to mediate conflict, not by the holistic reduction of "one-
> world morality" or through cross-cultural value homogeneity, but by in-
> telligent behavior based on inquiry and the transformational possibilities
> that result from the repudiation of fixed essences and all ontological log-
> ics. (180–81)

It is not just that philosophy *ought* to have a practical function over and
above its theoretical abstractions but that it cannot proceed properly—
that philosophers do not and cannot know what they are doing as philosophers, that they cannot know what they mean—without a background in existential activities (if only of the broad sort characteristic
of metaphysics, attuned at least to ongoing developments in the sciences). Philosophy has its origins and thus its background in existential activities no less than does mathematics. But according to Sleeper,
Dewey's meliorism has a broader significance as well. Dewey is ultimately concerned with "the reconstruction of a culture divided against itself" (193)—and more specifically, with the dissolution of fallacious
oppositions between theory and practice, science and ethics, politics and
aesthetics that are deeply ingrained and continue to bedevil contem-

porary culture. To fully understand Dewey's logical theory, Sleeper argues, one must position it properly with respect to this binding theme of meliorism in his philosophy as a whole.

All eight chapters of the book end with critical bibliographies surveying a broad range of relevant secondary literature and with comments that are often as interesting and informative as the central text. Sleeper presses home the fact that a firm grasp of history is essential to interpreting and developing Dewey's thought. He meticulously traces the philosophical roots of Dewey's logical theory in the works of Aristotle, Kant, Hegel, Mill, Peirce, James, and others, while explaining its crucial significance for later twentieth-century analytical philosophy. The book paints a vivid picture of the importance of logical theory in Dewey's thought and builds a solid and expansive foundation for a critical analysis and evaluation of his philosophy as a whole.

This book is about Dewey's logic and metaphysics. It also says a lot about Ralph Sleeper as a perceptive, insightful, thorough, evenhanded scholar, historian, and philosopher. And it establishes Sleeper as a force to be reckoned with when it comes to interpreting Dewey's philosophy properly. Reading Sleeper, one quickly realizes that to pursue these issues one has to mine the mountain of texts on which he draws. Many writers in a pragmatist vein lead one to think that enough spadework has been done, as if the gold were all mined out. It may be comforting to think one need not put effort into digging for oneself, but one would then miss what is valuable in the classical texts. Sleeper offers no such comfort. He compels one to face the fact that there is work still to be done to complete a renaissance in American philosophy—a revival to which this book greatly contributes.

Notes

1. Alfred North Whitehead and Bertrand Russell, *Principia Mathematica,* vol. 1 (Cambridge: Cambridge University Press, 1910), 71–72.

2. John Dewey, *Logic: The Theory of Inquiry,* in John Dewey, *The Later Works, 1925–1953,* ed. Jo Ann Boydston, 17 vols. (Carbondale: Southern Illinois University Press, 1981–90), 12:4.

3. John Dewey, *Art as Experience,* in ibid., 10:286.

4. Ibid.

Preface

Philosophers are inclined to turn the prefaces to their books into cameo autobiographies. There are precedents for this among the classics of the field, of course, the moving preface to the reader that Descartes wrote for his *Meditations* and the opening passage of Spinoza's essay "On the Improvement of the Understanding" being memorable instances. But they are examples of the genre so rarely equaled as to deter imitation rather than inspire emulation. My own view is that the reader is better served by a few remarks outlining the context and intent of a book, rather than by an account of its personal provenance.

John Dewey rarely used the prefaces of his books for any other purpose. He wanted his reader to see the relevance of his thought to the world in which he was writing. He had little interest in addressing posterity, nor was he the sort of philosopher who delights in devising definitive solutions to the kinds of problems that philosophers are always putting to themselves. He was far more interested in the troubled times in which he lived and in the human problems of those times. It is not that he neglected the classic problems of philosophy exactly, only that he wanted us to see them in relation to our own lives and culture, our own problems, not just those of the past. He wanted us to see how different our own world is from that of the past, as well as how it has emerged from that past and is indissolubly linked with it. He tried to present the reader with a context in which his own project could be seen to make sense.

Dewey argued that philosophy should have an impact on the world. He thought that the critical work of philosophy should have consequences in the conduct of our lives and in the culture in which we live. He wanted us to see that philosophy has the power to influence social change through criticism and inquiry. It is this conception of philosophy that drew Dewey to pragmatism and that comprises his distinctive contribution to it. In my estimation it is a contribution so substantial as to constitute a radical reconstruction of pragmatism as he found it. It is the aim of this study to trace that reconstruction and to elicit its central characteristics and claims.

In an important address to the Eastern Division of the American Philosophical Association in 1984, John McDermott argued that we are witnessing a renascence of classical American philosophy, a renascence that will restore pragmatism to its proper place among the classic sources of our tradition. Yet it was a memorable moment indeed when the commentator on McDermott's thesis referred to its author as a "hip Utilitarian." We are, perhaps, some distance from Bertrand Russell's insistent characterization of pragmatism as an expression of the American free enterprise system and our national habit of exploiting private property for the exclusive benefit of the individual. But as distinguished a historicist as Alasdair MacIntyre can still so misjudge the history of pragmatism in America as to suggest, in *After Virtue,* that it was merely a *preparatio evangelica* for the conversion to ethical emotivism. We are still not far from the misunderstanding that prompted A. J. Ayer, in his *Origins of Pragmatism* of 1968, to dismiss John Dewey, along with F. C. S. Schiller and "the Italian Papini," as mere "publicists of the movement."

Richard Rorty warned against these misreadings of our intellectual history in his presidential address to the Eastern Division in 1979. He urged us to focus our attention on the hints that William James and Dewey offered as to how our lives might be changed, a suggestion that was given sharper definition by Stephen Toulmin, in his introduction to volume 4 of Dewey's *The Later Works.* Toulmin urged that we stop thinking of Charles Sanders Peirce, James, and Dewey as members of a single school of pragmatists. He wanted us to see how much Dewey's philosophical methods and arguments differed from those of his predecessors, and how much closer they were to those of his younger contemporaries Ludwig Wittgenstein and Martin Heidegger. Like McDermott and Rorty, Toulmin argued that until we recognize just how different Dewey's thinking is from that of his predecessors, we will go on misjudging it and misappropriating it to our own philosophical considerations.

It is in this light that the present study of Dewey's contribution to pragmatism is undertaken. But I should not conceal from the reader that, while I share in the assessment outlined above, there have been some surprises along the way. Having all too readily acquiesced in Russell's judgment that Dewey's logical theories do not belong to logic at all, but to "psychology," I was surprised to discover how central a role Dewey's concern for the genesis and function of formal logic plays in the development of his conception of philosophy. Long in the habit of regarding Dewey's contributions to philosophical logic as either badly outmoded or limited to the development of instrumentalism, I had difficulty conceding that Dewey had mounted a powerful argument against the direction taken by logic under the influence of Frege and Russell. Nor was it easy to accept that Dewey's dissent after *Principia Mathematica* was based on a theory of language that he had worked out by combining elements of Peirce's semantics and semiotics with a reformulation of James's doctrines of belief and truth. The realization that it is this theory of language that powerfully links Dewey's conception of logic with his metaphysics was not one that could be readily taken on board. Having thought of Dewey as not having anything important to say regarding the philosophy of language, it seemed counter-intuitive to ascribe so much importance to a theory of language and communication. Yet this conclusion made sense. It helped to explain the fact that Dewey's work comprised something like a system—a fact that seemed to surprise even Dewey himself. It is not that we should have been reading Dewey as having taken the so-called linguistic turn ahead of Oxford and analytic philosophy; it is just that we should have been reading him as a philosopher of culture all along. For what could be more central to the understanding of culture than an adequate understanding of the language in which its affairs are conducted?

Acknowledgments

I have been aided and abetted along the way by all sorts of persons and institutions. I am embarrassed by my riches in this respect and list my creditors somewhat indiscriminately, for there seems no way in which I can fairly evaluate just how much of my enormous debt is owed to each. What is clear to me is that without their individual and collective help, the results would have not only been much less adequate than they are, they would not have been reached at all. Those persons are: Alan Rosenberg, Peter Manicas, and John McDermott—friends, colleagues, and critics whose encouragement from the outset comprises what Dewey would call a *vera causa* of the project itself; my colleagues at Queens College upon whose expert knowledge I have called at various points where my own was deficient— Gene Fontinell, Gerry Myers, Jack Noone, and Edith Wyschogrod; Fred Purnell and Nick Jordan for assistance in making available an early version for use by my graduate classes; Abraham Edel, Jim Campbell, Peter Sylvester, Ron Jager, John Stuhr, Drew Christie, Tom Olshewsky, and Konstantin Kolenda—colleagues scattered across the country who have commented on various parts of the whole at various points; and Willard Quine and Jaakko Hintikka for comments on portions read at meetings of the Northern New England Philosophical Association.

Acknowledgment should be made, as well, to Sidney Hook for his kind permission to use Dewey's letter to him at the beginning of Chapter Two, and also for his support and encouragement; to the Morris Library at Southern Illinois University for access to the Dewey and Hook archives; to Jo Ann Boydston, Director of the Center for Dewey Studies and General Editor of Dewey's collected works; to Baker Library of Dartmouth College; and to the Lamson Library of Plymouth State College of the University of New Hampshire.

The words of this project have been efficiently processed at various points by the Word Processing Unit at Queens College, and have been put in final processed form by Kae Page of Wentworth, New Hampshire, whose care and personal interest belies the impersonality of the computer. I am especially grateful to her for this final touch.

My indebtedness to Jeanne Ferris, my Editor at the Yale University Press, deserves special acknowledgment, as does my incalculable debt to my private "in-house" editor Louise C. Sleeper.

R. W. S.

Sanbornton, New Hampshire
September 1985

1: *On Interpreting Dewey*

Patience, to use Frank Kermode's word, is a mark of the classic. We have only to think of Plato's work, or Hegel's, to grasp the point. The classic endures adaptation to times and places far removed from those of its origin. It demands to be heard but does not ask to be interpreted in one way only. We respond to it in terms of our own condition.[1]

Richard Rorty reminds us that Dewey's work is like that. "For some years," he tells us, "whenever I thought I had something general and useful to say, it sounded like an echo of something I had once read. When I tried to run it down, I was constantly led back to Dewey."[2] Thus Rorty sees Dewey as pivotal in the conversation now going on about the future of philosophy and its role in culture. He credits Dewey, along with Wittgenstein and Heidegger, with helping to bring the "foundational" era of philosophy to a close. It is as a consequence of pragmatism, Rorty thinks, that we are now in an era of "post-philosophical" culture.[3]

The trouble comes, not with Rorty's recognition of Dewey's pervasive "antifoundationalism," but with his construal of its consequences. We are left, he tells us, with "ungrounded social hope" and a philosophy that can provide us with nothing more than occasional illumination to dispel the gathering gloom. Philosophy, according to Rorty, is to give "edification," and there doesn't seem to be anything very edifying in Rorty's attenuation of philosophy's function to the point where it becomes indistinguishable from that of literary criticism. What rankles is Rorty's insouciant reductionism. Pragmatism—at least Dewey's sort—had seemed to offer us more than that. It had seemed to be teaching us how to transform the culture that is decaying around us, rather than just how to "cope" with its collapse.[4]

It is not an easy task to discover just where Rorty's reading of the contemporary philosophical scene goes wrong. We have already been given a variety of diagnostic analyses, and more are sure to come.[5] My own sense is that Rorty starts to go off the rails when he takes as a consequence of pragmatism that we can at last forget about metaphysics and epistemology. That is not at all the point of its antifoundational stance, it seems to me. What we should be doing, as a consequence of pragmatism, is assigning new functions to these old disciplines, not dismissing them altogether—not building up new foundations, of course, but discovering what metaphysics and epistemology can do for us once they have been relieved of their old foundational responsibilities. It is this task that engaged Dewey throughout his life, and I see Dewey's achievement as his thoroughgoing reconstruction of these ancient disciplines, one that the future of philosophy must take into account.

In the chapters that follow I shall be examining the character of pragmatism from the perspective of Dewey's contribution to it. I adopt this approach because Dewey brought to pragmatism a very different conception of philosophy from that of either Charles Sanders Peirce or William James, the so-called founders of pragmatism. Although Dewey drew liberally on both Peirce and James in working out his own version, he traveled a different path from the outset. In the end it is this different conception of philosophy that gives Dewey's pragmatism a unity and coherence lacking in the work of his predecessors, a consistency of perspective and development that is all his own.

For the sake of clarifying the controlling nature of Dewey's conception of philosophy, this introductory chapter is followed by two chapters that trace and interpret the early development of Dewey's work. Chapter Four analyzes the content of Dewey's thought in the first decade of this century, a crucial stage in the evolution of his mature philosophy. Chapters Five and Six are expositions of that mature philosophy as found in the two texts that have determined my interpretation of Dewey's work as a whole, *Experience and Nature* and *Logic: The Theory of Inquiry*. Chapter Seven sketches the consequences of this mature philosophy for value theory, religion, aesthetics, and politics. In the last chapter I try to show the integrity of Dewey's work and some of its ramifications.

That Dewey had difficulty articulating the central conceptions that control and unify his work is well known.[6] But an occasional lucid passage, such as the following, from the central chapter of *Experience and Nature*, allows us a glimpse of what he was up to: "When communication occurs all natural events are subject to reconsideration and revision; they are re-adapted to meet the requirements of conversation, whether it be public discourse or that preliminary discourse termed thinking. Events turn into objects; things with a meaning" (*LW*1:132).

In a later chapter of the same book Dewey tells us that philosophy is criticism, and that metaphysics provides us with a "ground-map of the province of criticism" (*LW*1:308–9). These are hints that Rorty regards as neither very original nor useful, and he brushes them aside. But seen in the perspective that I shall try to develop, they are significant clues to the conception of philosophy that Dewey spent most of his life working out. They are indicative of Dewey's commitment to philosophy in general as a force for social change, and to a particular philosophy in which language and communication are the essential means by which culture develops and in which our conversations take place against a metaphysical background of crucial importance.

It is commonly accepted that Dewey's conception of philosophy led him to think of knowledge as something to be sought, not for its own sake, but for the sake of action. According to this view, Dewey's pragmatism is a form of instrumentalism. What is less commonly recognized is that his conception of philosophy required him to think of action itself as instrumental, as a means of ontological change. From this perspective, which I accept, Dewey's pragmatism is seen to be a radical form of realism—a transactional realism in which instrumentalism plays a subordinate role. Knowing thus takes the place of knowledge, and thinking entails active involvement with independent reality, an involvement that is causally efficacious. Even reflection is a means of conducting transformational transactions with the world, a means of changing, or reconstructing, the world.

I shall argue that it is this transformational conception that shapes the development of Dewey's philosophy. I find it even in his earliest work—in the publications that antedate his studies at the Johns Hopkins University, as well as those of his idealist period, when he was teaching at the University of Michigan. It is this conception of philosophy as transformational that accounts for Dewey's commitment to philosophy itself, and to the version of Hegelian idealism in which he first tried to express his ideas, as well as for his later use of the vocabulary of pragmatism and the sharp differences between his thought and that of both Peirce and James.

It is a conception of philosophy that has its origins in Hegel's conception of logic, but one that differs from Hegel's in being antifoundational from the outset. Even in his most Hegelian writings, Dewey never embraced the Absolute nor the pervasive teleology of Hegel's work. From the beginning he rejected those elements of Hegel's thought that attracted Peirce and drew him constantly in the direction of "objective idealism." What interested Dewey in Hegel's work was the account of the transformational consequences of thought on culture, the idea that thinking is an active force in social change. This interest, which Dewey expressed in both his teaching at Michigan and his early essays on logic published in *Mind* and elsewhere, took root in a conception of logic as different from Hegelian dialectic as from the modal logic that Peirce was trying to work out. Dewey rejected outright the architectonic role for metaphysics found in Peirce. Nor was he attracted to Peirce's conception of the relationship between logic and scientific method. From the start Dewey was skeptical of the a priori forms ascribed to "logical necessity" and set out to base his own philosophy of logic on the a posteriori success of experimental science. He rejected the dualism implicit in the traditional disjunction between the analytic and the synthetic, and argued for a theory of language in which this duality was no longer a controlling factor.

What Dewey did learn from Peirce—chiefly through Peirce's early essays "The Fixation of Belief" and "How to Make Our Ideas Clear" in *The Popular Science Monthly*—was a way of interpreting the achievements of science. Dewey quickly adapted this to what he was learning from James, reworking James's theory of the organic basis of human behavior, as described in *The Principles of Psychology*, to fit his own conceptions of philosophy and logic. Whereas James seemed bent on "practicalizing intelligence," Dewey was intent on "intellectualizing practice."[7] He rejected James's account of "necessary truths" in the final chapter of the *Principles*, just as he rejected Peirce's conception of the foundational character of formal logic. Dewey found himself compelled to work out his own ideas regarding necessity in logical relations and in the practice of inquiry. His thesis, presented in his contributions to the 1903 University of Chicago publication *Studies in Logical Theory*, was welcomed by James, who seems not to have noticed the difference between his own earlier account and that of Dewey. Peirce noticed Dewey's defection, however, and called him to task for committing the "philosopher's fallacy." He recognized that much more than instrumentalism was involved in Dewey's all too "intolerant" "genetic method." In fact, Dewey was already at work on the metaphysics that he subsequently elaborated in *Experience and Nature*, and had already rejected Peirce's account of logical necessity and the ontology underlying it.[8]

Dewey's contributions to the *Studies* of 1903 are conventionally understood as the platform from which his mature work was launched. It is

doubtless for this reason that countless critics have found little development in Dewey's philosophy beyond instrumentalism. What little remained to be done could be summed up in what Sidney Hook called the
"metaphysics of the instrument."[9] But in my view, the 1903 *Studies* are
just the beginning of Dewey's development of what he called the "logic of
experience," a development that would not be brought to completion
until his 1938 *Logic: The Theory of Inquiry*. By fastening on "instrumentalism" as a tag for Dewey's philosophy of logic, critics have been misled
into thinking that he was either unaware of, or did not understand, the
direction in which mainstream logic was going. Because Dewey aimed his
criticism of formal logic in the *Studies* at Lotze, a logician already scorned
by Frege and his successors, philosophers have been left with the impression that Dewey's work on logic was outmoded almost before it began.
But, in my view, Dewey had already embarked on a powerful critique of
formal logic at the very time that Frege, Russell in his 1903 essay on *The
Principles of Mathematics,* and Carnap in his 1928 *Der Logische Aufbau der
Welt* were developing it.

It is customary to view Dewey's philosophical logic as almost solely
concerned in this period with his attempt to work out a theory of scientific
method. Nor do I reject that view. It is just that I think we are bound to
misconstrue Dewey's understanding of science if we persist in thinking of
his 1938 *Logic: The Theory of Inquiry* as having little or nothing to do with
Principia Mathematica and the subsequent history of "logical atomism" in
Russell's work and the "positivism" of the Vienna Circle. We must amend
Rorty's observation that Dewey was "waiting at the end of the dialectical
road which analytical philosophy traveled" by the observation that Dewey
was trying to block that road from its beginning.[10]

Conventional wisdom acknowledges, of course, that Dewey's conception of logic diverges sharply from that of Frege and his successors. But it is
inclined to dismiss Dewey's logic as vestigial "psychologism," in the manner of Russell, or to brush it aside—as Nagel did—as hopelessly out of date
because of its failure to make use of the powerful new "symbolic" techniques. The conventional wisdom fails to recognize that Dewey was working out a full-scale theory of discourse, a philosophy of language, of the sort
required for understanding how the symbols we use relate to the world in
which we use them. We have paid scant attention to Dewey's carefully
worked out semiotic and the bearing of that semiotic on his semantic
theory. We are aware, as Quine has remarked, that Dewey was already
maintaining that "meaning" is "primarily a property of behavior," while
Wittgenstein "still held his copy theory of language."[11] But we are rela-

tively unaware of Dewey's efforts in the direction of "naturalizing" mathematics, or of his anticipation of Quine's own theory of "natural kinds." The present essay is an attempt to show what is lacking in the conventional approach.

It is a central tenet of Dewey's conception of philosophy that an adequate "general theory of language" is an essential precondition of the philosophy of logic and inquiry, and that the development of such a general theory is as much a matter of metaphysics as of logic itself.[12] It is for this reason that Dewey assigns the central chapters of both *Experience and Nature* and *Logic: The Theory of Inquiry* to the philosophy of language. The role assigned to metaphysics in this undertaking is that of providing a background theory that shows why communication is possible and necessary, a role that is fulfilled by the denotation of the "generic traits of existences of all kinds" (*LW*1:308). The role assigned to logic is that of showing how the generic traits of individual existents (objects) provide warrants for knowledge and for the propositional forms by means of which that knowledge is acquired and expressed.[13]

Because of all the confusion in the literature as to what Dewey's metaphysics is all about and how it relates to his logic, I shall first clarify their different subject-matters, insisting on the importance of retaining Dewey's own early designation, in the 1903 *Studies*, of experience as the subject-matter of logic. And to distinguish this logic of experience from the metaphysical background theory that lies behind it, I shall use the phrase "metaphysics of existence." In Dewey's philosophical logic, experience is what logic is all about, an emphasis that is lost when we think of logic as a matter of a priori principles and the demonstrations and "proofs" that they validate. By the same token, I shall be strongly critical of the almost universal habit of taking it for granted that experience is the subject-matter proper of his metaphysics.

As indicated above, I believe that Dewey's conception of pragmatism assigns a new role to epistemology as well as to metaphysics. The foundational function of epistemology is denied by assigning the task of accounting for what explains knowledge jointly to logic and metaphysics—that is, to the theory of inquiry and the theory of existence, as well as to the theory of language that links them. If we are to see how Dewey's work hangs together, we must recognize that Dewey is not attempting to work out a theory of knowledge on the Kantian paradigm of the metaphysics of experience. It would be better to say that Dewey's metaphysics is not a metaphysics of experience at all than to risk assuming that it is just another species of the kind of metaphysics embodied in Kant's *Critique of Pure Reason*. All the same, since Dewey clearly includes experience and its generic features in the subject-matter of his metaphysics, it would be wrong to say that Dewey had no metaphysics of experience at all.

The solution to this problem of perspective, of how Dewey conceives the new role of epistemology, is deceptively simple. It consists in noting the distinctively Aristotelian turn taken by Dewey's thought after he left Chicago for Columbia in 1904. Under the influence of Woodbridge and other so-called realists engaged in promoting an Aristotelian revival, Dewey began to think of his conception of logic as an organon of inquiry. As it developed during the Columbia years, it began to take on more and more of the characteristics of realism. Although Dewey condemned the fallacy of what he called "ontological logics," he became more and more concerned with the ontological implications of his own conception. Thus he became as much engaged in the reconstruction of realism as he had previously been in the reconstruction of idealism.

In effect, what Dewey worked out was a reconstruction of both the Kantian and the Aristotelian deposits in the tradition. If I stress the reconstructional aspect, it is because the result was no mere synthesis by a dialectic of compromise, but rather something far more radical, in that it penetrated to the roots of Kant's conception of reason and Aristotle's conception of nature. It is clear that in *Experience and Nature* and *Logic: The Theory of Inquiry* Dewey is trying to salvage both Kant's emphasis on the mind's contribution to the process of knowing and Aristotle's insistence on the natural genesis of that process. If we see Dewey as trying to make everything scientific, as Rorty does,[14] we lose sight of this attempt at radical synthesis of these classical elements of the epistemological and metaphysical traditions. For though there is a sense in which Dewey is always taking into account what science can tell us, he is not trying to put scientific method in the place once occupied by classical metaphysics and epistemology.[15] He is not trying to overcome tradition, but rather to transform it.

John McDermott has reminded us that Dewey once said that it is only by "sufficient preliminary conversation" that catastrophe can be averted, that, "apart from conversation, from discourse and communication, there is no thought and no meaning, only just events, dumb, preposterous, destructive."[16] This, as I see it, is precisely what Dewey's conception of philosophy is all about. It accounts for Dewey's pervasive sense that we are always on the brink of disaster, but it also accounts for his equally pervasive sense of social hope. It accounts for his meliorism and his dedication to the instruments of democratic reform; his historicism and his commitment to education; his theological agnosticism and his lifelong struggle to affirm the "religious" qualities of everyday life.

Few philosophers have enjoyed conversation with their critics as much as Dewey did. And few philosophers have been afforded so much opportunity. In his own time, as well as ours, Dewey's critics have been as prolific as Dewey himself.[17] I cannot hope to do justice to this torrent of criticism in an essay the size of this one; all I can do is to select what I consider to be most significant, either because it had some impact on the way in which Dewey's work developed, or because it has strongly influenced the way in which we interpret that work and assess its meaning and merit. Such criticism I shall consider in the body of the text. The rest will be given the admittedly short shrift of relegation to the relevant bibliographic essay. In a few cases, I have included in the bibliographical essays some harsh criticism of my own, criticism that is necessarily brief, but not altogether one-sided, I hope.[18]

The character of pragmatism as a philosophy is as little understood in our day as it was in Dewey's. Rorty sees it as giving us a way of treating the "past as material for playful experimentation rather than as imposing tasks and responsibilities upon us."[19] In the mid-1920s Lewis Mumford, in his romantic evocation of preindustrial America in *The Golden Day,* saw pragmatism much as Rorty does when he talks of "coping" with the social changes going on around us. Mumford accorded pragmatism the role of promoting acquiescence to the decline of values consequent on the Civil War and the rise of industrial and entrepreneurial capitalism.[20] Writing in the pages of *The New Republic,* Dewey responded as follows:

> The implied idealization of science and technology [by pragmatism] is not by way of acquiescence. It is by way of appreciation that the ideal values which dignify and give meaning to human life have themselves in the past been precarious in possession, arbitrary, accidental and monopolized in distribution, because of lack of means of control; by lack, in other words, of those agencies and instrumentalities with which natural science through technologies equips mankind. Not all who say *Ideals, Ideals,* shall enter the kingdom of the ideal, but only those shall enter who know and respect the roads that conduct to the kingdom.[21]

Pragmatism thus conceived is a philosophy rooted in common sense and dedicated to the transformation of culture, to the resolution of the conflicts that divide us. Thus conceived it is a philosophy that honors the past through its commitment to improving the present upon which our social hope for the future depends. It was to express the necessity of this kind of pragmatism that Dewey wrote: "The life of all thought is to effect a junction at some point of the new and the old, of deep sunk customs and unconscious dispositions, that are brought to the light of attention by some conflict with newly emerged directions of activity. Philosophies which emerge at distinctive periods define larger patterns of continuity which are woven in, effecting the enduring junctions of a stubborn past and an insistent future."[22] In my view, Dewey's pragmatic philosophy is of this kind. It emerged at a critical point in our deliberations about the future of our philosophy and our culture, a philosophy worth paying attention to, one that can survive our interpretations and that has the enduring quality that is the mark of a classic.

CRITICAL BIBLIOGRAPHY

Prefatory Note on Citations. Citations of Dewey are to the editions of the collected works published by Southern Illinois University Press under the editorship of Jo Ann Boydston: *The Early Works, 1882–1898,* 5 vols.; *The Middle Works, 1899–1924,* 15 vols.; *The Later Works, 1925–1953,* 15 vols. These are cited in the standard way, with the initials of the series followed by the volume and page numbers. At the time of writing, however, *The Later Works* are incomplete and do not extend beyond Dewey's work of 1932.

General

Each volume of the collected works contains an introductory essay that places the contents of the volume in historical and critical perspective. In addition, the cooperative research project at Southern Illinois University has published an invaluable volume, *Guide to the Works of John Dewey,* edited by Jo Ann Boydston (Carbondale: Southern Illinois University Press, 1970), which contains twelve essays by different authors on selected aspects of Dewey's work, each followed by an extensive bibliography. These essays and bibliographies are the point of departure for the study of the definitive editions of the collected works and, collectively, provide the best available overview of Dewey's work. Southern Illinois University Press has also published the only full-scale biography of Dewey: *The Life and Mind of John Dewey* by George Dykhuizen (1973), which is indispensable for keeping the chronology straight; its extensive footnotes also provide an excellent guide to the main currents of the critical literature.

Readers wishing to avoid all this scholarly apparatus may prefer to consult one of the various selections of Dewey's work. There is an excellent two-volume anthology edited by John J. McDermott: *The Philosophy of John Dewey* (Chicago: University of Chicago Press, 1973), which is also available in a paperback edition. McDermott's selection supersedes that of Richard Bernstein, *John Dewey: On Experience, Nature, and Freedom* (New York: Liberal Arts, 1960), which is now out of print. McDermott includes a selected bibliography, a sketch of Dewey's life, and a valuable essay giving a philosophical perspective of Dewey's work. Like Bernstein, however, McDermott gives the impression that experience comprises the extent of the subject-matter of Dewey's metaphysics. While this would have gladdened the heart of Shadworth H. Hodgson, whose four-volume *The Metaphysic of Experience* (London: Longmans, Green, 1898) takes a similar view of what metaphysics is all about, it threatens my own with embolism. I take the view, in opposition to both Bernstein and McDermott, that Dewey was not a forerunner of phenomenological analysis. His vocabulary is not phenomenological at all, but naturalistic. Accordingly, his approach to language is logical, rather than phenomenological. Dewey's phrase "the logic of experience," introduced in the 1903 *Essays,* is an indication that Dewey was already trying to work out a theory of language that would link it more closely with the vocabulary of natural science than with that of phenomenological discourse. He wanted to show the genesis of logic from natural science, and to place it in the context of existence. (For further discussion of this matter, see chapters Five and Six.)

In addition to these anthologies of Dewey's writings, there are several anthologies of writings about Dewey's work. Foremost among them is the volume in the Library of Living Philosophers series edited by Paul Arthur Schilpp: *The Philosophy of John Dewey* (Evanston, Ill.: Northwestern University Press, 1939). This contains Dewey's response to the criticism contained in that volume, as well as a biographical sketch put together by his daughter. It is perhaps the most convenient source from which to begin an investigation of the relationship between Dewey's conception of logic and that of Russell (about which, see Chapter Four below). Schilpp includes a bibliography in the later edition (New York: Tudor, 1951), pp. 609–86. Three celebratory volumes honoring Dewey's seventieth, eightieth, and ninetieth birthdays contain many valuable essays, not all of which can have added to the conviviality of the occasion for which they were written. By far the most useful of the Festschriften is *John Dewey: Philosopher of Science and Freedom,* edited by Sidney Hook (New York: Dial, 1950), although it is not, perhaps, as valuable as *Dewey and His Critics,* edited by Sidney Morgenbesser (New York: The Journal of Philosophy, Inc., 1977), a collection of articles from the *Journal of Philosophy* that constitutes by far the best source for tracing the effect of his critics on the development of Dewey's work after 1904.

Of the several full-length treatments of Dewey's work, I can recommend none wholeheartedly. The best is clearly Sidney Hook's early study *John Dewey: An Intellectual Portrait* (New York: John Day, 1939). A student of Dewey's, Hook had the advantage of long personal acquaintance; but the perspective obviously reflects its early date of publication. George Geiger's *John Dewey in Perspective* (New York: McGraw-Hill, 1964) suffers from myopia with respect to Dewey's logic, as does Richard Bernstein's *John Dewey* (New York: Washington Square Press, 1966), although the latter achieves a better balance. Because Bernstein saw Dewey's goal as the explication of a metaphysics of *experience* and thus failed to appreciate the significance of Dewey's logic and its relation to his metaphysics of *existence,* he could not grasp the theme of continuity that Dewey stresses in the *Logic.* It seems entirely plausible that at least some of Rorty's misreadings of Dewey are due to Bernstein's book, although Bernstein himself has expressed his own misgivings about Rorty's revisionism (cf. Bernstein's review listed below).

On balance, the best studies of Dewey's overall achievements are not to be found in the above-mentioned books at all, but in the more contextual studies that treat Dewey in relation to the history of American philosophy and the pragmatic movement in general. I have found two of these especially useful: in relation to the broad context of American philosophy, chapter 14 of *A History of Philosophy in America,* by Elizabeth Flower and Murray Murphey (New York: Putnam's, 1977; Indianapolis: Hackett, 1979), for which Flower is responsible, is especially good on the development of Dewey's views of psychology and their relation to James's changing views; and H. S. Thayer's *Meaning and Action: A Critical History of Pragmatism* (Indianapolis: Bobbs-Merrill, 1968), is especially strong on the theme of continuity (see particularly his Appendix 1). Thayer deals at length with the controversy between Dewey and Russell over the matter of truth, and with the problem of the analytic-synthetic distinction in the controversy between Dewey and C. I. Lewis.

In addition there are two useful general histories: Herbert W. Schneider, *A History of American Philosophy* (New York: Columbia University Press,

1946), and W. H. Werkmeister, *A History of Philosophical Ideas in America* (New York: Putnam's, 1949).

There are also several useful bibliographies in addition to those in the *Guide to the Works of John Dewey,* which are arranged topically. Only one is needed, however, to supplement those in the *Guide:* namely, the chronological bibliography of Milton Halsey Thomas: *John Dewey: A Centennial Bibliography* (Chicago: University of Chicago Press, 1962), which is particularly useful for its list of writings about Dewey on pp. 195–293. For a more complete list, however, see *Checklist of Writings about John Dewey, 1887–1973,* edited by Jo Ann Boydston and Kathleen Poulos (Carbondale: Southern Illinois University Press, 1974).

Concerning pragmatism in general, the best bibliography that I have discovered is in *Pragmatic Philosophy: An Anthology,* edited by Amalie Rorty (Garden City, N.Y.: Doubleday Anchor Books, 1966), but now out of print, unfortunately. This is one of the few attempts to trace the influence of pragmatism in recent philosophical work. "Part Three: Recent Reactions and Adaptations" of this anthology contains selections from a wide range of philosophers—from F. P. Ramsey to Hilary Putnam—who have, at one time or another, listened to Dewey.

Specific to Chapter One

In one respect at least Rorty faithfully emulates Dewey; he is extraordinarily prolific, contributing not only to the scholarly press but to popular periodicals as well. I list here a minimum of his writings pertinent to the points made in Chapter One: *The Linguistic Turn* (Chicago: University of Chicago Press, 1967), of which he was editor; *Philosophy and the Mirror of Nature* (Princeton: Princeton University Press, 1979); and *Consequences of Pragmatism* (Minneapolis: University of Minnesota Press, 1982). This introductory essay to *The Linguistic Turn* is the key to understanding his philosophical development. In it Rorty expresses a conception of philosophy that appears to shape his thinking in both *Mirror* and *Consequences,* although he ascribes it to linguistic philosophy in general. There are, he thinks, no philosophical problems as such: what seem to be problems of philosophy are merely linguistic confusions, which can be cleared up either by reforming the language or by attending more closely to how we use it. In *Mirror,* he applies this notion to those kinds of philosophy that he regards as using language as representational. It is here that he adopts Dewey, Wittgenstein, and Heidegger as his heroes, because he sees them as sharing both his antipathy to representational language and his antifoundational conception of philosophy. In his presidential address to the Eastern Division of the American Philosophical Association in 1979, which appears as the ninth essay in *Consequences,* he announced his adoption of pragmatism (as he understood it at the time). But, as the remaining essays in *Consequences* show, this did not affect his conception of philosophy at all. He continued to insist that philosophy had no problems of its own, that real problems are not solved by philosophers and should be turned over to others, and that philosophers should stick to what they are good at—namely, detecting pseudo-problems and "dissolving" them. The introductory essay is perhaps the most useful exposition of this conception of philosophy. The essay on Dewey's metaphysics applies this conception straightforwardly and shows why we should dismiss Dewey's work on metaphysics as a "mistake" (p. 85). It is also where Rorty reveals his conviction that Dewey was trying to work out a metaphysics of experience (p. 77). His disarming response to criticism by Abraham Edel and myself is contained in the "Symposium on Rorty's *Consequences of Pragmatism,*" *Transactions of the Charles S. Peirce Society,* vol. 21, no. 1 (1985): 1–48.

Because Rorty shares Bernstein's view that Dewey was attempting a metaphysics of experience, Bernstein's evaluation of Rorty's *Mirror* is a valuable source. It appeared under the title "Philosophy in the Conversation of Mankind," *Review of Metaphysics,* vol. 33, no. 4 (1982): 745–75. Bernstein says: "What Rorty leaves out—or fails to give its just due—is that Dewey was primarily concerned with the role that philosophy might play *after* one had been liberated from the obsessions and tyrannies of the problems of philosophy" (p. 768). (See also the review of *Mirror,* ibid., pp. 799–801.)

Two other studies are important. MacIntyre challenges Rorty's conception of philosophy in "Philosophy, the 'Other' Disciplines and Their Histories: A Rejoinder to Richard Rorty," *Soundings,* vol. 65, no. 2 (1982): 127–45. He puts his criticism in a completely different context from Bernstein: in trying to assess Rorty's understanding of analytic philosophy, MacIntyre places Rorty's work in the perspective of the history of *that* movement, rather than in the context of pragmatism. MacIntyre concludes that Rorty has provided a "millenarian consolation for analytic philosophers," but that all this means is that the history of analytic philosophy has not yet been "finally demythologized" (p. 144). The most complete and accurate account of Rorty's interpretation of Dewey's work yet to appear is James Campbell's essay on "Rorty's Use of Dewey,"

Southern Journal of Philosophy, vol. 22, no. 2 (1984), in which Campbell concludes that "Rorty offers us a portrayal of Dewey's thought lacking its core—its role in social reconstruction" (p. 185).

From sources that, although they do not pertain directly to Rorty's conception of pragmatism, are useful in putting his conception in perspective, I select two for mention here. The first is a volume of essays entitled *Pragmatism: Its Sources and Prospects,* edited by Robert J. Mulvaney and Philip M. Zeltner (Columbia, S.C.: University of South Carolina Press, 1981). The essays are by Thayer, Quine, and McDermott, whose other work has already been mentioned, and Ernest Gellner and James Gouinlock. Thayer's essay, "Pragmatism: A Reinterpretation of the Origins and Consequences," offers a contrasting view, much more firmly embedded in the historical context, which can be usefully contrasted with Rorty's view. Quine's essay, "The Pragmatists' Place in Empiricism," puts the movement in an empiricist perspective and shows how its various participants differ from each other in emphasis. Characteristically, Quine pays close attention to their treatment of analytic-synthetic dualism and concludes that they share only two distinctive tenets: "The two best guesses [regarding these tenets] seemed to be behavioristic semantics, which I so heartily approve, and the doctrine of man as truth-maker, which I share in large measure" (p. 37). Gellner's "Pragmatism and the Importance of Being Earnest" attempts to further the interpretation of pragmatism as "cheerfulness as a strategy or style [that], as defined, [stands] in opposition to a sense of crisis" (p. 45). This line is similar to Rorty's, but what Rorty praises in pragmatism, Gellner deplores. For the most part his essay is an attack on Quine's pragmatism, which he interprets as a way of doing epistemology. It is a very long way from Rorty's view, and also from Quine's. In his essay "From Cynicism to Amelioration: Strategies for a Cultural Pedagogy," McDermott characteristically contrasts the meliorism of Dewey with the social criticism of Herbert Marcuse and Norman O. Brown, and credits Dewey with recognizing who our "real enemies" are (p. 91). In a curious way the essay serves as a response to both Rorty and Gellner, though neither is its target. James Gouinlock, whose *John Dewey's Philosophy of Value* (New York: Humanities Press, 1972) is the best full-scale treatment of the subject, contributes an essay on "Philosophy and Moral Values: the Pragmatic Analysis." Gouinlock is one of the few writers on Dewey's ethics to attempt to set forth the relation of the metaphysics to problems of value judgment. In this essay he takes aim at the recent ethical theories of John Rawls and Robert Nozick, criticizing them from a Deweyan perspective. The collection is a valuable counterbalance to the other book that I want to mention, Morton White's *Pragmatism and the American Mind* (Oxford: Oxford University Press, 1973).

Together with Ernest Nagel, White seems to have decided early on that Dewey's *Logic* is not an important part of the Dewey canon, and in the section of the volume entitled "Pragmatism and Analytic Philosophy," he includes three critical essays designed to confirm this. In another section of the book, he, unlike Rorty, praises Dewey as "A Great Philosopher of Education"; and in yet another section approves Dewey's criticism of social Darwinism. I shall be dealing with White's estimate of Dewey's *Logic* in the critical bibliography to Chapter Six, so will make no further comment here except to say that he appears to follow Nagel's line in his early reviews of Dewey's book and in his essay on "Dewey's Reconstruction of Logical Theory," in *Sovereign Reason* (Glencoe, Ill.: The Free Press, 1954), pp. 118–40.

2: The Conception of a Philosophy

*L*ate in 1950 Dewey closed a letter to Sidney Hook with these words: "As I see it now, tho not at the time, ive spent most of years trying to get things together; my critics understand me only after they split me up again." The letter was accompanied by the partial draft of an article responding to criticism by various authors that had recently been published, under Hook's editorship, in observance of Dewey's ninetieth birthday. "The enclosed," Dewey writes, "is the first part of an article I propose if and when finished Ill send to the Journal."[1] It was never finished, but Dewey continued working. In the following year he wrote to Arthur F. Bentley of his intention to continue the project on which he had been working for most of his life: "If I ever get the needed strength, I want to write on *knowing* as the way of behaving in which linguistic artifacts transact business with physical artifacts, tools, implements, apparatus, both kinds being planned for the purpose and rendering *inquiry* of necessity an *experimental* transaction."[2] This project also remained unfinished. Dewey was ill, and his strength never returned. A few months later he was dead.

These letters suggest that Dewey was well aware of the fact that he had not been able to convince even his most sympathetic critics that he was, in the end, able "to get things together." They also suggest to the reader the task undertaken in this book. I want to show that Dewey *had* succeeded in pulling the various strands of his work together, that he *had* succeeded in developing a coherent perspective on the problems of philosophy and culture, that his conception of philosophy can be understood without "splitting" him up.

The letter to Hook suggests some of the facets of my task. Dewey complains that his metaphysics has been misconstrued because of his critics' failure to see how its subject-matter relates to the technical distinction made in logic between "generic and universal propositions." He complains that his work on ethics has been misunderstood owing to their failure to see how his emphasis on method furnishes a unifying factor. He complains that his critics generally remain "oblivious that according to my view all judgment is 'practical' and what they take as practical can be understood only as one species of the whole genus." The letter to Bentley suggests some requirements to be met in what follows. The centrality of Dewey's analysis of the process of knowing as a transaction must be emphasized, as well as the role of language in the way of behaving that knowing manifests. Moreover, it must be shown how these crucial analyses relate to the analysis of judgment and the apparatus of culture, its artifacts and its implements. Both letters suggest that the task ahead will involve conceptual analysis and "hermeneutics," for it is clear that Dewey's work involves extensive consideration of the conceptual content of experience, as well as its empirical content, and that the relation between them is central to the interpretive judgment.

For now it is enough to remark that I shall try to present Dewey's conception of philosophy as controlling his pragmatism, a pragmatism made coherent and—in a sense—systematic. I want to show how central Dewey's work on logic is to the whole. So I shall give an unaccustomed emphasis to Dewey's work on logical matters from the outset, and in this chapter I will stress that this work began early on in Dewey's career. It comprises the central strand of that permanent deposit which Dewey said he retained from his early Hegelianism, one that remained integral to his conception of philosophy to the end. It constitutes the means by which Dewey conducted his systematic reconstruction of pragmatism, a reconstruction that exhibits the character of pragmatism as a coherent and logical perspective on the fundamental problems of philosophy and of human experience.

Dewey has intimated, somewhat disingenuously, that he "drifted away" from Hegelianism during the fifteen years that marked the early stages of his professional career before he had found a way to make the perspective of pragmatism his own.[3] His published writings during this period show a direction that can scarcely be described as "drifting," however. In an article written even before he undertook his graduate work at Johns Hopkins (1882–84), he set forth a prescient statement of his trajectory: "the problem of philosophy", he wrote, "is to determine the meaning of things as we find them."[4] While at Johns Hopkins he pressed forward in this direction, outlining a conception of the task of philosophy that, although stated in

Hegelian terms, would lead him to a lifelong emphasis on inquiry, on method as the unifying factor. "On its subjective side," he wrote, "philosophy comes into existence when men are confronted with problems and contradictions which common sense and the special sciences are able neither to solve nor resolve. There is felt the need of going deeper into things, of not being content with haphazard views or opinions derived from this or that science, but of having some principle which, true on its own account, may also serve to judge the truth of all besides."[5] In the end, this would lead Dewey to the principle of inquiry, to the logic of experience.

From the outset, Dewey's Hegelianism was not based on the metaphysics of the Absolute. In fact it was not based on metaphysics at all. From the beginning Dewey appears to have had a conception of philosophy in which metaphysics has been demoted from its traditional position as "first philosophy." For Dewey the appeal of Hegelianism rested, rather, on the logic of synthesis, which "supplied a demand for unification that was doubtless an intense emotional craving, and yet was a hunger that only an intellectualized subject-matter could satisfy. . . . Hegel's synthesis of subject and object, matter and spirit, the divine and human, was, however, no mere intellectual formula; it operated as an immense release, a liberation. Hegel's treatment of human culture, of institutions and the arts, involved the same dissolution of hard-and-fast dividing walls, and had a special attraction for me."[6] Or so Dewey said in 1930. At the time the method of synthesis, as Dewey understood it, was not that of logic at all. It was what follows from adopting what was then called the "psychological standpoint" in approaching Hegel.

Dewey was first introduced to the psychological standpoint at Johns Hopkins, in the teaching of George Sylvester Morris. Of his teachers at Hopkins, only Morris is mentioned as an "enduring influence" in Dewey's autobiographical reflections, although Morris was there for only "a half year of lecturing and seminar work." But it is perhaps worth cursory notice that among Dewey's unmentioned graduate teachers was Charles Sanders Peirce, whose instruction in logical matters Dewey appears to have taken, albeit without significant effect. The psychological standpoint was what would be the unifying factor for the moment, though by the time Dewey wrote and published his first book, the *Psychology* of 1887, in which that method was explicated as the proper approach to philosophy, he had already moved away from it. But for the time being, Morris's particular viewpoint and approach to Hegel served, and Dewey set to work to prove that Hegel's method was not really one of logic at all, but of psychology.

In a series of articles published in *Mind*, Dewey argued again and again that "in truth, we do not go from logic to nature at all. The movement is a reverse movement."[7] He was trying to show that Hegelianism could be unimpeachably scientific, as Morris maintained, insofar as it adopts the systematic study of experience, which is psychology, or "more definitely," that "Psychology, and not Logic, is the method of Philosophy." Thus the path to pragmatism that Dewey was following had reached the point at which the method of inquiry was paramount, but the method at this stage was that of psychology. The explanation is a simple one, in Dewey's view: since Hegel had shown that the world is mind, and since psychology is the study of mind, then psychology, rather than metaphysics, is the study of reality—thus the *Psychology* of 1887.

By the time of the revised editions of 1889 and 1891, Dewey was already undercutting his own arguments in a series of articles on the nature of logic. Psychology, he was now beginning to argue, is not itself a method but uses a method. It uses—or should use—the method of science, hence both logic and psychology are now seen as scientific. The shift, stimulated no doubt by the publication of William James's great *Principles of Psychology* in 1890, is not sufficient to eject Dewey from the Hegelian orbit,[8] but it is a very different Hegel that Dewey now presents. Dewey's own words are worth quoting at length, for although Dewey was still a long way from embracing any form of empiricism—let alone pragmatism—the curve of the trajectory is now unmistakable:

> This, then is why I conceive Hegel—entirely apart from the value of any special results—to represent the quintessence of the scientific spirit. He denies not only the possibility of getting truth out of formal, apart thought, but he denies the existence of any faculty of thought which is other than the expression of fact itself. His contention is not that 'thought' in the scholastic sense, has ontological validity, but that fact, reality is significant. Even, then, were it shown that Hegel is pretty much all wrong as to the special meanings which he finds to make up the significance of reality, his main principle would be unimpeached until it is shown that fact has not a systematic, or interconnected, meaning, but is a mere hodgepodge of fragments. Whether the scientific spirit would have any interest in such a hodge-podge may, at least, be questioned. [*EW*3:138–9]

While still articulated in the language of Morris's and Thomas Hill Green's objective idealism, the realism implicit in Dewey's emphasis on the meaning of fact itself, as it emerges from the application of the scientific spirit, is ready to break through. Only two years earlier Dewey had been citing with approval Green's contention that "there is no standard *external* to experience." Now, even thought must not be "apart thought," but must be the "expression of fact itself" (*EW*3:22). The psychological standpoint is rapidly seceding in favor of the standpoint of the scientific spirit. What remained was for the scientific spirit to settle down into the experimental laboratory.

That process was already taking place at Michigan, where Dewey had been given his first academic appointment by Morris, and where he had returned, after a year at the University of Minnesota, to succeed Morris as chairman of the Department of Philosophy. It was given recognition by Dewey's success in convincing the university to appoint someone to teach physiological psychology. The person invited turned out to be George Herbert Mead, who arrived late for the fall semester of 1891. He had previously done graduate work at Harvard with Josiah Royce and James, attracted there by the growing reputation of James's psychological laboratory, and had gone on to Germany for further study at Berlin.[9] Familiar with the work of the pioneers in "Phys. Psy.," as he called it, Mead was eager to apply what he had learned from Dilthey, Zeller, Wundt, Hering, Helmholdt, Stumpf, and the rest to philosophy. He was to teach a course in the history of philosophy and to take full responsibility for instruction in his specialty. As it turned out, that specialty was at the center of Dewey's attention; Mead was at once caught up in the trajectory of Dewey's developing conception of philosophy. They would, in the event, become pragmatists together.

Mead signaled the tenor of collaboration with Dewey in a letter to his in-laws in Hawaii in the spring of 1892. Mead's wife had already left to spend the summer with her parents, and it had been expected that Mead would follow. Instead, he decided to remain at Ann Arbor, explaining that it "has been a difficult and most trying decision." But, he continues:

> For me in Physiological Psychology the especial problem is to recognize that our psychical life can all be read in the functions of our bodies—that it is not the brain that thinks but our organs in so far as they act together in the processes of life. . . . This is quite a new standpoint for the science and has a good many important consequences—especially does it offer new methods of experiment which must be worked out and I can't do this if I do not have the summer here for study and the arrangement of the laboratory. . . . What I am at work on has all the meaning of social and religious life in it.[10]

Among the important consequences, it is now clear, were Dewey's land-mark paper of 1896, "The Reflex Arc Concept in Psychology." For it was that paper, more than any other, that marked Dewey's final break with idealism.

The 1892 spring term at Michigan was decisive for Dewey in other ways too. Relieved of any feeling of responsibility for carrying on the Morris tradition, Dewey exercised his initiative, as well as his emerging vision of philosophy, by inaugurating a new introductory course in philosophy. The syllabus of the new course, known as "Course 5," is dated February 1892, and its first "Section" says it all:

SECTION I.—Philosophy (science) is the conscious inquiry into expe-rience. It is the attempt of experience to attain to its own validity and fullness; the realization of the meaning of experience.
Science and philosophy can only report the actual condition of life, or experience. Their business is to reveal experience in its truth, its reality. They state what *is*.
The only distinction between science and philosophy is that the latter reports the more generic (the wider) features of life; the former the more detailed and specific. [*EW*3:211]

Dewey had been working this out in a series of essays in which logic and science were portrayed as being on convergent historical paths. He was trying to reconcile the empirical logic descended from Mill with the transcendental logic stemming from Kant. He seems, in the course of these essays, to have completely abandoned psychology as method, though he would later return to it in reconstructed form.

The series begins in January 1890 with the publication, in *Open Court,* of "Is Logic a Dualistic Science?" After a cursory discussion of several propo-nents of the "Newer Logic"—mentioning Lotze, Sigwart, Wundt, Jevons, Bosanquet, and Bradley—Dewey zeroes in on what he calls "Venn's Empirical Logic."[11] Venn assumes, Dewey says, that we must take for granted a certain duality between the outside world and the observing and thinking mind. Logic is concerned with judgments of the latter about the former; it operates as a kind of "third thing," mediating between the other two, or bringing the one to bear upon the other. Dewey rejects this idea that logic should concern itself with the "correspondence" between the two worlds, or with the relation between perception and conception, observa-tion and thought. He pushes the notion that "logical processes enter equally into both perception and conception, so that, from a certain standpoint, each has a logical character" (*EW*3:77–8).

What Dewey is addressing here is the old dogma of the bifurcation of the universe. His target is the rigid distinction between a priori and a posteriori elements of knowledge. He is working out an account of knowing as a process in which analysis of the given is continuous with the synthesis that emerges as knowledge. He is challenging both Venn's account of experience as divisible into perception and conception and the analytic-synthetic distinction presupposed in both empirical logic after Hume and the transcendental logic of neo-Kantians and objective idealists. He does this from what he is now calling the "logical standpoint"—but later simply calls "inquiry"—as shown by this rhetorical query: "Whence the whole chemical theory of combustion, and what is the need of it, unless the first judgment that 'fire burns' is, after all, only a tentative and crude *analytic-synthetic* process, needing to be carried farther, to be corrected, and, finally, transformed into a hypothesis more nearly agreeing with facts?" (*EW*3:79; emphasis added.)

Dewey goes on, in the same article, to deny that perception lacks logic in the required sense. He attacks the idea that it has no formal qualities at all: "Knowledge from the first, whether in the form of ordinary observation or of scientific thinking, is logical; in ordinary observation, however, the logical process is unconscious, dormant, and hence goes easily and inevitably astray. In scientific thinking the mind knows what it is about; the logical functions are consciously used as guides and as standards."[12] This is the view that Dewey holds throughout his life; in expanded form it is a major theme of *Logic: The Theory of Inquiry,* of 1938. It is a key to understanding his ontology as well, for the passage continues: "But knowledge, experience, the material of the known world are one and the same all the way; it is one and the same world which offers itself in perception and in scientific treatment; and the method of dealing with it is one and the same—logical. The only difference is in the degree of development of the logical functions present in both." Dewey is arguing not only against mind–body dualism, but also against the dualism of commonsense objects versus scientific objects. He is arguing forthrightly for a logic *with* ontology, a logic capable of expressing and clarifying our ontological commitments, one that takes its cues from natural science, and for realism in science.[13]

Dewey picked up the argument again a few months later in "The Logic of Verification," in the April issue of *Open Court.* He no longer uses Venn as a foil, preferring to face questions of truth head on. For, once the duality of logic is set aside, what is the criterion for judging truth? Once the correspondence theory is abandoned, what do we have to go on? Dewey dismisses coherence theories as hopeless, since theories that are perfectly coherent can have absurd consequences. Although this argument reveals an almost pragmatic thrust, Dewey passes at once to an approach to verification that he returns to again and again in his later work, doing so without a flicker of recognition that he is traveling paths already trodden by Peirce and James. He begins with a consideration of how it is that we sometimes know that we have been wrong, have made a mistake, and so start over. In this situation, he says, it is not that our concepts fail to square with the facts, for at such a juncture we cannot even be sure of the facts. Indeed, we are as unsure of the facts as we are of our concepts. We come, like children, to the realization that our ideas are merely ideas, and we begin, like savages, to distinguish between the real and the apparent facts that surround us. The projectibility of ideas on to facts helps, and the realization that facts themselves are transformed—become more meaningful—when viewed in relation to different ideas helps even more.[14]

In this, Dewey is heading toward realism again, but this time it is clear that he wants to avoid the scholastic form, in which the real is what it is in complete and utter disregard of inquiry. Unlike traditional realists, he is not arguing against nominalism, but, in Hegelian fashion, for the role of the knower in determining the character of the known. He is arguing for a transaction between the knower and the known—in a word, for a kind of transactional realism. The argument goes this way: "if the idea, the theory, is tentative, if it is pliable and must be bent to fit the facts, it should not be forgotten that the 'facts' are not rigid, but are elastic to the touch of theory." In sum, "the distinction between the idea and the facts is not between a mere mental state, on the one side, and a hard rigid body on the other. Both idea and 'facts' are flexible, and verification is the process of mutual adjustment, of organic interaction. It is just because the 'facts' are not final, settled facts that the mind frames its hypothesis or idea; the idea is the tentative transformation of these seeming facts into more real facts" (*EW* 3:87). This, of course, is a fundamental thesis of what was to become a pragmatic theory of truth, one that would be enunciated as such by Peirce and James. But Dewey's argument implies an ontology that is clearly his own, one that emerges from his early devotion to Hegel's ontological logic. Dewey had arrived at pragmatism by a different itinerary, but he did not yet know it.[15]

The last major article of the series, the 1891 *Monist* essay on "The Present Position of Logical Theory," continues to defend Hegel's logic on one central point. Or, to put it more accurately, it defends Hegel's logic on one central point against the new empiricist logic derived from Mill, as well as against the transcendental logic resulting from Green's reconstruction of Kantianism. That point is Hegel's denial of the Kantian doctrine of the a priori, that is, the denial of what Dewey calls "apart thought" in logic. What Dewey wants to retain is Hegel's contention that the so-called a priori element in knowledge is nothing apart from experience, that it is somehow embodied in the structure of experience itself. The a priori, Dewey argues, is not given by the mind or thought somehow supervening upon experience; it must be residually present in the knowing process as such, not imported into that process from outside. Here is Dewey's reading of Hegel's point:

> Now when Hegel talks of relations of thought (not that he makes much use of just this term) he means no such separate (Kantian *a priori*) forms. Relations of thought are, to Hegel, the typical forms of meaning which the subject-matter takes in its various progressive stages of being understood. And this is what *a priori* means from a Hegelian standpoint. It is not some element *in* knowledge; some addition of thought to experience. It is experience itself in its skeleton, in the main features of its framework. [*EW*3:137]

The "Reflex Arc" essay would later describe the structure of experience in psychological terms, using empirical and denotative description. But here it is described in logical terms, for Dewey conceives the subject-matter of logic as the formal character of experience that is inherently present as its skeleton or framework.[16]

In this essay Dewey is clearly trying to bring the empiricist and transcendentalist strains of logical theory together, to show that they both involve a similar mistake. It is the mistake of assuming the independence of the *a priori* from the *a posteriori*, the analytic from the synthetic in the logical calculus. What Hegel had united, Dewey argues, the neo-Kantian idealists have separated. These objective idealists have given short shrift to Hegel's logic precisely because they have failed to see how Hegel derives the formal elements of reasoning from the actual processes of inquiry; they have gone back to the scholastic separation of formal thought from sense experience, the Kantian separation of pure and practical reason, the duality of Venn's logic—and that of Green, Bosanquet, and Bradley. It is the same flaw that vitiates the conception of logic descended from empiricism—from Mill and from Hume—the flaw that prevents empiricist logic from following through on the implications of its own inductive methods. It is the failure to see that the norms of logical form are derived from the inductive method, that they are not supervenient forms descending on experience like a *deus ex machina*. Empiricist logic is no less scholastic in its dogmatic separation of a priori and a posteriori elements than is transcendentalist logic as interpreted by the neo-Kantians.[17]

Dewey is searching for a synthesis between induction and deduction, between empiricism and transcendentalism, for a logic that will ultimately incorporate the actual lessons of science, rather than continuing the pretense that the formal principles of analytic reason somehow control scientific method. He is arguing that the norms and criteria of verification are not derived from the formal canons of logic, but rather from the structures of the actual process of verification. He is arguing that formalistic logic is unable to account for the actual successes of science, that what is actually going on is the reverse. But he continues to frame his arguments in the language of Hegelianism and to defend Hegel's conception of logic, something he would continue to do until after the turn of the century. It is only with the appearance in 1903 of *Studies in Logical Theory* that he finally abandons the vocabulary that he had inherited from Morris and Green. John Herman Randall, Jr., has recorded Herbert Schneider's shrewd observation of what Dewey was up to in these years: "Dewey formed his own instrument of language in the midst of nineteenth-century idealism, in a world eager to talk the new tongue of evolutionary thinking. As our colleague Herbert Schneider has acutely pointed out, Dewey used the language of philosophical idealism to direct evolutionary thought against its conclusions. This proved a most effective technique for undermining and reconstructing idealism" (*EW*3:xviii). Even so, there are passages in the early writings in which all traces of idealism seem to disappear, passages in which Dewey seems almost to have adopted the language and posture of positivism, of Comte and Spencer, as in this example:

It will be seen that logic is no revived, redecked scholasticism, but a complete abandonment of scholasticism; that it deals simply with the inner anatomy of the realm of scientific reality, and has simply endeavored, with however much anticipation, to dissect and lay bare, at large and in general, the features of the subject-matter with which the positive sciences have been occupying themselves in particular and in detail.

That we are almost at the point of such conflux, a point where the general, and therefore somewhat abstract lines of critical logic will run into the particular, and therefore somewhat isolated, lines of positive science, is, in my opinion, the present position of logical theory. [*EW*3:141]

But, Dewey argued, this would not bring the task of metaphysics down to the level of meaninglessness anticipated by Comte.

"The scientific spirit," Dewey writes, "is not antagonistic to the task of metaphysics at all." And in a passage prescient of his own work in *Experience and Nature*, no less than in *Logic: The Theory of Inquiry*, he foresees not only a new logic based on natural science, but a metaphysics set free of all "transcendent entities and forces," a metaphysics of the sort anticipated not by Comte, but by Renan as early as 1848, in his essay on the *Future of Science*. In that essay, as Dewey points out, Renan envisaged the replacement of the category of 'being' by the category of 'evolution.' In Dewey's own words of 1891 it looks like this:

> Science freed from its fear of an external and dogmatic metaphysic, will lose its fear of metaphysic. Having unquestioned and free possession of its own domain, that of knowledge and of fact, it will also be free to build up the intrinsic metaphysic of this domain. It will be free to ask after that structure of meanings making up the skeleton of the world of knowledge. The moment this point is reached, the speculative critical logic worked out in the development of Kantian ideas, and the positive, specific work of the scientific spirit will be at one. [*EW*3:141]

Dewey has arrived at the conception of the relation between logic and metaphysics that he was to maintain until the end. It is the conception of logic as the critical theory of experience, of experience as pedagogical, and of metaphysics as the critical theory of existence, the "ground-map of the province of criticism," which is sustained by logic, as inquiry.[18]

Until now, I have been writing of Dewey's early departure from Hegelianism as if it were exclusively a matter of escape from idealist logic and metaphysics, a plunge into pragmatism by way of logical considerations and the embrace of the scientific spirit at home in the psychological laboratory. But other concerns abetted the transition and contributed to the shift in Dewey's thinking, and in retrospect seem to hang together with Dewey's central concern with the logic of experience, the logic of inquiry and method.

Reflecting on these early years some three decades later, Dewey recalled that, for him, the appeal of Hegel's thought—like that of Plato's—lay not simply in its systematic unity of logic and metaphysics, but also in the fact that the system always came down, in the end, to the concrete problems of actual life. In "From Absolutism to Experimentalism," he says:

> I imagine that my development has been controlled largely by a struggle between a native inclination toward the schematic and formally logical, and those incidents of personal experience that compelled me to take account of actual material. . . . There were "subjective" reasons for the appeal that Hegel's thought made to me; it supplied a demand for unification that was doubtless an intense emotional craving, and yet was a hunger that only an intellectualized subject-matter could satisfy. It is more than difficult, it is impossible, to recover that early mood. But the sense of divisions and separations that were, I suppose, borne in upon me as a consequence of a heritage of New England culture, divisions by way of isolation of self from world, of soul from body, of nature from God, brought a painful oppression—or, rather, they were an inward laceration. [*LW*5:150–3]

This inward laceration that he sees as stemming from his New England background can be pinned down to an even more proximate cause. For it is clear that, like so many young philosophers of the period, he was engaged in a personal struggle with the problem of religious faith and commitment. Not only were all of Dewey's philosophical mentors professed Christians, but the vast majority were ordained ministers, and access to university positions in philosophy were largely under their control, since they occupied key positions in all the major universities. It was an important turning point in Dewey's life when, after succeeding Morris in the chairmanship at Michigan, he felt free to publish in secular journals like *Open Court* and the *Monist*, rather than in theologically oriented periodicals such as the *Andover Review*. At this time too, he felt free to institute an introduction to philosophy course in which theological concerns were treated as historical anachronisms, and to argue—as he did in a Sunday morning address to the Student Christian Association at Michigan in 1892—that "democracy thus appears as the means by which the revelation of truth is carried on" (*EW*4:9).

There is reason to believe that Dewey's somewhat distant relation to matters of faith and theology during these early years was a reflection of the fact that he had already come to terms with his own religious qualms. Max Eastman has quoted Dewey to the effect that these had been resolved as far back as 1879–80, when Dewey was teaching high school in Oil City, Pennsylvania, as the result of a "mystical experience." Just how mystical

that experience was may be judged from Dewey's account of it to Eastman:
"What the hell are you worrying about anyway? Everything that's here is
here, and you can just lie back on it. I've never had any doubts since then,
nor any beliefs. To me faith means not worrying. . . . I claim I've got
religion, and that I got it that night in Oil City."[19]

Whatever that experience meant to Dewey, it is plain that by 1892 he
was little concerned to follow in Morris's footsteps—or those of the neo-
Kantians generally—in working out a reconciliation of traditional supernaturalism and empirical science. Nor was Dewey prepared to follow
Hegel in this regard. Even in the flush of Dewey's most Hegelian writings,
it is never the Hegel of the Absolute that shines through, never the Hegel of
orthodox supernaturalists, but the naturalistic Hegel of the *Phenomenology
of Mind*, the pantheistic Hegel of the early *Lectures on the Philosophy of
Religion*, the Hegel that inspired Feuerbach's *The Essence of Christianity*
and, later, Karl Marx's "Theses on Feuerbach," and Friedrich Engels's "On
the History of Early Christianity." For already Dewey was working out his
own conception of the relation of the actual to the ideal—the latter
becoming, in his 1934 *Common Faith*, a possible name for God—a relation
in which faith takes a "social and practical turn," a matter to which we will
return in Chapter Seven.

Here is his own account:

> Social interests and problems from an early period had to me the
> intellectual appeal and provided the intellectual sustenance that many
> seem to have found primarily in religious questions. . . . I seem to be
> unstable, chameleon-like, yielding one after another to many and
> diverse and even incompatible influences; struggling to assimilate
> something from each and yet striving to carry it forward in a way that
> is logically consistent with what had been learned from its predeces-
> sors. . . . I like to think, though it may be a defense reaction, that with
> all the inconveniences of the road I have been forced to travel, it has
> the compensatory advantage of not inducing an immunity of thought
> to experiences—which perhaps, after all should not be treated even by
> a philosopher as the germ of a disease to which he needs to develop
> resistance. [*LW*5:154–6]

It is not all that easy to discern from these words what was actually going on
as regards Dewey's relationship to organized religion during his years at
Michigan. Lewis S. Feuer writes that these were years of outward conformity, years in which Dewey apparently remained a "devout Congregationalist."[20] And the record does show him participating in Bible in-

stitutes, teaching Sunday school classes, and giving courses on the life of
Christ, the Epistles of St. Paul, and Church history. But according to Jane
Dewey's account of her father's life, that outward conformity may have
masked an inner struggle. For she points out that Dewey's parents lived
with the young philosopher's family at Ann Arbor during those years, and
that "while his father was hurt at his son's recreance to the Republican
party, associated in his mind with the preservation of the union, and his
mother at their defection from the religious teachings of their boyhood,
both were sufficiently liberal in their views and had sufficient confidence in
their children to keep the family relation a close one."[21]

Dewey's father had been an abolitionist and had served in the Quarter-
master Corps of the Union Army. Dewey's mother was rather more than a
"devout Congregationalist," it seems, for it is recorded that her customary
greeting, even during the years at Michigan, was: "Are you right with
Jesus?" It is recorded that Dewey's response to a question following an
address to the Ministerial Band at Michigan in 1893 on the subject of "The
relation of Philosophy to Theology," in which he was asked about the
nature of prayer, was: "Prayer is the 'seek and ye shall find,' the inquiry of
science. . . . The scientist seeks and finds something,—results. 'Pray always,' must have meant that the essence of prayer is in a certain attitude"
(*EW*4:365).[22] It is hard to see that this response is consonant with anything less than a severely reconstructed version of Hegelianism, if of
Hegelianism at all. Dewey seems already to have adopted the attitude of an
unregenerate and whole-hearted naturalism. Perhaps, as Max Eastman has
suggested, it was all worked out back in Oil City.

Jane Dewey's reference to Dewey's recreance to the conservative politics
of the Republican party signals another feature of Dewey's concerns
during this early period, concerns that are of a piece with his philosophical
trajectory in the direction of pragmatism. As early as 1888, in an address to
the Philosophical Union at Michigan on "The Ethics of Democracy,"
Dewey was taking a political stance that was not only thoroughly democratic, but that pointed toward something more radical in the way of a
critique of the concept of individualism underlying the system of indus-
trialized capitalism. Dewey was already using the vocabulary of Hegelianism in support of the socialist ideas of the "back-to-the-people" movement
then taking hold in literature, social theory, and economics. In an article
published in the *International Journal of Ethics* in 1891, he works out an
ethical justification for strikes. And in his *Outlines of a Critical Theory of
Ethics,* his first major book since the *Psychology,* he illustrates what he means
by a moral law by reference to the problems of labor and suggests that

ethics must involve a principle of action that will result in a movement toward the solution of those problems. Although in the *Outlines* of 1891 Dewey makes a sharp distinction between the general theory of ethics and political philosophy, he also makes it clear that there is a continuity between them that must be maintained. To make sure that his principle of action is not equated with "rugged individualism" but is conducive to "the satisfaction of the entire moral order, the furthering of the community in which one lives," he frames his "Ethical Postulate" in terms of a principle of social welfare, and states it in bold capitals: "IN THE REALIZATION OF INDIVIDUALITY THERE IS FOUND ALSO THE NEEDED REALIZATION OF SOME COMMUNITY OF PERSONS OF WHICH THE INDIVIDUAL IS A MEMBER: AND, CONVERSELY, THE AGENT WHO DULY SATISFIES THE COMMUNITY IN WHICH HE SHARES, BY THAT SAME CONDUCT SATISFIES HIMSELF" (*EW*3:322). Although this formulation employs terms that are still recognizably Hegelian, it is evident that what Dewey had been teaching in his introduction to philosophy course was not far from his mind. For he immediately compares the ethical postulate with the similar postulate underlying all science, which he defines, in somewhat cavalier fashion, as "the conviction of the thoroughgoing and permanent unity of the world of objects known—a unity which is sometimes termed the 'uniformity of nature' or the 'reign of law'." He then goes on to say that "without this conviction that objects are not mere isolated and transitory appearances, but are connected together in a system by laws or relations, science would be an impossibility" (*EW*3:323).

Dewey is here giving full rein to his confessed propensity for schematic thinking, prescient not only of the ethics that he would later work out with his colleague J. H. Tufts at the University of Chicago, but of the *Logic* of 1938 as well. For he goes on to lay out the relation of ethics and science to logic, subsequently bringing them together in the context of the further inquiry belonging to the kind of metaphysics that he would work out in *Experience and Nature*. The passage, retrospectively, seems a clear foreshadowing of the pragmatic turn still to come. For the whole web of relations begins with the problem of practice and the need to discover a principle of action. Here, in attenuated form, is a vision of a metaphysics, what Dewey would later think of as a "background theory":

> Moral experience *makes for the world of practice* an assumption analogous in kind to that which intellectual experience makes for the world of knowledge. And just as it is not the affair of science, as such, or even of logic (the theory of science) to justify this presupposition of science,

or to do more than show its presence in intellectual experience, so it is
not the business of conduct, or even of ethics (the theory of conduct)
to justify what we have termed the "ethical postulate." In each case the
further inquiry belongs to metaphysics. [*EW*3:323]

Readers of Dewey's *Outlines* in 1891, of course, would have had little
reason to think that this represented a departure from the ethics of Green,
Bradley, or Caird. But Dewey himself was ready to move on, as a second
book on ethics, published only two years after the *Outlines,* makes clear.

The Study of Ethics: A Syllabus, Dewey asserts in his preface, is "in no sense
a second edition of the previous book"—an assertion that in my view ranks
as the understatement of the year 1893! For the *Syllabus,* as it soon came to
be known, marks a sharp and unmistakable departure from the method and
perspective of the earlier book. No longer does Dewey express any indebtedness to Green and Bradley, or even to James, despite the adoption of a
Jamesian vocabulary throughout. Where the *Outlines* had proceeded by
means of a dialectical comparison of the great historical antitheses in ethical
theory, which Dewey then tried to reconcile, the *Syllabus* inaugurates a new
approach altogether. Abjuring dialectics from the start, Dewey adopts the
genetic method that characterizes his procedure in ethics henceforth, the
method that he expounds as "the logic of experience" a decade later in his
contribution to the *Studies in Logical Theory,* and that he elaborates in his
1938 *Logic: The Theory of Inquiry.* It is the same method that he employs in
his valedictory against "noncognitivism" in ethics in his 1939 contribution
to the International Encyclopedia of Unified Science, the *Theory of Valuation,* the method that Peirce called "intolerant" in 1905 and chided Dewey
for adopting. But it is also the method that James welcomed in 1903 as a
contribution to radical empiricism.

Moreover, the *Syllabus* adopts a perspective that is wholly naturalistic, a
perspective that dominates his contributions to the *Ethics* published jointly
with Tufts in 1908 and revised in 1932, and that provides the background
for his 1920 *Reconstruction in Philosophy* and his 1929 Gifford Lectures,
published as *The Quest for Certainty.* It is what we have come to regard as an
antifoundational perspective, one that controls Dewey's conception of
metaphysics in *Experience and Nature* and, as he wrote to Bentley, renders
"*inquiry* of necessity an *experimental* transaction."

Critics of Dewey's work, both early and late, have had difficulty in
grasping just how much of Dewey's conception of the transformational
power of philosophy is expressed in the *Syllabus.* His contemporaries

almost all saw the move as an attempt to, in effect, place idealism on an experimental basis, though they later saw it as anticipating the instrumentalism that they took to be the next stage in his development. Later critics have pointed to Dewey's adoption of an evolutionary perspective, and to the influence of James's *Principles of Psychology* of 1890. But almost alone among Dewey's critics, early *and* late, Josiah Royce discerned the central nerve of Dewey's argument. He saw that Dewey had abandoned idealism altogether and had adopted what he called "ethical *realism*."[23] As far as Royce was concerned, this was a serious mistake on Dewey's part, not so much because realism in ethics cannot be defended, but because it needs a metaphysical foundation of the sort that Dewey fails to provide. As Royce puts it, the *Syllabus* lacks the "whole" context "for which Professor Dewey so frequently contends." Without that context, which metaphysics alone can provide, Dewey's ethical realism remains an "essentially partial doctrine." Royce had spotted the antifoundational perspective of the *Syllabus* but had failed to see that Dewey was already putting ethics in a historicist perspective, a "whole" of the sort for which he contends. Dewey was already arguing for the kind of background theory for ethics that he later elaborates in *Experience and Nature,* a holistic and contextualist approach to ethical realism.

The *Syllabus* reformulates the ethical postulate of the *Outlines* in terms that reflect Dewey's growing interest in social change and his "progressive" concern with moral and political freedom. The goal of the moral life is the freeing of that life "through knowledge of its real nature and relations." The theory of the moral life will therefore conceive of "conduct as the normal and free living of life as it is" (*EW*4:221). From the perspective of the individual, "conduct is the co-ordinating or bringing to unity of aim and interest, the different elements of a complex situation," whereas from the standpoint of the social "scene of action, . . . conduct is co-ordinating, in an organized way, the concrete powers, the impulses and habits, of an individualized agent." So the ethical postulate is recast in terms more apposite to social psychology than Hegelian metaphysics: "The conduct required to truly express an agent is, at the same time, the conduct required to maintain the situation in which he is placed; while, conversely, the conduct that truly meets the situation is that which furthers the agent" (*EW*4:234). This is already the contextual approach that Dewey takes in his 1922 *Human Nature and Conduct,* the most explicitly sociological of Dewey's works, as well as in his more political analyses, *The Public and Its Problems* (1927) and *Individualism, Old and New* (1930). But it is also the approach that he takes in the development of his educational theory

throughout. In the *Syllabus* this comes out most forcefully in connection
with the discussion of obligation.

Dewey frames the argument in the context of historical progress. He
wants to show the roles of social structure and social function as means of
change that respond to both individual and social needs. Progress requires
both definite individualization and specific organization. Every individual
as instrument, he says, must assert a "specific, differentiated character, or
relapse into uselessness." At the same time, every such instrument must be
"truly instrumental," serving the ends of the whole. It is when individual
habits fail to serve the ends of the whole that consciousness of obligation
arises (*EW*4:314). Dewey suggests the parallel with organic evolution that
Social Darwinists subsequently turned into a kind of social determinism,
but he goes on to show why the latter is defective—namely, because the
habits and impulses of the self, unlike the instincts of the more primitive
organism, are subject to self-control. His argument is that the habits and
impulses of individualized selves, being not entirely fixed, have attained
individualization only because of their history of constant interaction with
all those factors outside the self to which the self responds by readjusting
the pattern of its conduct. To achieve a unified self, conduct must be
constantly re-formed to meet the enduring needs of the self in a changing
world. "A new end comes in, and demands a rearrangement, a reform, of
older habits and interests" (*EW*4:317).

The demand comes not from the external character of the situation
alone, but from the reciprocity of the self–world relation. The whole
situation demands reconstruction, even if the consciousness of obligation
arises as a consequence of the self's individuality. The need of the individual is not for conformity to a pattern of conduct prescribed from outside,
nor for the world to be reorganized so as to meet the existing needs of the
self and to conform to the habits and interests already established for
meeting those needs. The normal and free living of life necessitates that the
transformation be reciprocal, that the whole scene of action be changed.
Unlike Social Darwinists, Dewey is not talking of progress in purely, or
even primarily, social terms. He is talking principally in terms of the
individualized self, and of the sense of obligation that comes to consciousness in such a self in "critical periods, periods of greater or less readjust-
ment, of adaptation of old habits to new needs" (*EW*4:316). Thus:

This connection of obligation with the periods of reconstruction in
moral progress also accounts for the relativity, or better, the individuality of duty. Let theorists deal with the facts as they may, the fact

remains that no two persons have or can have the same duties. It is only when we are dealing with abstractions that they appear the same. Truth-telling is a duty for all, but it is not the duty of all to tell the same truth, because they have not the same truth to tell. [*EW*4:317–8]

A passage telling us that Dewey is not just dealing with the old philosophical conundrums about truth or with the ethics of the self follows immediately. He frames a sharp criticism of the "modern moral methods" of society in this context:

> Any other conception is like the pedagogical theory which has mechanized our schools—that all the children are to recite the history, the geography, the arithmetic lesson in the same way. It is only the abstraction, the text-book, which is the same. The truth to each child is this abstract fact assimilated to his own interests and habits, and proceeding from them vitalized—free. The great underlying contradiction, the lie, in modern moral methods, is the assertion of individuality in name, and the denial of it in fact. [*EW*4:318]

It is in passages like this that we see how thoroughly naturalistic Dewey's approach had become by 1893, and how completely the ethical realism that Royce detected necessitates that naturalistic context, despite the label "experimental idealism" that Dewey was still willing to accept (*EW*4:264). It is not that we can "read all of Dewey's later outlook into his 1893 comments," the danger that Wayne A. R. Leys has warned us against (*EW*4:ix). It is just that the *Syllabus*—and the rest of Dewey's work in 1893—displays how clearly the trajectory of Dewey's philosophical development is controlled by a conception of philosophy itself, a conception that is antifoundational from the outset, even as it seeks a new role and function for philosophy.[24]

From his very earliest works—"The Metaphysical Assumptions of Materialism" (*EW*1:1) and "The Pantheism of Spinoza" (*EW*1:9)—there is a continuous and, I believe, conscious effort on Dewey's part to work out the linkage between common sense and the abstractions composing the stock-in-trade of the profession as he found it. It is a conception of philosophy that accepts the necessity of change, and that aims at the transformation of the tradition, rather than its defeat or elimination. Dewey conceived of philosophy as itself a force for change, as instrumental in both the progress necessary for the development of personal moral character and the reciprocal progress necessary for social and political reform. It is a philosophy that can be articulated as advocacy as well as protest, one that can suggest changes to be accomplished, not merely explain changes that have already occurred. Dewey sees philosophy as something to be worked out with the past clearly in mind, but also in full consciousness of the problems of the present. It is to be melioristic in its consequences, committed to working out the problems that confront us and the conflicts that divide us. This is the conception of philosophy that Dewey himself expressed as controlling the path that he was "forced to travel."[25]

I shall close this chapter by reference to an essay which, to my way of thinking, shows Dewey's perspective on the character of logical theory to be as naturalistic as that controlling his approach to ethics in the *Syllabus*. It is an essay which is prescient, not only of the logic of experience that Dewey subsequently propounded in the *Studies in Logical Theory* of 1903, but of the 1938 *Logic* as well. For, in "The Superstition of Necessity," Dewey attacks the whole problem of the relationship between logical form and the reality of objects. It marks a decisive beginning in what became a lifelong effort to naturalize both logic and epistemology.

When "The Superstition of Necessity" was published in 1893, Dewey was struggling to express the realism that he had already come to recognize as a necessary element in any genuinely experimental science, one that he had been groping toward in his critical attempt to synthesize the empiricist logic descended from Mill and the transcendentalist logic of the neo-Kantians. He was trying to salvage the "one central point" of Hegelian logic that he valued—its denial of the Kantian a priori—and at the same time account for the projectibility of knowledge obtained from the empiricist description of induction. In so doing, he was trying to work out a conception of logical necessity that would accord with our actual experience of inquiry in the natural sciences, one that would not invoke the transcendental at all. In "The Superstition of Necessity" he reached the conclusion that the concept of necessity arises from the practice of inquiry, that it is, in a sense, the a posteriori product of thought rather than its a priori principle. He got there by denying it the ontological status that it held in Hegel's system.

A routine objection to the Hegelian world system had been that it incorporates the formal principle of logical necessity into the world order, importing it from Kantian transcendental logic, and that it does so gratuitously, given that there is no empirical evidence of the presence of such logical necessity in nature as such. The denial of this presence, accordingly, undercuts the entire conception of the Hegelian Absolute and of the *logos* that is thought to be unfolding itself in the dialectical processes of nature and history. It is an important feature of Dewey's most Hegelian writings that he accepted the implications of that denial from the outset. When he argues that the a priori must not be understood in terms of "apart thought," or as Kantian "forms of intuition," or when he argues against the metaphysical presuppositions of deterministic materialism, Dewey takes the denial of the ontological logic of necessity almost for granted. It is doubtless this taken-for-granted denial that influenced his early decision to argue for logic, rather than metaphysics, as the way in which we should approach nature. And it was just as surely a factor in his later decision to adopt the psychological standpoint as the best position from which to view both logic and philosophy. By the time he had completed his analysis of the two competing schools of logical theory, between 1890 and 1893, Dewey was ready to articulate the denial of all ontological logics directly. He did so in an attack on the importation of the principle of logical necessity into the ontological order. In "The Superstition of Necessity" he argues the thesis that necessity is never a feature of actual relations, the only function of logical necessity being a strictly logical one—namely, that necessity is *only* a feature of judgment, an instrumental abstraction useful in the practice of inquiry.

Dewey then advances another thesis, closely connected with this one, that links this treatment of necessity with the subject-matter of the *Syllabus* and with the ethical realism that Royce discovered there. It is a thesis that anticipates the *kind* of metaphysics that Dewey would eventually be compelled to work out as background for his ethical naturalism. It attacks the notion of objects as fixed essences and of knowledge of objects in terms of such essences. Dewey argues that the process of knowing an object is a matter of developing judgments that progressively change the "value" of the object. He argues that our epistemological concern is not, and cannot be, with the object in itself, but rather with the known object. In conclusion, he states that: "If this be so, truth, however it be metaphysically defined, must attach to late rather than to early judgments" (*EW*4:22). It is significant that Dewey acknowledges that the topic of his essay was suggested by an earlier article by Peirce. And it is equally significant that he also points out that "my thought takes finally a different turn" (*EW*4:19).

He begins by alluding to all sorts of old ideas that stand in the way of progress, to superstitions that have become obstructions. He wants to show that the doctrine of necessity is just such an unwanted survival, a holdover from an earlier, less developed period of knowledge that must somehow be eradicated because it has become an almost intolerable burden, one that tends to paralyze science. He then suggests that we can rid ourselves of this burden by realizing that necessity has no reference to objective things or events, and that it comes into play only in regard to the development of judgment. He argues that strict necessity is wholly conceptual and never a matter of empirical fact, whether the fact in question is single and isolated, or a whole made up of many particulars. Thus:

All science can ultimately do is to report or describe, to completely state, the reality. So far as we reach this standpoint regarding any fact or group of facts, we do not say that the fact *must* be such and such. There is no necessity attaching to the fact either as a whole or as parts. *Qua* whole, the fact simply is what it is; while the parts, instead of being necessitated either by one or another or by the whole, are the analyzed factors constituting, in their complete circuit, the whole. In stating the whole, we, as of course, state all that enters into it; if we speak of the various elements as *making* the whole, it is only in the sense of making it *up*, not of causing it. The fallacy of necessitarian theory consists in transforming the determinate in the sense of the wholly defined, into the sense of something externally made to be what it is. [*EW*4:20]

What Dewey wants to show is that we arrive at the notion that any particular event has been "necessarily" caused owing to the fact that we always begin our search for an explanation of the event by considering "fragments" of information, "piecing together these fragments" until, by "transformation of them" in new combinations, "the recognition of the unity begins to dawn upon us." We have then, Dewey says, reached the stage at which judgment enters; what was simply a collection of independent facts we now judge to be held together by "necessary" ties that account for the event as a whole. The only necessity is that pursuant to the judgment that the event has thereby been accounted for; but the explanation has not so much been "discovered" as "produced" by the process of inquiry. The character of "necessity," therefore, is "purely teleological" and "contingent."

In this Dewey is not far from the controversial opening statements of *Experience and Nature,* still thirty years in the future. He is arguing that we can have no knowledge of the antecedently real, that known objects and events are not, and never can be, thoroughly independent of the knower. He is arguing, of course, in the vein of Peirce's fallibilism, but with his own metaphysical twist. The following passage reveals his relationship both to Peirce's view and to the position of conventional idealism:

There are certain points upon which there is now *practical* agreement among all schools. What one school has got at by a logical analysis of science, another school has arrived at by the road of a psychological analysis of experience. What one school calls the unity of thought and reality, another school calls the relativity of knowledge. The metaphysical interpretation further given to these respective statements may be quite different, but, so far as they go, they come to the same thing: that objects, *as known,* are not independent of the process of knowing, but are the content of our judgments. One school, indeed, may conceive of judgment as a mere associative or habitual grouping of sensations, the other as the correlative diversification and synthesis of the self; but the practical outcome, that the "object" (anyway as known) is a form of judgment, is the same. This point being held in common, both schools must agree that *the progress of judgment is equivalent to a change in the value of objects*—that objects as they are for us, as known, change with the development of our judgments. If this be so, truth, however it be metaphysically defined, must attach to late rather than to early judgments. [*EW*4:21–2]

Dewey is here responding to the *metaphysical* implications of Peirce's fallibilism, not just the doctrine itself. But where Peirce was concerned with the implications of tychism associated with the theory that evolution takes place by fortuitous variation—which he called, somewhat confusingly, "tychasm"—Dewey, as he himself says, takes a different turn. For Dewey is concerned to show that *all* judgment is practical, that there is no gulf between intellectual and practical judgment, and therefore that all judgment is, in effect, value judgment.

He tries to do this by showing that the notion of necessity is imported into judgment to serve a teleological purpose, that it is simply a way of acknowledging the relationship between a given end and the means by which it is produced. He thus introduces into the discussion the very notion of ends–means relations that is central to his logic and metaphysics throughout his life, and that connects them with his ethics and aesthetics. Moreover, the way in which he does so does not merely suggest the direction that his future work will take; rather, it amounts to a preliminary sketch of the entire ground-map of the province of criticism that he continued to work on for the rest of his life:

The practical value, the fruit from the tree, we pick out and set up for the entire fact so far as our past action is concerned. But so far as our *future* action is concerned, this value is a result *to be* reached; it is an end to be attained. Other factors, in reality all the time bound up in the one concrete fact or individual whole, have now to be brought in as means to get this end. Although after our desire has been met they have been eliminated as accidental, as irrelevant, yet when the experience is again desired their integral membership in the real fact has to be recognized. This is done under the guise of considering them as means which are necessary to bring about the end. Thus the idea of the circumstances as external to the "fact" is retained, while we get all the practical benefit of their being not external but elements of one and the same whole. Contingent and necessary are thus the correlative aspects of one and the same fact; conditions are accidental so far as we have abstracted a fragment and set it up as the whole; they are necessary the moment it is required to pass from this abstraction back to the concrete fact. Both are teleological in character—contingency referring to the separation of means from end, due to the fact that the end having been already reached the means lost their value for us; necessity being the reference of means to an end *which has still to be got.* Necessary means *needed;* contingency means no longer required— because already enjoyed. [*EW*4:29]

In another passage he tries to show "how completely necessity and chance are bound up with each other." He argues that chance, or accident, is not a matter of ignorance but of relationship: "Chance, in other words, stands for irrelevancy as the matter at first presents itself to consciousness; necessity is the required, but partial negation of this irrelevancy. Let it be complete, instead of partial, and we have the one real activity defined throughout. With reference to this reality, conditions are neither accidental nor necessary, but simply constituting elements—they neither may be nor must be, but just are" (*EW*4:33). With respect to explanatory hypotheses and predictions, Dewey finds both symmetry and a certain asymmetry. The symmetry consists in the supreme importance that we attach to our practical interests and the correlation of means and ends with causes and effects. The asymmetry consists in the difference between past and future, and the fact that necessity can no longer be viewed as equivalent to fixed uniformities in nature. Thus:

The effect is the end, the practical outcome, which interests us; the search for causes is but the search for the means which would produce the result. We call it "means and end" when we set up a result to be reached in the future and set ourselves upon finding the causes which put the desired end in our hands; we call it "cause and effect" when the "result" is given, and the search for means is a regressive one. In either case the separation of one side from the other, of cause from effect, of means from end, has the same origin: a partial and vague idea of the whole fact, together with the habit of taking this part (because of its superior practical importance) for a whole, for a fact. [*EW*4:36]

Dewey closes the essay with the hope that "this discussion has not been irrelevant, but the sure basis for going further" (*EW*4:36).

That this *is* such a basis has been the thesis of this chapter. The account of philosophical necessity sketched here introduces a theme that Dewey pursues for the rest of his life. It is the basis for his reconstruction of both idealism and empiricism, of the traditions in logic and metaphysics handed down from both Kant and Mill. And, in the immediate context, it is the basis on which Dewey began his reconstruction of the pragmatism that he was encountering in the writings of Peirce and James. It shows how different Dewey's conception of philosophy is from that of either of his predecessors. In the chapter that follows I shall address those differences and argue that an understanding of them is critical for the interpretation of the character of pragmatism as Dewey conceived it.

CRITICAL BIBLIOGRAPHY

The letter of Dewey to Sidney Hook from which the opening of this chapter quotes is one of a considerable number deposited by Hook in the Special Collections division of the Morris Library at Southern Illinois University. This library also contains the collection of Dewey's papers assembled by his widow, Roberta, and letters from Dewey that are among collections of papers of a number of Dewey's correspondents, including James H. Tufts, Henry N. Wieman, Paul Weiss, George S. Counts, Edward S. Ames, and Joseph Ratner. Since Dewey did not usually retain copies of his own letters, these collections are a significant source of otherwise unobtainable material on Dewey's development, a source concerned mostly with developments of the Chicago period and later.

The only extensive philosophical correspondence available is that between Dewey and Arthur F. Bentley, a comprehensive selection from which was put together by Sidney Ratner, Jules Altman, and James Wheller in *John Dewey and Arthur F. Bentley, A Philosophical Correspondence, 1932–1951* (New Brunswick: Rutgers University Press, 1964). It is a rich source for understanding how Dewey interpreted his own work. The letter quoted at the beginning of this chapter indicates, for example, that he viewed language both as behavior and as artifact. This suggests that he saw language as both natural in origin and artifactual in at least some of its applications. This insight, if correct, can be of considerable help in interpreting the theory of communication linking his philosophy of logic with his existential metaphysic.

The most complete account of Dewey's early years is given by Neil Coughlan in *The Young John Dewey* (Chicago: University of Chicago Press, 1975). Coughlan relies heavily on earlier research done by Dykhuizen and Lewis S. Feuer, both of whom published articles on the early years in *The Journal of the History of Ideas* in the late 1950s. Coughlan allows himself to be side-tracked by his interest in George Herbert Mead, eventually ascribing to Mead the greater influence on the course of American philosophy, but his account of the Dewey–Mead relationship in the early 1890s is extremely useful. Coughlan also gives us an account of Dewey's relationship with James R. Angell, son of Michigan's president, James B. Angell. The younger Angell was Dewey's student at Michigan, worked with Mead, and later joined them as a faculty member at Chicago. Their joint work in physiological psychology clearly forms the basis for Dewey's important 1896 essay on "The Reflex Arc Concept in Psychology" (*EW*5:96–109). Among Angell's papers, collected and deposited in the Sterling Library at Yale University, is a letter that Dewey wrote to Angell, who was then studying at Harvard with James, that he was ready to abandon the psychological standpoint that he had adopted from Morris. Thus the basic concept of the reflex "circuit" was already part of Dewey's thinking as early as 1891. It is also, in my view, the Dewey–Mead–Angell relationship that explains the introduction of the new course at Michigan in the spring term of 1892, in which science becomes the method of philosophy, thus replacing the method of psychology.

A very different account of Dewey's development is given by Morton G. White in his Columbia Ph.D. dissertation subsequently published as *The Origins of Dewey's Instrumentalism* (New York: Columbia University Press, 1943). Although White's account has never been seriously challenged, I regard it as defective in its failure to give adequate weight to Dewey's involvement in the work of Mead and Angell. The latter were not, as Dewey had been, under Morris's influence; they were simply trying to be scientific experimenters. They had none of Dewey's debts to mentors such as G. Stanley Hall, who, along with Morris, represented the establishment view in psychology. White fails to account for the rather abrupt change in Dewey's thought after Mead's arrival at Michigan, a change that cannot be fully explained by Morris's departure. I view the introduction of Course 5 as indicative of the naturalistic standpoint and vocabulary that Dewey had adopted at that point and that he would henceforth articulate. White's failure, later on, to grasp the connections between Dewey's philosophy of logic and the kind of ethics that he developed, beginning with the *Syllabus* of 1894, is no doubt due to his misreading of this early stage in Dewey's development (see White's essay on "Valuation and Obligation in Dewey and Lewis," in his *Pragmatism and the American Mind,* cited in the bibliography for Chapter One). I shall be commenting on White's criticism of Dewey's 1938 *Logic* in Chapter Five.

In my view, Sidney Hook's Columbia Ph.D. dissertation on Dewey's early philosophy, published as *The Metaphysics of Pragmatism* (Chicago: Open Court, 1927), is much more valuable than White's, although it has been less often cited in the literature. It was done under Dewey and bears his endorsement in an Introductory Word, and Hook has the advantage of close acquaintance with Dewey's work during the period in which Dewey was expanding his 1922 Carus Lectures into *Experience and Nature* of 1925. Even though, unlike White, he was writing before the publication of *Logic,* he surely comes closer to an understanding of the "metaphysics of the instrument," as he calls it, than White ever does.

Brief accounts of Dewey's early development are given by Elizabeth Flower, in *A History of Philosophy in America,* and Lewis Hahn, in the *Guide to the Works* (both cited in the bibliography for Chapter One). I recommend both, although both authors seem to have accepted White's account without serious criticism and to have accepted White's view that Dewey remained an unreconstructed idealist throughout his years at Michigan, and both undervalue the impact of Mead and Angell on Dewey's thinking. It is a feature of both accounts, too, that the influence of James on Dewey from 1890 is stressed, but that of Peirce is neglected, a matter to which I shall return in Chapter Three.

Coughlan, Flower, and Hahn, along with Dykhuizen, all give their own versions of Dewey's religious commitments and theological views during the early period. There has been much speculation about just when it was that Dewey turned his back on Christianity. The assumption that this is what happened, of course, implies that at some point he was a Christian. There may be room for doubt about this, however. If Eastman got Dewey's story right, Dewey may not have believed in the Christian God at all after leaving his teens. (The Oil City experience occurred, after all, when Dewey was either twenty or twenty-one.) Harry M. Campbell, in *John Dewey* (New York: Twayne, 1971), maintains that Dewey dropped Christianity suddenly in the middle of his years at Michigan

(1884–94), citing a change between his 1884 address to the Student Christian Association (*EW*1:61–3) and his 1893 talk to the Ministerial Band (*EW*4:365–8). In my opinion, it takes a good deal of imagination to see much change between the two. Even in 1884 Dewey was employing the word *God* for the Hegelian all-unifying World Spirit, rather than the Absolute Idea. By 1893 it is clear that Dewey is trying to portray Christianity as an important institutional and historical force, but one that is more than a little anachronistic; thus: "The function of the church is to universalize itself, and thus pass out of existence" (*EW*4:367). Campbell denounces Dewey for his early "apostasy," and berates him for his disloyalty to his mother. John Blewett, S.J., in an essay which he contributed to the volume that he edited on *John Dewey: His Thought and Influence* (New York: Fordham University Press, 1960), takes a more sympathetic viewpoint, arguing that Dewey early on realized that he could not accept the fundamentalism of his parents, and that he was working out a way of dealing with his relationship with them during the years that they lived with Dewey and his wife at Ann Arbor. He regards Dewey's problem as one of conflict between supernaturalism and science, a conflict that Dewey tried to resolve by collapsing his religious concerns into a fervent defense of democracy.

That Dewey, during the Michigan years, was becoming ever more concerned with economic, social, and political matters is evident. Lewis Feuer brings this out very clearly in his article on "John Dewey and the Back to the People Movement in American Thought," *Journal of the History of Ideas,* vol. 20, no. 4 (1959): 545–68. Feuer's research is used by Coughlan in his dramatic account of Dewey's involvement with Franklin and Corydon Ford and the abortive plan to publish at Michigan a periodical called *Thought News*. Although that plan was stillborn, its conception shows Dewey's early interest in applying philosophical insights to practical and political matters. Feuer's research shows that Wayne A. R. Leys is not quite correct when he states, in his introduction to volume 4 of the *Early Works,* that the "publicist and social critic" of the "Roaring Twenties and the Threadbare Thirties" was not evident in the John Dewey of 1893 (*EW*4:ix).

3: *The Logic of Experience*

*I*n April of 1905 Dewey wrote to Peirce complimenting him on his recently published essay entitled "What Pragmatism Is." Peirce wrote back that he was pleased but puzzled by Dewey's praise, explaining that Dewey's conception of logic as set forth in the 1903 *Studies* "certainly forbids all such researches as those which I have been absorbed in for the last eighteen years. That is what I like least in those four papers." Peirce had reason to be puzzled. He was well aware of the fact that Dewey's logic of experience, if pursued, would undermine the very foundations of the system that he had been trying to construct for those last eighteen years.[1]

The essay that gave rise to Dewey's letter announced Peirce's farewell to the term *pragmatism,* which he had "invented," as he put it, to "formulate the theory that a *conception,* that is, the rational purport of a word or other expression, lies exclusively in its conceivable bearing upon the conduct of life."[2] Finding the term as used by James and F. S. C. Schiller to have vastly outgrown its original purpose, Peirce now proposed to "kiss his child good-bye and relinquish it to its higher destiny." In its place, to "serve the precise purpose of the original definition," Peirce announced the birth of the word *pragmaticism,* which, he said, "is ugly enough to be safe from kidnappers." The essay concluded with an elucidation of what Peirce had intended by the original definition, together with the new intention of submitting a "proof that the doctrine is true." This proof, he went on to say, "would essentially involve the establishment of the truth of synechism."[3] But it was this doctrine, Peirce recognized, that would be undermined by Dewey's logic of experience.

Peirce had given a tentative formulation of synechism in his essay on "The Law of the Mind," a sequel to the essay on "The Doctrine of Necessity" that had stimulated Dewey's response in "The Superstition of

Necessity." In that essay, the first in which the term appears, synechism was invoked to explain how the several elements of Peirce's developing system hang together. It united Peirce's logical realism with his objective idealism, and the tychism of objective chance "with its consequent thoroughgoing evolutionism."[4] In "What Pragmatism Is," Peirce elaborates the point that synechism is intended to connect the real—which he defines as "being as it is regardless of what you or I may think about it"—with what is "destined" to be believed as a consequence of the continuity of experimental inquiry. He wants to show that the real is a physically efficient constraint on the direction and process of inquiry. Thus synechism was to vindicate Peirce's long-standing commitment to "Scotistic realism," as he styled it, which held to the fixed reality of general objects (universals), by linking that realism to his objective idealism through the process of evolutionary development. It is a process, he says, "whereby the existent comes more and more to embody those generals which were just now said to be destined." It would replace the Hegelian dialectical process with "evolutionary love," a feature that Peirce himself recognized as meaning that synechism is "closely allied to the Hegelian absolute idealism."[5]

Now, responding to Dewey's compliments, Peirce complains that Dewey's logical theory, when adopted, as Dewey proposed, to the exclusion of all other methods, is intolerant. He concludes on a chastening note, and with a reminder to Dewey of what the doctrine of synechism entails: "The first maxim of my 'Synechism' runs: 'Let us not precide our conclusions beyond what our premises definitely warrant.' What you had a right to say was that for certain logical problems the entire development of cognition and along with it that of its object became pertinent, and therefore should be taken into account. What you do say is that no inquiry for which this development is not pertinent should be permitted."[6] Peirce was right about what Dewey had said in the *Studies in Logical Theory:* Dewey was trying to block the road that Peirce was traveling, whether he had a right to do so or not.

At that stage, Dewey may not have been entirely clear as to just how Peirce would get his final system together. What he *was* clear about, however, was that Peirce's version of logical realism would not work. What was at issue between Dewey and Peirce was a matter that Peirce identified as of extreme importance, and rightly so. Dewey had been arguing that all those who think of formal logic as somehow normative for scientific method are guilty of imposing apart thought on experiential materials, to which it does not belong. In the *Studies* he had argued that logical norms are to be derived from the procedures of science, a thesis that Peirce was correct in seeing as intolerant of his own methods. For it was central to Peirce's conception that the function of philosophy is to set the stage for science, clear away the "metaphysical rubbish," and, by means of logical analysis, make explicit the criteria for proof. For Peirce, then, logic is a normative science, a self-correcting discipline involving the self-discipline of thought itself. Its normative rules, therefore, are not to be derived from science, as Dewey was maintaining. As Peirce was quick to see, Dewey was already at work on the reconstruction of pragmatism, almost before he had applied for enrollment in the school or been accepted by the membership.

Evidence that Dewey had been accepted, at least on a probationary basis, is contained in a letter of 1903 from James to Schiller. Basing his acceptance on the same *Studies in Logical Theory* that Peirce would criticize for its intolerance, James, with typical enthusiasm, wrote to Schiller of the emergence "under Dewey's inspiration" of "a flourishing school of radical empiricism."[7] Later in the same year James wrote of the Chicago school as "splendid stuff, and Dewey is a hero. A real school and real thought."[8] By the time he published his *Pragmatism* in 1907, James was putting references to the *Studies in Logical Theory* and no fewer than four other articles by Dewey at the head of his list of references—ahead of his references to Schiller, even—although he was also confessing "that there is no logical connexion between pragmatism, as I understand it, and a doctrine which I have recently set forth as 'radical empiricism.' The latter stands on its own feet. One may entirely reject it and still be a pragmatist."[9]

Why this dramatic difference of opinion over the 1903 *Studies*? Why was Peirce ready to condemn as intolerant the very method that James was praising to the skies? Are we to assume that the explanation lies simply in the different personality traits of the two men; that Peirce was simply exhibiting the acerbity for which he was notorious, and James his equally well-known generosity? Or was James, already aware of the approaching rift between himself and Peirce, welcoming Dewey and his Chicago school because they were traveling a different path from Peirce, one heading in the direction of radical empiricism, rather than the pragmatism that Peirce would soon abandon? What are we to make of James's startling assertion that "in America, John Dewey's 'Studies in Logical Theory' are the foundation," even though he went on to credit Peirce with the origin of the term *pragmatism*? Was James a less perceptive reader of the *Studies* than Peirce? Or was he, perhaps, just as perceptive?

In response to such questions, I would say that Dewey was already at work, in the *Studies,* on the project of reconstructing the pragmatism of both Peirce and James. In what follows, I will try to show that Dewey was intolerant not only of Peirce's claims for the doctrine of synechism, but also of James's claims for the doctrine of necessary truths in *The Principles of Psychology*. For Dewey, the necessity of pragmatism rested on neither of these doctrines, but rather on the concept of necessity that he had already set forth in response to Peirce in "The Superstition of Necessity" of 1893. It was this account of the logic of necessity that set Dewey on the path of the genetic method that he subsequently adopted in the *Studies,* that controls his logic of experience and the instrumentalism that emerges from it. Dewey's conception of logic differed from that of Peirce less in terms of how each understood the methods of experimental science than in the ontology each thought those methods to be based on. And Dewey's conception of experience differed from that of James less in terms of ontology than in terms of the relationship between psychology and logic. In the *Studies in Logical Theory* Dewey shows how our logical norms emerge from the process of inquiry and reflect the ontological structures encountered in that process. He demonstrates the emptiness of the ontology of Scholastic realism and shows how completely our experience of the real can account for the success of inference without calling in a priori forms or the supposedly self-evident truths of logical relations. He attacks both Peirce's commitment to an ontology of fixed essences and James's commitment to intuitive necessary truths. We ought to get our logic from our ontology, Dewey maintains, not our ontology from our logic. Nor should we get our logic from psychology, for it is not the psychology of experience that matters, but its logical forms.

Conventional wisdom has it that pragmatism is a philosophy that issued from the joint efforts of Peirce and James. Peirce in the role of logician and James in the role of psychologist join forces to work out the plot, with the help of supporting actors like George Herbert Mead, Friedrich Schiller, and John Dewey. But once Dewey is seen to have been reconstructing pragmatism virtually from the outset, changes in role are inevitable. For in Dewey's reconstruction the role of psychologist is as often played by Peirce as by James, and the role of logician as often by James as by Peirce. I shall begin with Peirce in order to show that what Dewey appropriated from Peirce was psychological rather than logical and shall then turn to James to show that what Dewey took from James was as often as not logical as psychological.

Peirce, according to Dewey's reckoning, always conceived of logic using the formalist model, redolent of logic's Aristotelian and Kantian origins. This model takes for granted the distinction between the formal analysis of conceptual materials and the synthesis involved in associative sense experience. It is this distinction that accounts for the purely formal character of the Aristotelian syllogistic, in which logic deals exclusively with objects by means of their concepts, the conceptual nature of an object being taken to be its essential nature and therefore the basis of inference. It is this same distinction that accounts for Kant's theory of the "perfected form of the syllogism," arrived at through the doctrine of a priori forms of intuition, by means of which the phenomenal world of appearance is rendered intelligible to pure reason. It is this remnant of formalism that remains as an element in Peirce's logic—even after Peirce abandoned the syllogistic Kantian logic of subject-predicate in favor of the logic of relations—that Dewey cannot accept. In a different context and form he had argued against it in his criticism of Venn's logic. He would argue against it yet again in the *Studies,* this time in criticism of Lotze's logic. It was this remnant in Peirce's method of attack on "necessitarianism" in "The Doctrine of Necessity Examined" that stimulated Dewey's attack in "The Superstition of Necessity." Comparison of the two quickly exposes their differences.[10]

Peirce's article is a powerful attack on the necessitarian doctrine that all natural events are subject to the reign of universal and absolute law. He begins with an argument designed to show that the order of nature cannot simply be postulated as necessary unless the necessity implied is either "provisional" or such that it would "present itself in experience." Since experience itself is provisional, the only valid claim that can be made is contingent on its being denied by "possible experience." Peirce then goes on to considerations of the evidence of the sciences, which, one after another, point to chance as a genuine feature of nature—the feature that he elsewhere calls "tychism."

What is not questioned in Peirce's article is the origin of the concept of necessity. What Peirce seems to assume is either that the idea of necessity is a priori in something like the Kantian sense, or that it is analytic. Since he excludes it as a postulate in inductive reasoning that would allow inductions to produce certitude—and therefore a kind of naturalistic determinism in the natural sciences—it seems likely that he was already thinking of it in terms of the logic of relations and hence as an analytic relation, one that has no part in the synthetic relations stated in scientific conclusions. In any case, the purely formal character of the concept of necessity remains outside Peirce's examination. It never comes under attack, and if it did, it would presumably be defended as essential to Peirce's conception of the relationship of logic to the empirical sciences.

Here it is important to recognize that, although his theories of knowledge went through several stages, at no time did Peirce describe logic as a theory of inquiry. When he makes his attack on the doctrine of necessity, he is clearly applying the theory of inquiry that he had worked out earlier, in the series of six papers in the *Popular Science Monthly,* which included the essays entitled "The Fixation of Belief" and "How to Make Our Ideas Clear."[11] It is this theory, identified as *pragmatism* both conventionally and by James, that I shall call Peirce's doubt–belief theory. For Peirce, logic had little to do with either doubt or belief, or with the process by which the former is resolved into the latter. Logic is part of Peirce's theory of signs, in which it is defined as the relation of signs to their conceptual objects. In other words, Peirce places logic more in the context of what can be thought of as his (semiotic) theory of truth, whereas the doubt–belief theory of inquiry belongs to his (semantic) theory of meaning.

It is in the context of the doubt–belief theory that Peirce can be seen as playing the role of psychologist for Dewey. And the point of Dewey's attack on necessitarianism in "The Superstition of Necessity" is to bring Peirce's doubt–belief theory to bear on the very point that Peirce neglects: the concept of necessity as such, its genesis and its role. The theory was developed in the domain of psychology in the first place, Peirce's goal being to explain the role of human psychology in the evolutionary success of the human organism. Survival, he argues, depends on the capacity of the organism to develop modes of behavior that are at once adapted to the environment and adequate to the satisfaction of organic needs. Peirce called these modes of behavior "habits" and, in the case of the human organism, such habits, when thoroughly engrained, comprise what he calls "beliefs." What he attempts to show is that the possession of beliefs involves the cessation of doubt through transformation of the whole situation of the organism from an initial precarious state into one that is secure. "Inquiry" is defined as the process of transformation, and the most satisfactory method of inquiry will be that which leads to behavior patterns—beliefs—that are most reliable in the long run. Doubt, accordingly, is the initiator of inquiry. Doubt is not just the absence of belief; rather, it is that state of uncertainty as to what to do next that characterizes the existential situation that we sometimes call "anxiety," at other times simply "frustration."

Dewey takes over this pattern of inquiry virtually intact, but he interprets it more liberally than Peirce intended. He reconstructs it into something more than a psychology of inquiry accounting for "fixation of belief." For him it becomes a logic of scientific method. He goes beyond belief to knowledge and the process that he ends up calling, in the *Studies,* the "logic of experience." What Peirce had intended primarily as a psychological adjunct to his logical theory, Dewey turns into the substance of logic itself. Henceforth he would be unable and unwilling to draw any hard-and-fast lines between logic and scientific method; his philosophical logic thus serves as his philosophy of science. Moreover, it also serves as first philosophy in the sense that it occupies for Dewey the role played by metaphysics in classical thought. And he does all this in the context of his attack on "The Superstition of Necessity."

In his critique of Venn's logic, Dewey had already articulated his conviction that the process of knowing is logical throughout, that there is no sharp break between the a posteriori and the a priori, but at that stage he was articulating this conviction in the language of Hegel. In "The Superstition of Necessity" he articulates it in the language of James. The "logical and the practical consideration of necessity," he says there, shows that "logical necessity rests upon teleological" (*EW*4:33). It is this thesis of logic that Dewey derives from James's *Principles of Psychology*.[12]

I have been construing Dewey as already understanding that Peirce would never be able to bring together the two fundamental themes of his philosophy unless he could exorcise the formalist ghost from his conception of logic. I have presented Dewey as already seeing the contradiction between Peirce's tychism and the fallibilism of his doubt–belief theory of inquiry and his contrasting commitment to what he liked to call his "Scotistic Realism" and his conviction that the object of eventual knowledge consists in the "permanent possibility of sensation." According to this construal, Dewey already recognized the flaw in both Peirce's conception of logic and his metaphysics. Stated simply, that flaw was Peirce's implicit commitment to an ontology of fixed essences. That Dewey was already prepared to give up Scholastic logic in all its forms, including the Scotistic one to which Peirce clung, was, at the time, as we have already seen, a consequence of Dewey's reluctance to abandon the one central point of Hegel's logic, the denial of any role to the Kantian a priori element in knowledge that Dewey tagged as "apart thought." Now, in "The Superstition of Necessity," Dewey waxes polemical on this theme, attacking it directly as "a standing still on the part of thought; a clinging to old ideas after those ideas have lost their use, and hence, like all superstitions, have become obstructions" (*EW*4:19). He is taking direct aim at the whole classical and Scholastic doctrine of fixed essences as the foundations of all eventual knowledge; he is attacking the dogma of the analytic-synthetic distinction as a foundational error of both empiricism and neo-Kantian idealism. And he is using a strategy learned from James, a strategy of logical analysis clothed in psychological garb—of conceptual analysis of experience designed to account for the genesis of the notion of fixed essences and a priori forms of intuition.

The strategy was suggested by James in the *Principles* under the heading of "Necessary Truths and the Effects of Experience" (pp. 1215–80). There James attacks not only the Kantian account of the a priori, but that assumed by Spencer as well; both the pure reason doctrine and the "brain structure *cum* frequency of impression" doctrine of associationist psychology are shown to be inadequate in accounting for the relations subsumed under the laws of logic or the systems of classification in mathematics. According to James, the "large body of *a priori* or intuitively necessary truths" are, in general, to be accounted for as "truths of *comparison* only" and as expressing relations "between merely mental terms." He then observes that "nature . . . acts as if some of her realities were identical with these mental terms. So far as she does this, we can make *a priori* propositions concerning natural fact. The aim of both science and philosophy is to make the identifiable terms more numerous. So far it has proved easier to identify nature's things with mental terms of the mechanical than with mental terms of the sentimental order" (p. 1269).

Implied here is the whole strategy of Dewey's argument in "The Superstition of Necessity," and, it can be argued, an outline of Dewey's project in his *Studies in Logical Theory* and *Experience and Nature* as well. For what Dewey took James to mean is that we can account for the origins of our most stable and reliable norms of inquiry without postulating any source other than experience. He was showing that we have no need for what Dewey called "apart thought," that Peirce's doubt–belief theory of inquiry is not only adequate, as Peirce supposed, for grounding a behavioristic theory of meaning, but that the logic of experience is an adequate basis for a theory of truth. Even metaphysics could be seen as a consequence of experience, since in its task of showing both why science is possible and why it is necessary, it could look to science for its norms and procedures. In other words, even metaphysics could be seen as getting its ontology from the experience of inquiry.

James himself, of course, drew no such sweeping conclusions from his account of experience in the *Principles*. He was not yet ready to propose either the epistemology of radical empiricism or the metaphysics of the 1909 treatise, *A Pluralistic Universe*. While the *Principles* contains a remarkable number of hints at both this later epistemology and later metaphysics, James digs in his heels on the matter of necessary truths. Earlier in the

Principles, in his treatment of reasoning, he had pointed to the fallacy of thinking of the essence of a thing as something that is fixed and immutable, of thinking that "a thing's essence makes it *what* it is" (p. 960). He had credited Locke with trying to lay this fallacy to rest: "Locke undermined the fallacy. But none of his successors, so far as I know, have radically escaped it, or seen *that the only meaning of essence is teleological, and that classification and conception are purely teleological weapons of the mind.* The essence of a thing is that one of its properties which is so *important for my interests* that in comparison with it I may neglect the rest" (p. 961).

Now, this time with respect to necessary truths, James succumbs to the temptation to "flourish the name of the immortal Locke" again. Such truths are not, as Dewey would argue, the a posteriori consequences of experience; nor are they, like concepts of essence, the "teleological weapons of the mind." Rather, they are both a priori and the fixed meanings that the mind discovers by examining its own contents—not apart thought, perhaps, but still not what can be obtained by a process of abstraction from experience. They are, by contrast, *purely* abstract, a sense of "abstract" that James holds, indifferently, as intuitive or innate (p. 1255).

In what must be one of the strangest turns ever taken by a philosopher in defense of the a priori status of logical forms, James invokes a passage of Locke's "fourth book" that offers an alternative to the doctrine of innate ideas as an explanation of how we acquire general knowledge. Here is a portion of Locke's text as quoted by James:

> All general knowledge lies only in our own thoughts, and consists barely in the contemplation of our own abstract ideas. Wherever we perceive any agreement or disagreement amongst them, there we have general knowledge; and by putting the names of those ideas together accordingly in propositions, can with certainty pronounce general truths. . . . What is once known of such ideas will be perpetually and for ever true. So that, as to all general knowledge, we must search and find it only in our own minds, and it is only the examining of our own ideas that furnish us with that. Truths belonging to essences of things (that is, to abstract ideas) are eternal, and are to be found out by the contemplation only of those essences. [p. 1256]

It is not that James fails to acknowledge Locke's distinction between mental truth and real truth, or even that he fails to recognize that "logic does not say whether Socrates, men, mortals, or immortals *exist.*" It is rather that he uses Locke's account of abstract ideas as drawn from experience in defense of his own "nativist" account of the a priori, not noticing, it appears, that in his own genetic account, the teleological weapons of the mind would have done for the eternal verities what they had done for fixed essences.[13]

In any event, it was not James's account of the a priori forms of thought that impressed Dewey. It was James's account of experience, which he saw as providing for the kind of logic of necessity that he himself made the central contention of "The Superstition of Necessity," the conception of the logical connections that we regard as necessary arising *"as needed"* during the course of inquiry. The account of experience offered by James in the *Principles* was precisely what Dewey had needed all along—a viable alternative to the traditional bifurcation between the realism of the Scholastics and the idealism that he was trying to leave behind. Dewey saw that James's account avoided the subjectivism that characterized the psychologistic logics which he had been criticizing. He saw, too, that it avoided the inevitable dualism that he regarded as the fatal flaw in the empiricist logics descended from Mill and that he had rejected in his analysis of Venn's logic. It may not be going too far to say that Dewey saw in James's account of experience the way out of the blind alley of the so-called problem of induction, a way he began to map in the *Studies in Logical Theory,* for already in James's text a preliminary sketch of that map can be found in the account of our experience of "natural kinds."

In James's treatment of the capacity of the organism to perform the function of comparison involved in "judging, predicating, or subsuming," there are texts that provide for just the ontology of logic toward which Dewey was groping: "Comparisons result in groups of like things; and presently (through discrimination and abstraction) in conceptions of the *respects* in which the likenesses obtain. The groups are *genera* or *classes,* the respects are *characters* or *attributes.* The attributes again may be compared, forming genera of higher orders, and their characters singled out; so that we have a new sort of series, *that of predication, or of kind including kind"* (p. 1242).

Again, in a text that reaches even further into the ontology of a natural science, into the objects and relations of nature:

> This world *might* be a world in which all things differed, and in which what properties there were were ultimate and had no further predicates. In such a world there would be as many kinds as there were separate things. We could never subsume a new thing under an old kind; or if we could no consequences would follow. Or, again, this might be a world in which innumerable things were of a kind, but in

which no concrete thing remained of the same kind long, but all objects were in a flux. Here again, though we could subsume and infer, our logic would be of no practical use to us, for the subjects of our propositions would have changed whilst we were talking. In such worlds, logical relations would obtain, and be known (doubtless) as they are now, but they would form a merely theoretic scheme and be of no use for the conduct of life. But our world is no such world. It is a very peculiar world, and plays right into logic's hands. [p. 1246]

But the text goes on to show that logical inference is not mere psychologism masquerading as logistic, and that no genetic fallacy is involved in deriving the norms of inference from experience, in their being learned norms, rooted in trial and error:

Some of the things, at least, which (the world) contains are of the same kind as other things; *some* of them remain always of the kind of which they once were; and some of the properties of them cohere indissolubly and are always found together. *Which* things these latter things are we learn by experience in the strict sense of the word, and the results of the experience are embodied in "empirical propositions." Whenever such a thing is met with by us now, our sagacity notes it to be of a certain kind; our learning immediately recalls that kind's kind, and then *that* kind's kind, and so on; so that a moment's thinking may make us aware that the thing is of a kind so remote that we could never have directly perceived the connection. [pp. 1246–7]

It is from texts like these that Dewey drew the conception of logic that drives the argument in "The Superstition of Necessity" and that provides the scaffolding of the *Studies in Logical Theory* of 1903.

But more than James's influence is needed to account for the conception of logic that emerges in the *Studies in Logical Theory*, as we shall now see, and neglect of this fact flaws many an account of Dewey's development between 1890 and 1903 (see the critical bibliography to this chapter for examples).

By 1906, when he delivered his presidential address to the American Philosophical Association at Cambridge, Dewey had already put together James's vocabulary of characters and kinds and Peirce's doubt–belief theory of inquiry:

Beliefs look both ways, towards persons and toward things. . . . They form or judge—justify or condemn—the agents who entertain them and insist upon them. They are of things whose immediate meanings form their content. To believe is to ascribe value, impute meaning, assign import. The collection and interaction of these appraisals and assessments is the world of the common man,—that is, of man as an individual and not as a professional being or class specimen. Thus things are characters, not mere entities; they behave and respond and provoke. In the behavior that exemplifies and tests their character, they help and hinder; disturb and pacify; resist and comply; are dismal and mirthful, orderly and deformed, queer and commonplace; they agree and disagree; are better and worse. [*MW*3:83]

But it is a reconstruction of Peirce and James, as is also evident. For, Dewey goes on to say, it is by means of beliefs that characters are changed as well as comprehended. Characters are not only the means employed by understanding to regulate life's choices, to make judgments; they are also transfigured in the process.

Thus the human world, whether or no it have core and axis, has presence and transfiguration. It means here and now, not in some transcendent sphere. It moves, of itself, to varied incremental meaning, not to some far off event, whether divine or diabolic. Such movement constitutes conduct, for conduct is the working out of the commitments of belief. That believed better is held to, asserted, affirmed, acted upon. The moments of its crucial fulfillment are the natural "transcendentals"; the decisive, the critical, standards of further estimation, selection and rejection. That believed worse is fled, resisted, transformed into an instrument for the better. Characters, in being condensations of belief, are thus at once the remainders and prognostications of weal and woe; they concrete and they regulate the terms of effective apprehension and appropriation of things. This general regulative function is what we mean in calling them characters, forms. [*MW*3:83–4]

Dewey was already building his theory of values into his theory of knowledge, his metaphysics and ontology, his theory of the individual and society. The address concludes: "But beliefs are personal matters, and the person, we may still believe, is social. To be a man is to be thinking desire; and the agreement of desires is not in intellectual conclusion, but in the sympathies of passion and concords of action:—and yet significant union in affection and behavior may depend upon a consensus in thought that is secured only by discrimination and comparison" (*MW*3:100).

The amalgam of affection and behavior as contingent on consensus in thought is what Peirce had called "community welding." But in making it clear that such a consensus is obtained only by discrimination and comparison, Dewey was invoking a concept of logic drawn from James. He was invoking the notion of "kinds" and of "that kind's kind" which James had said that we learn by experience. Dewey was not arguing that "fifty thousand Frenchmen can't be wrong." He was arguing that value appraisals and judgments are every bit as empirical and objective as factual estimates and the conclusions of science. He was arguing that what James referred to as the "sentimental order" is as much a matter of natural fact as is the mechanical. He was offering the logic of experience as a basis of social science—and social hope.[14]

During the decade from 1894 to 1904, Dewey served the University of Chicago in the triple role of head of the departments of philosophy, psychology, and pedagogy. The joint appointment was apt recognition of Dewey's flourishing reputation in all three fields, and the relative youth of the university rendered the task of administering three departments within the capacity of one individual. Moreover, in the standard academic curricula of the period, all three subject-matters were closely related. Dewey's assignment was to develop all three areas, to recruit faculty and students, and to put the new university on the map in terms of academic standing. His success in carrying out this assignment was remarkable, even taking into account the relatively munificent character of the new institution.

Dewey's appointment to Chicago was urged on its president, William Rainey Harper, by James H. Tufts, who, along with Mead, had been recruited to the Michigan faculty by Dewey in 1891 but had left in 1893 for further study at Freiburg. Tufts had been one of Harper's students in theology at Yale prior to the Michigan appointment, and Harper had brought him to Chicago. In urging Dewey's appointment to President Harper, Tufts stressed Dewey's great productiveness at Michigan and made much of the fact that Dewey could be expected shortly to publish a definitive book on "instrumental logic." That may have been the project which eventually took shape as the *Studies in Logical Theory* of a decade later. For the time being Dewey's work took the form of the writings on education; the founding of the lab school, in which his wife, Alice Chipman Dewey, was also involved; an increasing concern with social problems that brought him into close contact and collaboration with Jane Addams and Hull House; the parenting of his own children; and research in psychology and sociology. In the latter, Dewey worked closely with Mead, whom he had brought to join him at Chicago soon after his own appointment had been secured. It can easily be seen that Dewey's project was carried forward consistently and coherently in addressing the multiple problems of all these areas. For the project involved working out much more than the instrumental logic anticipated by Tufts, much more than his own epistemology and theory of "education as philosophy," as he sometimes put it. He was working out a logic of experience that would bring together the whole diverse multiplicity of problems facing him. He was beginning to work out the conception of philosophy that would allow him—much later, to be sure—to say that he had a system.[15]

In Chicago, as a consequence of his ongoing observation of children, both in the lab school and at home, Dewey was finally ready to offer his own amendment to James's theory of conceptual learning and to bring it into conformity with the logical perspective that he had adopted in his critique of Venn's logic. He did this in a number of papers, the best-known of which is "The Reflex Arc Concept in Psychology," first published in the *Psychological Review* in 1896, a paper that "remained for decades one of the most influential works in the science of psychology," as McKenzie put it.[16]

It builds a bridge between the radical empiricism of James and the pragmatism of Peirce, the two doctrines that James, in 1907, was still maintaining had "no logical connexion" with each other. It is precisely such a logical connection that Dewey had anticipated already in "The Superstition of Necessity" and his Michigan papers on logical matters. For it is the thesis of "The Reflex Arc Concept in Psychology" that the cognitive process does not break down into a duality of stimulus and response, but is a continuous process—not an arc but a full circuit. Dewey uses the same logical argument that he advanced against Venn's duality in logic, now clothed in psychological terms, against the prevailing interpretation of the reflex mechanism supposed to be involved in acquiring knowledge of the external world. He attempts to show that the organism harbors no a priori mechanical reflex mechanisms of its own that would control action and form the basis of belief and habit—no reflexes, in other words, that would signify the organic presence of anything like the Kantian a priori forms of thought—but rather, that all forms of thought are the result of transactions between the organism and its environment. He was thus attempting to purge James's empiricism of its last vestige of subject–object duality by unifying in a continuous and active process of coordination what he finds still disjointed in James's account of mental terms as contrasted with the way nature acts.[17]

Dewey closes his paper on the reflex arc with the suggestion that this bit of psychology has broader implications than he has been able to discuss within the narrow confines of the paper itself:

It is the co-ordination which unifies that which the reflex arc concept gives us only in disjointed fragments. It is the circuit within which fall distinctions of stimulus and response as functional phases of its own mediation or completion. The point of this story is in its application; but the application of it to the question of the nature of psychical evolution, to the distinction between sensational and rational consciousness, and the nature of judgment must be deferred to a more favorable opportunity. [*EW*5:109]

The *Studies in Logical Theory,* of course, was one such opportunity. Others were articles that appear both before and after the reflex arc paper of 1896. In the guise of a discussion of the role of intelligence in the critical development of social institutions, Dewey employed the reflex circuit concept in all his educational writings of the period: earlier in "The Psychology of Infant Language" (1894), later in *The School and Society* (1899); earlier in his review of Lester Ward's *Psychic Factors in Civilization* (1894), later in his "Interpretations of Savage Mind" (1902); earlier in *Interest in Relation to Training of the Will* (1895), later in his presidential address to the American Psychological Association (1899) on the topic of "Psychology and Social Practice."

At the same time Dewey missed no opportunity of applying the concepts of learning theory to topics as wide-ranging as law, ethics, aesthetics, and metaphysics—in papers collected together in the fifth volume of the *Early Works*—and to the development of logic itself. With regard to the latter, two of his writings stand out: a slim volume on *The Significance of the Problem of Knowledge* (1897) and an article entitled "Some Remarks on the Psychology of Number" (1898).[18] In the first, Dewey reviews the history of the problem of knowledge in much the same fashion as he does later in *Quest for Certainty,* arguing that the many misconceptions that have arisen over the years have their genesis in philosophy's perennial tendency to set theory apart from practice, knowledge from action. It is an attack on both idealist metaphysics and the denial of all metaphysics by Comte and his followers, showing how both sides get off on the wrong foot:

The distinctions which the philosophers raise, the oppositions which they erect, the weary treadmill which they pursue between sensation and thought, subject and object, mind and matter, are not invented *ad hoc,* but are simply the concise reports and condensed formulae of points of view and of practical conflicts having their source in the very nature of modern life, and which must be solved if modern life is to go on its way untroubled, with clear consciousness of what it is about. As the philosopher has received his problem from the world of action, so he must return his account there for auditing and liquidation. [*EW*5:5–6]

This essay, first delivered as an address to the Philosophical Club at Michigan, is important in regard to the reflex arc paper, for it includes a response to some of the criticism that had already been directed at the latter and places that criticism in historical perspective.

What Dewey wanted to show is the historical impact on philosophy of the struggle between formalism and reductive behaviorism, how we have oscillated with regard to whether we place the emphasis on structure or function and have usually adopted one to the exclusion of the other in attempting to decipher the conundrum of how knowledge is possible. Dewey would have us start with *de facto* examples in which cognitive structures emerge from action, as needed, to comprise the conceptual furniture of thought. The reciprocal nature of structure and function may then be seen in the application of knowledge in the control of behavior—in action. What Dewey was already responding to in 1897 was the criticism that he was erecting a theory of the psychology of learning that was strictly functionalist in character, a criticism that had been powerfully launched by Tichener from the structuralist camp. Dewey was rejecting the dualism of structure versus function that would continue to plague the social sciences for generations to come, and rejecting it on the basis of the view of the process of inquiry that he had already outlined and would continue to flesh out for the rest of his life. For we meet the thematic content of *The Significance of the Problem of Knowledge* once again in the final chapter of *Logic: The Theory of Inquiry,* "The Logic of Inquiry and Philosophies of Knowledge."

The essay on the psychology of number carries the same theme over into the field of number theory and is important as one of Dewey's rare excursions into the somewhat esoteric regions of the perennial problem of the foundations of mathematics. This 1898 article reiterates and clarifies the thesis as to how numerical concepts are formed that he and James Alexander McLellan had worked out earlier and had published under the title *The Psychology of Number and Its Application to Methods of Teaching Arithmetic* (1895). In it Dewey reaffirms his conviction that formal concepts originate in action, arising always in the context of some problem-solving activity. Thus the number idea has its genesis in the counting process undertaken as a means to some practical end (like the idea of necessity in "The Superstition of Necessity"). Once the *use* of numerical concepts is established—and the value of such use is confirmed—numbers are discovered to have many other uses besides simple enumeration of instances. But such other uses—in the concept of ratio, for example—are made possible only by the abstraction of numerical concepts from the original experience of setting off discrete instances.

Dewey is not arguing that numbers as such are reducible to the activity of counting, but that the formal concept of number arises from an activity instituted to satisfy a need. (He repeatedly uses the example of the need to count the number of horses in a herd.) He does not pretend that he has discovered the foundation of mathematics and elsewhere remarks on the difference between his own work and that undertaken by mathematical theorists:

> Without pretending to a knowledge of numerical theory which I do not possess, I may say that it seems to me that the work done by Gauss is at precisely the opposite pole from that which the educator needs from the psychologist, i.e., Gauss was attempting to reduce to its ultimate simple numerical generalizations the developed mathematical structure. Dr. McLellan and myself were engaged upon a much humbler task of finding out what sort of a mental condition creates a demand for number, and how it is that number satisfied that demand.
> [*EW*5:427–8]

In making this confession Dewey was addressing an earlier criticism of his work with McLellan that had troubled him sufficiently that he wrote a reply to the reviewer, H. B. Fine, a professional mathematician and collaborator with Peirce on matters of formal logic, that was published in *Science* in 1896. In that reply he signaled to Fine that he was perhaps more aware of what was going on in pure mathematics and mathematical logic than Fine had supposed. The reference to Gauss is indeed somewhat surprising, for it is to Karl Friedrich Gauss (1777–1855) that we owe the term *non-Euclidean* as applied to modern geometry. Dewey's point was to make clear that he was not attempting to undermine the structure of higher mathematics, merely that he had worked out his own theory to account for the ultimate origins of its abstract concepts. He was saying that if mathematics has any logical foundations, those foundations are to be found in the logic of experience.[19]

It might be expected that, given all this preparation, the *Studies in Logical Theory* would hold few surprises. Indeed, it is usually assumed that in the *Studies* Dewey was finally pulling together the scattered elements of his thought into something like a systematic theory of knowledge. Such a reading caused James to see in the *Studies* the emergence of a new school of radical empiricism, and Peirce to denounce the book as intolerant of that whole dimension of science with which he was concerned in his response to Dewey—namely, "pure mathematics, dynamics and general physics, chemistry and physiology proper." This same reading of the *Studies* has led two generations of critics to think of Dewey's logic as instrumentalist and his theory of knowledge as functionalist. Nor is there any reason to take exception to this reading, as far as it goes, for the genetic account of thinking that Dewey presents in the *Studies* is clearly in line with the view that "thinking is instrumental to action" and that "structures can be understood only in terms of their functions." But if we think of the *Studies* only in terms such as these, we are likely to miss some of the surprising turns in Dewey's argument.

What I shall offer is a reading which suggests that Dewey was already anticipating the metaphysical perspective that he would set forth in *Experience and Nature,* which evolved from the Carus Lectures of 1922, and that he would continue to work on for the rest of his life. For, once it is recognized that Dewey was intent on reconstructing the philosophy of pragmatism as understood by Peirce or James, then the *Studies* can be seen to entail a concept of metaphysics as well as a theory of inquiry. Looked at from this standpoint, it makes sense to regard Dewey's logic of experience as the foreground against which the background of his metaphysics of existence takes shape. This reversal of grounds is, as I see it, Dewey's distinctive "Copernican Revolution" (*LW*4:229). For what Dewey means is that it is inquiry itself that shapes our concept of 'being,' and not our concept of 'being' that should be allowed to shape our theory of inquiry. He is rejecting the whole idea of metaphysics as foundational to the rest of philosophy; rather, he is reconstructing it as the ground-map of the province of criticism, the background that shows both why inquiry is necessary, and why it is possible.[20]

The fundamental theme running through the four sections of the *Studies* is the contention that thought must be understood as an activity that is undertaken in specific contexts and that has specific kinds of subject-matter, data, meanings, and consequences. And as a counterpoint to this theme is the secondary theme that every specific context and every specific kind of subject-matter, datum, meaning, and consequence is a limiting condition of thought. It is, of course, this secondary theme that delineates the metaphysical perspective and background of the foreground account of the whole thought process. In the first section Dewey examines the subject-matter of thought in order to show that it is rarely thought itself, but the existential situation in all its qualitative uniqueness and cognitive and affective aspects. In the second section he sets forth the conditions of the existential situation that stimulate thought and comprise its effective limits. He wants to show the extent to which the antecedent reality of the situation admits the possibility of transformation of the situation, as well as how far it restricts it. In the third section, "Data and Meanings," Dewey takes up the whole question of the construction and selection of a theory, the problem of transforming immediate experience into meaningful hypotheses and solutions. It is in this section also that he discusses the forms of thought that permit inference and implication. In the final section he considers the "objects of thought"—that is, meanings—as the "means of controlling action" and the "movement of experience" toward the ends of integrated, harmonious experience and effective performance.

In all four sections the considerations taken up are presented as continuous threads in a single fabric, woven into the complex whole of the inquiry process, so that each reinforces the others. Each stage of thought is implicated in every other stage, and it is in this respect that the "organicism" of the Hegelian conception of philosophy reveals itself as a permanent deposit in Dewey's *Studies,* there being no mention of dialectic.

I shall not attempt a detailed recapitulation of the contents of the stages, for, to a considerable extent, they involve reiterations of the several elements that have already been touched on: the character of the problematic situation that both provokes inquiry and gives rise to habits that are transformed, the teleological character of the formal concepts employed in reaching the desired results, the instrumental character of thinking, and the functional character of knowledge. Instead, I shall try to show how Dewey handles the instrumental and functional aspects of his theory in the perspective of the whole. In this way, by concentrating on the theory as a whole, rather than on its constituent details, the gradually emerging ontology on which the theory of logic is based can be seen. Like the ontology from which it emerges, the philosophy of logic that is developed in the *Studies* is unfinished. It is itself in the process of growth toward the mature theory that Dewey would expound thirty-five years later in *Logic: The Theory of Inquiry.* The central themes of the mature theory, however, are unmistakably present.

Indeed, they are stated quite explicitly in the preface, in which Dewey takes the trouble to list the points of agreement shared by the various contributors:

> All agree, the editor takes the liberty of saying, that judgment is the central function of knowing, and hence affords the central problem of logic; that since the act of knowing is intimately and indissolubly connected with the like yet diverse functions of affection, appreciation, and practice, it only distorts results reached to treat knowing as a self-enclosed and self-explanatory whole—hence the intimate connections of logical theory with functional psychology; that since knowledge appears as a function within experience, and yet passes judgment upon both the processes and contents of other functions, its work and aim must be distinctively reconstructive or transformatory; that since Reality must be defined in terms of experience, judgment appears accordingly as the medium through which the consciously effected evolution of Reality goes on; that there is no reasonable standard of truth (or of success of the knowing function) in general, except upon the postulate that Reality is thus dynamic or self-evolving, and, in particular, except through reference to the specific offices which knowing is called upon to perform in readjusting and expanding the means and ends of life. And all agree that this conception gives the only promising basis upon which the working methods of science, and the proper demands of the moral life, may cooperate. All this, doubtless, does not take us very far on the road to detailed conclusions, but it is better, perhaps, to get started in the right direction than to be so definite as to erect a dead-wall in the way of farther movement. [*MW*2:296]

A clearer statement of the radical ontology from which the theory of logic set forth in the *Studies* emerges could hardly be asked for. Reality is always in process and is not fixed in character, which means that judgment is efficacious in the reconstruction and transformation of the real. In specific situations of judgment the "means and ends of life" are thus reconstructed and transformed: no means are permanent, and no ends are absolute. "Knowing" is a thoroughly natural process that emerges from experience and, through judgment, contributes to the natural "evolution of reality." Dewey's commitment to a radical naturalism is as complete as his commitment to a radical empiricism. These are commitments that, as Dewey cautiously suggests in the preface, have a "more ultimate philosophical bearing" than could possibly be exhausted by the *Studies*. Dewey would be working them out for the rest of his life.

It has long been thought that Dewey's contributions to the *Studies in Logical Theory* suffer in clarity for being framed as a running commentary and critique of Lotze's 1874 *Logik,* which had been translated by Bosanquet and published in two volumes in 1888. What has not been recognized is that Dewey's contributions are also framed as a criticism of formal logic as such, that they are directed as much at Peirce's conception of the relation of experience to logic as at Lotze's transcendentalism, that they are a direct attempt to show that what James calls "necessary truths" are among the effects of experience, and, accordingly, that James was mistaken in accepting the Lockean dualism of mental versus real truth. Neither Peirce, in his criticism of Dewey's intolerance, nor James, in his praise of Dewey's radical empiricism, appears to have realized what Dewey was up to. In attacking Lotze's conception of logic, Dewey was attacking the a priori in *all* systems of logic, across the board.

Peirce, in his letter to Dewey, put the whole problem with Lotze's logic this way: "Your reasoning generally is that either Lotze or you must be right, now Lotze isn't, etc. But you in no case, or *one* at most, convince me at all that these are the only alternatives. In short, I think that you could have made a stronger argument if you had let Lotze alone." As Peirce goes on to point out, Lotze's defense of transcendental logic had already been disposed of by Henry Jones, in *A Critical Account of the Philosophy of Lotze,* in 1895. Why then, Peirce asks, did Dewey bother with Lotze? But what Peirce fails to recognize is that Jones criticized Lotze from the standpoint of idealism, whereas Dewey was working out a whole new set of arguments, not only against Lotze, but against idealism and all its metaphysical presuppositions. It is perhaps also worth mentioning that Peirce seems not to have been aware of Frege's attack on Mill's logic in *Die Grundlagen der Arithmetik* (1884), which had seconded Lotze's earlier distinction between the act of thinking and the content of thought. This distinction remained a central thesis of formalist logic as developed by Frege's successors, and was already an integral component of Bertrand Russell's *The Principles of Mathematics,* published in the same year as the *Studies.* It was just this distinction in Lotze's *Logik* that Dewey attacked in the *Studies,* the distinction he later attacked in Russell.[21]

What Dewey was groping for was an account of logic that would avoid both Peirce's formalism and James's psychologism. He was concerned much less with Lotze's version of neo-Kantian transcendentalism than with his running critique of psychologism. For it was in Lotze's critique of empiricist logic that Dewey was searching for flaws that would demonstrate how a more radical empiricism than that of Mill—or of Venn, for that matter—might avoid the necessity of postulating any a priori element in thought at all. Dewey was searching for a way to avoid psychologism—including the version that James had embraced in the final section of the *Principles*—which would simultaneously provide an escape from the logic of transcendentalism. Peirce was right in saying that the method worked out by Dewey was intolerant. It was intolerant not only of synechism, but equally so of James's nativist explanation of logical necessity. It was intolerant of *all* superstition of necessity.

It is a central argument of the *Studies* that instrumentalism is not just a theory of the utility of logical concepts—Lotze had already agreed to that. Dewey argues a deeper-rooted theory of the instrument, one that links the reality of the instrument with the reality of the object. He argues a logic of concepts as emergent from the ontological encounter with the real in the course of experience. He is trying to reverse the accepted order, in which *a priori* forms "legislate" over experience, as Kant put it. He does this by showing how the ontological divorce of thought from its object leaves reason ontologically isolated from its objects. He then shows how this isolation can be overcome by restoring reason and thought to the same ontological plane as objects and things. He argues the case for thought as functioning on the same ontological level as action, and for thinking and acting as continuous events. He shows that thinking is not merely instrumental, as Lotze had conceded, but that it issues in practical knowledge that is ontologically consequential.

What Dewey is arguing against is any theory of inquiry or knowledge that presupposes a hard-and-fast distinction between pure thought and its application; he fully recognizes that Lotze is affirming "the strictly instrumental character of thinking" while holding to the isolated character of pure thought. The problem with such dualistic commitment, Dewey says, lies not with instrumentalism as such, "but in the nature of the instrument." Here is a specimen of the kind of argument that Dewey employs again and again in the *Studies* against the ontological dualism that sets thought on one plane of existence and its objects on another:

I do not question the strictly instrumental character of thinking. The problem lies not here, but in the interpretation of the nature of the instrument. The difficulty with Lotze's position is that it forces us into the assumption of a means and an end which are simply external to each other, and yet necessarily dependent upon each other—a position which, whenever found, is thoroughly self-contradictory. Lotze vibrates between the notion of thought as a tool in the external sense, a mere scaffolding to a finished building in which it has no part nor lot, and the notion of thought as an immanent tool, as a scaffolding which is an integral part of the operation of building, and which is set up for the sake of building-activity which is carried on effectively only with and through a scaffolding. Only in the former case can the scaffolding be considered as a *mere* tool. In the latter case the external scaffolding is *not* the instrumentality; the actual tool is the action of erecting the building, and this action involves the scaffolding as a constituent part of itself. The work of building is not set over against the completed building as mere means to an end; it *is* the end taken in process or historically, longitudinally, temporally viewed. It is no mere accident of language that "building" has a double sense—meaning at once the process and the finished product. The outcome of thought is the thinking activity carried on to its own completion; the activity, on the other hand, *is* the outcome taken anywhere short of its own realization, and thereby still going on. [*MW*2:362–3]

Casting Dewey's metaphor aside, it can easily be seen that Dewey is talking about the ontological status and function of the logical instruments of inquiry, about the ontological continuity of thought and action. He is attacking not merely the epistemological dualism of the empiricist's distinction between perception and conception, which lies at the heart of the correspondence theory; he is also attacking the ontological dualism implicit in the apart thought of the pure theory of logic. It is not enough, he is arguing, to think of the relation between ends and means as merely rational or proportionate, as a purely conceptual relationship; it is an *actual* relationship, ontologically rooted in specific existential contexts and situations.

Dewey's continual emphasis in the *Studies* on the importance of the specific circumstances in which thoughtful deliberation arises has sometimes been taken as indicating little more than reinforcement of his more general contention that the various shifts in the history of thought and culture must be viewed in terms of how the problems being addressed were conceived and defined. It is true that in the *Studies* (and later in *Reconstruction in Philosophy* and *The Quest for Certainty*), Dewey does claim that his genetic method accounts for great changes in the evolution of thought and culture as specific and distinctive responses to alterations in the social and political, as well as intellectual, environment. He argues that these transformational responses represent critical turning points in the history of philosophy which can best be explained in terms of radical shifts in the ways problems are defined and the resultant, equally radical shifts in the ways philosophical answers are sought. But Dewey is not interested in stressing the specific and situational origins of inquiry merely in order to confirm, once again, the doubt–belief theory of inquiry that he shares with Peirce; he wants to show that the whole conceptual apparatus of formal logic can be accounted for by this genetic method, that conceptual relations of the type involved in implication, generalization, and inference are generated during the actual process of inquiry into the specific character of the particular situation that stimulates it. He wants to go deeper into the specific in order to lay bare its generic elements. Inquiry, he says, "seizes upon *certain* specific conditions and factors, and aims to bring them to clear consciousness—not to abolish them." In this process, comparison of "various situations which are antecedent or primary to thought and which evoke it" may yield some common denominator. Inquiry may show how "typical features in the specific antecedents call out diverse typical modes of thought reaction." Finally, inquiry may disclose ways in which the validity of thought is judged: "All the typical investigatory and verificatory procedures of the various sciences indicate the ways in which thought actually brings to successful fulfillment its dealing with various types of problems" (*MW*2:303–4).

Dewey contrasts this procedure with that employed by the epistemological logician, who moves directly to what Lotze calls the "universal forms and principles of thought which hold good everywhere both in judging of reality and in weighing possibility, *irrespective of any differences in the objects.*" This move, Dewey says, "defines the business of *pure* logic." Its results are "not so much either true or false as they are radically meaningless—because they are considered apart from limits." And in a brief passage he goes on to suggest the metaphysical perversity of one who would make such a move, as if to forewarn Bertrand Russell of his folly: "Its results are not only abstractions (for all theorizing ends in abstractions), but abstractions without possible reference or bearing. From this point of view, the taking of something (whether that something be a thinking activity, its empirical stimulus, or its objective goal), apart from the limits of a historic or developing situation, is the essence of *metaphysical* procedure—in that sense of metaphysics which makes a gulf between itself and science" (*MW*2:304–5). For, of course, the problem of meaning and reference—of existential implication—would loom ever larger on the horizon of formal logicians in the years ahead. It would cause Russell to remain a "Platonic Idealist" for years to come and would be a major stumbling block for Peirce, accounting in the end for his failure to complete his final system. Dewey was arguing for the naturalizing of epistemology and metaphysics.

He was urging both logicians and metaphysicians to take their cues from science, instead of continuing their pretext of hegemony over the procedures and laws of scientific discovery.

What Dewey saw was that the specific subject-matters of science—even the particular and individual objects comprising those subject-matters—include common features that constitute important and indispensable limit conditions of inquiry. They are what comprise the subject-matter of taxonomy, the systems of classification that are a necessary ingredient of any science that seeks valid generalization. He was already convinced that what grounds induction and projectibility of knowledge is not to be found in the conceptual material of pure logic as such, any more than it is to be found in Kant's pure reason. Rather, it lies in the specific materials of unique instances insofar as those instances exhibit similarities and differences that can be experienced. He had already taken to heart James's injunction regarding comparison as the clue to the ancient mystery of essence. He was already thinking in James's terms: of natural kinds and of predication as "of kind including kind." And by so doing, it hardly needs pointing out, he was supplying the needed structural element for his functional theory of knowledge and meaning. He was showing that the nature of the instrument must conform to the nature of the object, that the generic features of specific instances are among the limiting conditions of inquiry.[22]

I have been trying to bring out the fact that Dewey rejects the whole idea of thought as constitutive of the limiting conditions of inquiry, which is the linchpin of pure logic, of logic without ontology. What Dewey recognizes in his insistence on specific instances as fundamental to valid inquiry is that the generic character of those instances can easily be seen as a donation of thought, rather than as an emergent property. Indeed, by referring to the "common denominator" of specific instances as a set of "attributes," we may be implicitly conceding that this common denominator is an endowment of thought, rather than a limiting condition imposed on thought by its subject-matter. We may be conceding tacitly that such common properties of the instances comprising a class are the result of our attribution of them to the whole collection, rather than being rooted in the ontological structures of the instances themselves. By denying that such a concession is necessary, that attributes exhibited in common are not extensional facts— his common denominators, in other words—Dewey is denying that they are the products of constitutive thought. In modern parlance we could say that Dewey is committed to the view that attributes and properties of particulars are intensional, in that they can be understood apart from their instantiation, but that there is no reason to think of them as *purely* intensional. For it is a decisive feature of Dewey's claim that intensional meanings are employed successfully only when they are rooted in extensional structures—what he calls the "limiting conditions"—of actual instances. In this, of course, Dewey casts his lot with realism as against idealism. But this realism is a far cry from either Peirce's realism of the permanent possibility of sensation or James's tenacious realism of "The Will to Believe." Where Peirce remains committed to essences as somehow both fixed and universal, despite the presence of chance in the process of evolutionary transformation, Dewey commits himself to a more piecemeal approach. He treats essences as provisional, rather than as permanent, "possibilities of sensation," to use Peirce's phrase. No fixed essences are to be allowed. Thus he veers in the direction of James's pluralism—but without going all the way.[23]

As I have suggested already, James seems to have been committed to the view that the only meaning of essence is teleological. He had characterized essence as a weapon of the mind, as "that one of [a thing's] properties which is so important for my interests that in comparison with it I may neglect the rest" (p. 961). But in Dewey's view, James was thereby flirting with subjectivism and was in danger of conceding that the whole notion of essence is a product of constitutive thought operating idiosyncratically. Indeed, at the point where James succumbs to "The Will to Believe," Dewey would side with Peirce's judgment that James had gone over the edge and had abandoned the method of "science" in favor of that of "tenacity" (see *MW*10:77). Dewey was ready to concede, in the *Studies,* that the emergence of a "common quality" during the course of inquiry into a particular sensory matter is due to its being "selected and set aside *as* present, as immediate" and "as useful for further thought." He is even ready to concede that this common quality that allows generalization is selected precisely because it meets some need that has stimulated inquiry in the first place, although he denies that the selection is merely a matter of expediency or convenience, for it must be made from what is actually there, or "given," to experience. In passages such as the one that follows, Dewey is groping toward a position of scientific realism somewhere between James's tendency toward nominalism and Peirce's Scotistic realism:

> To find out *what is* given is an inquiry which taxes reflection to the uttermost. Every important advance in scientific method means better agencies, more skillful technique for simply detaching and describing what is barely there or given. To be able to find out what can safely be taken as *there,* as given in any particular inquiry, and hence be fruitful

for hypothesis-making, for entertaining of explanatory and interpretive ideas, is one phase of the effort of systematic scientific inquiry. It marks its inductive phase. To take what is discovered to be reliable evidence within a more complex *situation* as if it were given absolutely and in isolation, or apart from a particular historic situs and context, is the fallacy of empiricism as a logical theory. To regard the thought-forms of conception, judgment, and inference as qualifications of "pure thought apart from any difference in objects," instead of as successive dispositions in the progressive organization of the material (or objects), is the fallacy of rationalism. [*MW*2:347]

The apparent circularity of this argument, in which Dewey seems to oscillate between treating evidence as first "given" and then "taken," is actually quite real. That he emphasizes the processive (temporal) character of inquiry, however, mitigates the charge of circularity. As Hilary Putnam has remarked of a similar characteristic of Nelson Goodman's procedures: "This is a circle, or better a spiral, but one that Goodman, like John Dewey, regards as virtuous."[24] Which helps explain, perhaps, why the version of realism that Dewey eventually worked out was as little understood as it was frequently attacked.

Thus the position that Dewey had reached by the time of the publication of the *Studies* was one of transition. His conception of philosophy that was still in the making was "barely there," to borrow Dewey's word for what is given to experience. It is a promissory note, not a finished transaction. This is not to say that Dewey achieved nothing in the *Studies,* however, for it was there that he embarked on the project of reconstruction that would, in the end, involve not only pragmatism, but the conception of philosophy overall. The task of philosophy, as construed in the *Studies,* is neither solely to understand the world nor solely to change it; rather, it is to change it by understanding it.

Joseph Ratner once selected the passage given below, which is from the first section of Dewey's contribution to the *Studies,* in order to illustrate this point.[25] Ratner saw it as signaling a commitment that Dewey would hang on to throughout his career. But it does more than that, for it also suggests how Dewey's conception of philosophy can be of value in tackling many apparently separate and distinct problems.

The value of research for social progress; the bearing of psychology upon educational procedure; the mutual relations of fine and industrial art; the question of the extent and nature of specialization in science in comparison with the claims of applied science; the adjust-ment of religious aspirations to scientific statements; the justification of a refined culture for a few in the face of economic insufficiency for the mass, the relation of organization to individuality—such are a few of the many social questions whose answer depends upon the posses-sion and use of a general logic of experience as a method of inquiry and interpretation. I do not say that headway cannot be made in such questions apart from the method indicated: a logic of experience. But unless we have a critical and assured view of the juncture in which and with reference to which a given attitude or interest arises, unless we know the service it is thereby called to perform and hence the organs or methods by which it best functions in that service, our progress is impeded and irregular. We take a part for a whole, a means for an end; or we attack wholesale some interest because it interferes with the deified sway of the one we have selected as ultimate. A clear and comprehensive consensus of social conviction, and a consequent con-centrated and economical direction of effort, are assured only as there is some way of locating the position and role of each typical interest and occupation. The domain of opinion is one of conflict; its rule is arbitrary and costly. Only intellectual method affords a substitute for opinion. A general logic of experience alone can do for social qualities and aims what the natural sciences after centuries of struggle are doing for activity in the physical realm. [*MW*2:313–4]

Dewey's achievement here is to offer an intellectual method appropriate to a changing world, a world always in transition—in James's words, an "unfinished universe." Or, as Dewey himself put it in the *Studies:* "Philos-ophy, defined as such a logic, makes no pretense to be an account of a closed and finished universe. Its business is not to secure or guarantee any particular reality or value. *Per contra,* it gets the significance of a method" (*MW*2:313).

In the chapters that follow, we shall see how Dewey applied that method.

CRITICAL BIBLIOGRAPHY

I follow the standard practice of citing passages from the *Collected Papers of Charles Sanders Peirce,* hereafter *CSP,* by volume and paragraph numbers; volumes 1–6 are edited by Charles Hartshorne and Paul Weiss, 7 and 8 by Arthur W. Burks. Of the letter to Dewey from Peirce, 8.243–4, Burks writes as follows: "Dewey had written from Columbia University, praising this (*Monist*, 1905) article. The letter, dated 11 April, 1905, is in Widener VB2a. The date of the article and the date of Dewey's letter establish the date of Peirce's letter as c. 1905 (see 239n1)." The letter is conveniently reprinted in *Pragmatic Philosophy*, ed. Amelie Rorty (cited in the bibliography for Chapter One), pp. 118–20.

Few critics have paid much attention to the relationship between Peirce's conception of logic and Dewey's, and unfortunately, Richard Bernstein, who is an exception in that he devotes a substantial section of his *Praxis and Action* to it in "Part III. Action, Conduct, and Inquiry: Peirce and Dewey," (Philadelphia: University of Pennsylvania Press, 1971), neglects Peirce's semiotic and devotes most of his attention to Peirce's theory of inquiry, rather than to the modal logic that Peirce was trying to work out. He is thus able to show a closer relationship between Dewey's instrumentalism and Peirce's philosophy of science than between Peirce's logic proper and Dewey's. By failing to draw attention to Dewey's criticism of Peirce's formalism, he thus appears to have missed the point of the exchange between Dewey and Peirce in 1905. Bernstein merely notes on p. 200 that "One of the sharpest criticisms of Dewey's *Studies in Logical Theory* (1903) was written by Peirce." But Peirce's published review of the *Studies* was much kinder to Dewey than the private correspondence would lead us to expect (see *CSP* 8.188–90, originally published in *The Nation*, 76 [1904]: 219–20). Bernstein goes on to say that "Peirce supplied the intellectual backbone to pragmatism, but Dewey perceived the ways in which Peirce's ideal of a self-critical community of inquirers had important consequences for education, social reconstruction, and a revitalization of democracy" (p. 201). This presents a curious notion of what comprises the intellectual backbone of pragmatism and may reflect Bernstein's opinion that Dewey "lacked Peirce's creative logical genius" (p. 201). In my view, however, it was Dewey's creative logical genius that allowed him to see the flaw in Peirce's conception of logic, the same flaw that he later saw in the Frege–Russell conception.

The best comprehensive treatment of Peirce's several attempts to create a system is that by Murray G. Murphey, *The Development of Peirce's Philosophy* (Cambridge, Mass.: Harvard University Press, 1961). I follow Murphey in his claim that Peirce's doctrine of synechism turns out to be a form of objective idealism and not at all the expression of the Scholastic realism that Peirce wanted. I believe that Dewey began to see Peirce as more idealist than himself after receiving the chastening letter. The charge of intolerance directed at the method of the *Studies* would be echoed later by Russell, as I shall indicate in Chapter Four. For now it is enough to note that Peirce was trying to work out a system of modal logic at the end of his life. That seems to me to be the work of a convinced essentialist, one who conceives of logic very differently from Dewey. Peirce was on a track that would lead him in the direction of the mathematical logic of Russell's *Principia Mathematica*, rather than to a logic of experience. In any case, it is perfectly clear that Peirce never could bring himself to accept James's conception of the meaning of essence.

The letters of William James are quoted from Ralph Barton Perry, *The Thought and Character of William James* (Boston: Little, Brown, 1935), which is still the best source for understanding the relationship between Dewey and James. But John McDermott's collection, *The Writings of William James* (New York: Random House, 1967; also available in a Modern Library edition, 1968), should also be consulted. McDermott's introduction is a superb overview of James and his work. I have used the excellent edition of *The Principles of Psychology* published by Harvard University Press in 1981, the eighth volume in *The Works of William James*, which has two introductory chapters, one by Gerald E. Myers on the philosophical context, the other by Rand B. Evans on the psychological context. In my attempt to untangle James's conception of necessary truths, I have also drawn on conversations with Professor Myers, a long-time colleague. The most useful bibliography of James's work is still that contained in McDermott's collection. Biographies of James are less useful, but those by Gay Wilson Allen—*William James* (New York: Viking, 1967)—and Jacques Barzun—*A Stroll With William James* (New York: Harper and Row, 1983)—are well worth reading. Barzun, in particular, seems to regard James from an angle similar to Dewey's, for he sees clearly that James is not the altogether "tender-minded" thinker he is sometimes taken to be. Barzun stresses James's contention that "the mind is not wholly adrift in experience" but is guided by the sense of "sameness in things" (p. 56), and he takes it that it is this sense that provides the "very keel and backbone of our thinking." This is the very point that Dewey borrowed from James, although Dewey construed it as a point of logic rather than psychology. If we must seek for the backbone of pragmatism, we are more likely to find it here, I think, than, as Bernstein suggests, in Peirce's synechism.

The *Studies in Logical Theory* was published as a joint effort by the members of the Chicago philosophy department, as part of the Decennial Publications of the university. By 1903 the department included not only Mead and James Angell (who had worked with Dewey at Michigan), but

Tufts, A. W. Moore, and E. S. Ames. Two excellent sources for this group's activities and influence are Darnell Rucker, *The Chicago Pragmatists* (Minneapolis: University of Minnesota Press, 1969), and Charles Morris, *The Pragmatic Movement* (New York: Braziller, 1970). A comparable source for the Harvard department is Bruce Kuklick's *The Rise of American Philosophy: Cambridge, Massachusetts, 1860–1930* (New Haven: Yale University Press, 1977).

Dewey's contribution to the 1903 *Studies in Logical Theory* did not, like Hume's radical attack on the conventional wisdom of his day, "fall stillborn from the press." Nevertheless, it failed to stimulate the kind of Copernican revolution that Dewey had envisaged. It encouraged instrumentalism, of course, but that approach to epistemology was already well on its way and scarcely needed any stimulus from Dewey. Pringle-Pattison, for example, thought that Dewey was just "biologizing" logic to accord with popular evolutionary views, missing entirely Dewey's emphasis on the social and ethical implications of the logic of experience ("On Truth and Practice," *Mind,* n.s., vol. 13 [1904], p. 309n). A. K. Rogers raised the question of Dewey's commitment to realism early on ("The Standpoint of Instrumental Logic," *Journal of Philosophy,* vol. 1 [1904], p. 208), and Dewey responded to this and other reviews in "The Postulate of Immediate Empiricism," *Journal of Philosophy,* vol. 2 (1905), (*MW*3:158 ff.). When Dewey's contributions to the *Studies* were reprinted, with additional material, under the new title *Essays in Experimental Logic* (Chicago: University of Chicago Press, 1916), a whole new batch of reviews and criticism ensued. I shall comment on these, in particular Russell's review, in connection with Chapter Four.

It is perhaps significant that the first serious study of the work to concentrate on the ontological roots of the logic of experience was not done until after the first edition of *Experience and Nature* was published in 1925. I refer to Sidney Hook's *The Metaphysics of Pragmatism* (cited in the bibliography to Chapter Two); Hook's treatment is sensitive to the changed role of metaphysics in the *Studies,* and he links it with Dewey's thesis that the logic of judgment is applicable to both science and ethics. It is unfortunate, therefore, that the most frequently cited critical source regarding Dewey's logical development as it culminated in the *Studies* is Morton White's *The Origins of Dewey's Instrumentalism* (also cited in the bibliography for Chapter Two). Originating as a Columbia doctoral dissertation under the supervision of Nagel, it reflects the perspective on Dewey's 1938 *Logic* that Nagel had been expressing in his various reviews of that book made retrospective to the 1903 *Studies*. White does not deal with either the ontology or the metaphysical background of the *Studies*. He treats Dewey's logical development almost entirely in terms of a move from idealism to evolutionism. He does provide a good account of James's influence on Dewey, however, and he does see the import of Dewey's early criticism of James's dualism in the *Principles of Psychology*, concluding that by 1893, "Dewey not only overtakes James but passes him" (p. 107). White clearly understands that by then Dewey was eager to connect ethics and the social sciences. However, he places his remark in the context of Dewey's alleged commitment to functionalism and of Dewey's acceptance of the evolutionary standpoint, thereby failing to grasp that the argument between James and Dewey was not only about psychology, but also about logic and its ontological roots. In this respect he quotes with approval Gordon Allport's comment: "So whole-hearted is his conversion to the functional position that Dewey accuses James of faint-heartedness" (p. 107).

What is perhaps most surprising about White is his failure to see how much Peirce's early work influenced Dewey. He seems to think that Dewey discovered Peirce's work only in 1904. Thus: "I say 1904, because in that year he wrote an article in which he said that some logicians, like Peirce, were interested in showing that logic was an instrument for arriving at warranted assertion" (p. 152). But this is not exactly what Dewey said in that article, in which he lists Peirce, along with his father, Benjamin Peirce, the Italian mathematical logician Peano, and Josiah Royce, under the general heading of "Mathematical Logic." After pointing out the tendency of these logicians to isolate formal logic from experimental inquiry, Dewey says of Peirce: "But, on the other hand, Mr. C. S. Peirce (if I interpret him aright) believes that one of the chief advantages of the mathematical, or symbolic statement is that logic may transcend thereby the limitations of mere formalism and become a potent instrumentality in developing a system which has inherent reference to the pursuit of truth and the validation of belief" (*MW*3:66). Dewey's reference to a system was clearly to Peirce's attempt to work out his doctrine of synechism, which would link the process of inquiry (the "validation of belief") with his modal logic of formal necessity. Given that this is all Dewey says about Peirce, it is hard to see how White gets Dewey's theory of warranted assertion out of this text.

In a recent article on "The Influence of William James on John Dewey's Early Work" (*Journal of the History of Ideas*, vol. 45, no. 3 [1984]: 451–63), Michael Buxton points out that White's thesis neglects any influence that James's writings may have had on Dewey prior to the publication of the *Principles of Psychology* in 1890. He offers evidence from Dewey's work in the 1880s that Dewey, independently of James, was already engaged in the process of reevaluating the psychological standpoint of idealism from the standpoint of biological functionalism. Buxton argues that Dewey held to a transcendental logic even *after* 1890, however, and that he was still trying to justify Hegel's dialectic by means of a Darwinian argument in late 1891 (p. 456). Even in "The Superstition of Necessity" of 1893, in which Dewey is arguing for the centrality of judgment in logic and for "the notion of reconstruction which was to be such a central aspect of his later philosophy," Buxton maintains that Dewey is not responding to either Peirce or James. He even suggests that Dewey used Venn's *Empirical Logic,* rather than the work of William James, to illustrate the idea of judgment as reconstruction (p. 459). In my opinion, of course, Dewey was using James's idea of the teleological concept of essences to reconstruct Peirce's conception of logical necessity and was already announcing his genetic account of logical forms. While Buxton does much to correct White's version of the development of Dewey's philosophical logic, he falls into the same error of neglecting Dewey's relationship to Peirce.

More surprising still, Buxton does not mention the sharp break in Dewey's work after the death of Morris. He fails to make use of Coughlan's account of the impact of Mead's arrival at Ann Arbor, of Dewey's institution of Course 5 in 1892, or of the clearly naturalistic standpoint of the *Syllabus* of 1894. Instead, he focuses almost exclusively on the development of Dewey's functionalism, in both his logical work and his ethics. It is a focus intended to show the origins of Dewey's later instrumentalism, of course, but it is too narrow to account for the conception of the ontological limits to inquiry that surfaces in *Studies in Logical Theory.* It thus fails to explain Dewey's developing ontology of the problematic situation that is such a centrally important element of the theory of philosophical logic set forth in the *Studies.* The only way of accounting for that element, it seems to me, is by reference to Peirce's doubt–belief theory, the impact of which seems to be about as clear as anything can be in this otherwise somewhat murky business.

The suspicion that Dewey remained attached to some form of idealism for much longer than White or Buxton think is given renewed currency by Wayne A. R. Leys's introduction to volume 4 of *The Early Works.* He compares Dewey's tortuous path from idealism to functionalism with G. E. Moore's rejection of idealism in favor of the precision and consistency of science; as a result, he sees Dewey as "still under the influence of an Idealist logic" in 1893, referring to "The Superstition of Necessity" as evidence (*EW*4:xiv). Leys seems to think that Dewey was following

Bradley at the time: "It had been consistent with this anti-intuitionist epistemology for Dewey to follow the ethical strategy of F. H. Bradley" (*EW*4:xv). He wants to show that both Dewey and Moore thought of ethics as a science, but that they meant quite different things by the word *science*. While Leys's conclusion regarding Dewey's ethical views in 1894 is not in question, it is hard to see why the argument that Dewey was still following Bradley in 1893 helps. The whole Bradley–Dewey relationship, which is also alluded to by Buxton, has been covered in much greater detail by Garrett M. Brodsky, in "John Dewey's Theory of Inquiry" (Yale University, unpublished Ph.D. dissertation, 1961). Brodsky sees Dewey's rejection of Bradley's conception of logic as having more to do with the conception of internal relations than with intuitionism. Dewey rejected Bradley's logic of internal relations for at least some of the same reasons as Moore and Russell; they were all looking for a logic that would square better with science. But Dewey's rejection was primarily a consequence of his rejection of a priorism in all its forms, which Moore's and Russell's was not. As far as Dewey was concerned, Sidgwick and Martineau were the "chief philosophical upholders of intuitionalism" in 1893, though he conceded that Green might also be "classed among the intuitionalists" if one extends the term "to include *a priorism* of the Kantian type" (*EW*4:131). Bradley may have been following an anti-intuitionist strategy in ethics, as Leys says, but it is hard to see how Dewey's anti-intuitionist strategy relates to that of Bradley. Dewey's antipathy to a priorism was well established by 1893, and I maintain that it is this antipathy that would have kept his strategy safely clear of the Bradleyan model.

4: Dewey's Aristotelian Turn

Dewey first met Russell at Harvard during Russell's triumphant tour of American universities in 1914. Russell was already a celebrity in logical and mathematical circles as a result of his 1903 work *The Principles of Mathematics* and as coauthor, with Alfred North Whitehead, of *Principia Mathematica*. These attempts to show that the foundations of mathematics are to be found in the principles and rules of purely analytical logic had already established Russell's reputation and were widely thought to represent the wave of the future as far as logical theory was concerned. Russell's philosophical logic represented the leading edge of philosophy as such, it was generally supposed, and even idealists like Josiah Royce were enthusiastic about its possibilities.[1] Clearly, if Russell was setting philosophy on the right path, Dewey was wandering down the wrong one. It might have been expected that they would clash at once, but they did not. Russell wrote to Lady Ottoline, his correspondent of the moment, that he had been favorably impressed by Dewey: "To my surprise I liked him very much. He has a slow moving mind, very empirical and candid, with something of the impassivity and impartiality of a natural force." By contrast he found Josiah Royce a "garrulous old bore."[2]

While Russell may actually have been acquainted with Royce's work, there is no evidence that he was familiar with Dewey's other than by hearsay. Not long after this first encounter Russell went to Columbia to deliver a paper on "The Relation of Sense Data to Physics." This was a problem that had first surfaced in Russell's 1912 book *The Problems of Philosophy*, one that comprises the central theme of his *Our Knowledge of the External World as a Field for Scientific Method in Philosophy* of the same year. Dewey was quick to see the direction in which Russell was moving and offered some objections which Russell, in his account of the event to Lady Ottoline, acknowledged to be the only ones worth considering. As Sidney

Hook observed: "This turns out to have been the high point of Russell's appreciation of Dewey."[3]

Shortly after the Columbia encounter, Dewey made clear his objections to Russell's whole modus operandi. In his essay on "The Existence of the World as a Philosophical Problem" (*MW*8:83–97), he made explicit his conviction that Russell was putting the cart before the horse.[4] He contended that the metaphysics of analytical realism that Russell was extrapolating from logic was headed for disaster, since it repeated the Cartesian blunder of starting with apart thought and then trying to construct a picture of the external world from the logical connections of purely abstract concepts. He saw Russell as making the mistake that vitiates all idealist logic and all systems of metaphysics that set out the principles and fundamental categories of 'being' as foundational to science and its subject-matter. It is the same mistake that Dewey had attacked in his critique of Venn's logic, and that he had pounced on as the central flaw in Lotze. Dewey argued in the same vein as he had in his commentary on Peirce's treatment of necessity, insisting that logical necessity exists only in the context of inquiry, as needed, and that it cannot be meaningfully ascribed apart from inquiry either to existence as such or to 'being.' He argued that we cannot use logic to justify scientific method, for the only justification of logic *is* that method, the logic of experience.

We cannot proceed, as Russell does in *The Problems of Philosophy*, from a first philosophy that consists of a logical construction of an unchangeable, rigid, exact world of 'being' to the external world of existence,[5] since it is from just this external world, despite its lack of permanence and stability, that we derive all that we know of existence, and all that we *can* know. It is clear, Dewey argues, that common sense is often misled, as Russell claims, by appearance. But this only goes to show that common sense is in need of the help of science. "It is not the common sense *world* which is doubtful, or which is inferential, but common sense as a complex of beliefs about specific things and relations *in* the world. Hence never in any actual procedure of inquiry do we throw the existence of the world into doubt, nor can we do so without self-contradiction" (*MW*8:96–7).

By the time Russell got around to replying to Dewey's objections, in an extensive review of Dewey's *Essays in Experimental Logic*, in 1919, he had already abandoned the extreme Platonistic realism that Dewey had attacked.[6] Nor was he defending the analytical realism that he had earlier worked out as a foundation for his work in logic and mathematics. He was already well into "The Philosophy of Logical Atomism," as he called it in his 1918 lectures, and his response is mostly taken up with a defense of that standpoint against Dewey's instrumentalism. He did not engage Dewey's objections at the level of either logic or metaphysics, but set the argument almost entirely in terms of the psychology of perception. He brushed Dewey's logic of experience aside thus: "What he calls 'logic' does not seem to me to be a part of logic at all; I should call it part of psychology."[7] Years later, after logical atomism had proved disappointing, Russell came around to a position of "neutral monism" that was much closer to Dewey's 1914 position. Here is Russell in 1924: "When I speak of 'simples' I ought to explain that I am speaking of something not experienced as such, but known only inferentially as the limit of analysis."[8] Later, he rejected even this remnant of his earlier atomism. In a move toward Dewey's contention that science should replace metaphysics as first philosophy, Russell confesses that "in science there are many matters about which people are agreed; in philosophy there are none. Therefore, although each proposition in a science may be false, and it is practically certain that there are some that are false, yet we shall be wise to build our philosophy upon science, because the risk of error in philosophy is pretty sure to be greater than in science."[9] Finally, reviewing his philosophical development in 1959, Russell sees the trajectory of his thinking as having moved progressively away from analysis and toward the synthesis that comprises the core logic of scientific knowledge: "I believed, originally, with Leibniz, that everything complex is composed of simples, and that it is important in considering analysis to regard simples as our goal. I have come to think, however, that although many things can be known to be complex, nothing can be *known* to be simple, and, moreover, that statements in which complexes are named can be completely accurate."[10]

In the meantime, of course, Dewey continued along the path to the reconstruction of pragmatism—and philosophy—that he had already mapped out in the syllabus for Course 5 in 1892. Russell was right: "He has a slow moving mind, very empirical and candid, with something of the impassivity and impartiality of a natural force."

I have offered this brief excursus on the relationship between Dewey and Russell, not to show their convergent trajectories, however, but to provide the context in which the discussion of Dewey's mature philosophy of logic should take place.[11] In this transitional chapter I want to show that Dewey's work on logical problems between 1903 and 1938—that is, between the *Studies in Logical Theory* and *Logic: The Theory of Inquiry*—took a metaphysical turn. I shall argue that Dewey gradually came to see his developing theory of philosophical logic as having ontological implications that he had not directly addressed in his early work. These implications were pushed to the foreground, not only by the skirmish with Russell, but by the failure of his critics in general to see that much more than instrumentalism as a method was involved in the conception of logic that he had been trying to work out. A very considerable part of Dewey's work during this period is given over to the ontological roots of knowledge reached by means of inquiry, the existential metaphysics that supplies the background theory for those ontological roots, and the theory of language that links the subject-matter of inquiry with that metaphysical background. It is in this period that the lineaments of a system start to emerge, in which it begins to be possible to see how it all hangs together.

It is important to my argument that Dewey's controversy with Russell not be dismissed as irrelevant to the development of Dewey's conception of logic in this period. While it is not possible, I believe, to argue that Russell was much affected by the clash with Dewey, it can certainly be argued that Dewey was deeply concerned with the issues that divided them. Moreover, it can also be maintained that all Dewey's work on logical matters after the 1914 encounter involves a critique of the direction in which mainstream logic was headed. It is this that justifies the observation that Dewey was not merely "waiting at the end of the dialectical road which analytical philosophy traveled" but was trying to block that road from the outset.

Dewey and Russell both set out on their philosophical travels from a common point of departure in Hegelian idealism. In their earliest work, both were under the domination of the idealist conceptions of their respective mentors. Where Dewey had George Sylvester Morris and Thomas Hill Green to contend with, Russell had Francis Herbert Bradley and John McTaggart Ellis McTaggart. But whereas Dewey was accompanied by Mead, Angell, and A. W. Moore in his departure from idealism, Russell's companion was G. E. Moore. Whereas Dewey was attracted by the *pragmatic* logic that he elicited from James's *Principles of Psychology*, Russell was attracted by the *formal* logic that he was uncovering in Frege's *Grundgesetze der Arithmetik* and *Die Grundlagen der Arithmetik*. By 1903, when Dewey's *Studies in Logical Theory* and Russell's *The Principles of Mathematics* were published, their divergent paths can be clearly discerned. It was G. E. Moore whom Russell credited with teaching him to think of propositions as logical entities that do not occupy space or time, as objects of thought independent of both mind and existence.[12] This was a very different release from idealism from that embraced by Dewey in the naturalized account of thought in James's *Principles*.

Although Moore's conception of logical entities can be seen to be what allowed Russell to get on with the task of philosophical analysis and the construction of the logical foundations of mathematics, it is somewhat less clear what role Moore played in persuading Russell that the distinction between 'being' and existence has a parallel in the distinction between facts and values. But Russell was evidently convinced of this distinction, a distinction the denial of which is a fundamental contention of Dewey's *Studies*. It was to be a divisive issue between analytic and pragmatic philosophy henceforth, one that Dewey would return to again and again in the years between the *Studies* and his 1939 *Theory of Valuation*. It would come to represent for Dewey the central difference between the consequences of proceeding from synthesis and those of proceeding from analysis, between the consequences of pragmatism as a philosophy and the consequences of analytical philosophy. [13]

In the meantime, while Dewey was working out his logic of synthesis, Russell was working out his logic of analysis. His first effort in that direction almost had to be aborted. Russell had been working through the pioneering efforts of Frege to establish the logical foundations of mathematics in the first volume of *Grundgesetze der Arithmetik* in preparation for his own try in *The Principles of Mathematics*. He had wanted, so he wrote to Frege, to present Frege's work to the English-speaking world. The trouble was that he had found a contradiction in Frege's logic, which should not have occurred, since Frege was working from self-evident principles, the truth of which was analytic. What Russell discovered was that one of Frege's self-evident principles implied a contradiction. He explained it to Frege in these words:

> You state (p. 17) that a function, too, can act as the indeterminate element. This I formerly believed, but now this view seems doubtful to me because of the following contradiction. Let w be the predicate: to be a predicate that cannot be predicated of itself. Can w be predicated of itself? From each answer its opposite follows. Therefore we must conclude that w is not a predicate. Likewise there is no class (as a totality) of those classes which, taken as a totality, do not belong to themselves. [14]

Frege, who had been about to publish the second volume of his *Grundgesetze*, wrote back to Russell that his discovery "has shaken the basis on which I intended to build arithmetic." And he quickly added an appendix to his forthcoming book that opened with these words: "A scientist can hardly encounter anything more undesirable than to have the foundation collapse just as the work is finished. I was put in this position by a letter from Bertrand Russell." [15]

The reason why Frege was quick to see that his foundation was flawed is that it consisted of a string of self-consistent set-theoretic rules of inference, the rule challenged by Russell being integral to the entire string. As he wrote to Russell, "not only the foundations of my arithmetic, but also the sole possible foundations of arithmetic, seem to vanish." Russell was undeterred by this foundational flaw, however, and took the position in both *The Principles of Mathematics* and *Principia* that it would be eliminated eventually. That it has not been, despite Russell's own tireless efforts and those of countless others, appears to be due more to the fact that it is not necessary to the ongoing viability of mathematics in use, than to the possibility that Frege and Russell had been looking for the foundations of mathematics in the wrong place. However, the latter is what Dewey was ready to claim. For it was part of Dewey's case against analytic realism that Moore and Russell were simply mistaken about the nature of their logical entities.[16]

Dewey's argument is consistent with the view of the nature of logic that he had been expounding all along: the normative rules must be discovered in and through the successes and failures of inquiry. They are not to be invoked from any outside source. Put in terms of his paper on "Logical Objects," delivered to the Philosophical Club at Columbia in 1916 but never published, the argument is given an explicit ontological context. It is an argument in support of realism and against idealism, of course, but a realism that is almost entirely new and different. Dewey argues that inference is existential: "Inference is a genuine thing, a *vera causa,* for which occurrence independent evidence can be adduced, while the rival conceptions refer to things the sole evidence of whose existence is the explanatory role they play in the particular theory in behalf of which they are invoked" (*MW*10:97). In other words, it is a realism that takes inference as a real event of transformational force and power, causally real in the emergence of new features of things "entering the inferential function." It takes inference as action, as behavior that causes changes in reality through interaction with things. It is transactional realism as the metaphysical background theory of the logic of experience.

Dewey sets his argument in motion by reviewing the three traditional ways of treating logical entities of the sort referred to by "common nouns, by words like 'between,' 'if,' 'or,' by numbers, or in general what are usually referred to as subsistences and essences." They have been treated, he says, "as (i) physical properties abstracted and grasped in 'rational apprehension'; as (ii) mental (i.e. psychical) existences; and (iii) as marking a peculiar type of Being, which is neither physical nor psychical, but rather 'metaphysical' in one of the most commonly used senses of that word." The latter is clearly intended to denote Russell's view of analytic realism, which Dewey wants to refute and against which he proposes a fourth point of view, "that logical entities are truly logical, while 'logical' denotes having to do with the occurrence of inference. In other words, logical objects are things (or traits of things) which are found when inference is found and which are only found then" (*MW*10:90). It is crucial to his argument, Dewey says, that inference be regarded as an event that is radically different from a psychical event. It is not just mental, although it may be accompanied by all sorts of mental and psychical conditions. It is independent and does not take place simply within the mind. Inference is an event "belonging to action, or behavior, which takes place in the world." Inference does not merely give us a picture of things, we might say; it gives us hands-on knowledge, or a way of proceeding. It is an activity: "It belongs in the category where plowing, assembling the parts of a machine, digging and smelting ore belong—namely, behavior, which lays hold of and handles and rearranges physical things" (*MW*10:91).

Once we begin to view inference as action, Dewey continues, it is easy to identify the fact of inference with the phenomenon of evidence. For it is in the use of evidence and only there that the fact is found. Only in use does inference have meaning, and only in use does it produce the logical entities in question as its own peculiar characteristic tools and results. Dewey's summary of this part of his argument is worth quoting in full:

> As long as method was treated as something to which instruments of physical analysis and recombination are extraneous, it was not easy to have any alternatives between thinking of dialectic (including of course definition, division and classification) as being in one to one correspondence with ultimate, non-empirical essences or forms, and thinking of reasoning as concerned merely with the products of the mental compounding of ideas. But if the method involves a technique of practical procedure, if discovery, ascertainment and prediction depends upon doing something to things and getting ready for what happens in relations may be purely methodological, and yet not "mental" in the traditional sense of mental. They may well be, I repeat, the tools of investigation. [*MW*10:93]

And of the results he has a note of critical importance: "A so-called immediate apprehension is a totally different sort of thing, logically speaking, according as it is or is not the outcome of prior technique of inquiry, even though immediate inspection should not be able to detect a difference in constituents" (*MW*10:93).

What Dewey wants to show is that "those lost souls of philosophical theory which go by the name of essences and subsistences" are both the instrumental "tools" of inquiry and the eventual objects that comprise its results. He is arguing for the existential reality of both the conceptual apparatus and its objects, for an existential logic and its ontology on the basis of inference as an existential event, something that happens as a *vera causa*, that is causally efficacious in generating changes in the antecedently real objects of inquiry. In this way the lost souls of traditional metaphysics are given new meaning, and the foreground of behavioral semantics is seen against a new background of empirical characteristics and generic traits.

The final section of Dewey's paper is a direct attack on Russell's logic, in which Dewey zeroes in on five distinct, but related, points. The first is simply a reiteration of his contention that the synthesis of the act of inference is temporally and logically prior to any analysis of the relation. Russell's "revival of the old question of the relation of the *a priori* and *a posteriori*," Dewey says, "seems an inevitable consequence of his method," one not calculated to please other realists. The second point challenges Russell's account of so-called molecular propositions and their connectives as not derived either from sense or by inference. Dewey argues that "they are not derived *by* inference, but *from* inference—from inference as itself an empirical occurrence." They are "not found till they are introduced by inference itself." The third challenges Russell's contention that the "points, particles and instants with which physics operates" are logical constructions, and very likely not existing things. Dewey argues that they must be either "esthetic fantasies or else tools of inference." As for the reality of points without extension and similar entities posited by physicists, Dewey simply argues that "the reality to which they refer is the specific reality which it is—namely, that of controlled inference." In other words, Dewey holds that these so-called conventions do have extensional reference, but it is to the procedures and operations of inquiry as events. Their meaning is in their use, and if that use is extensional, then they have extension (*MW*10:95).[17]

The fourth point relates once more to the foundations of mathematics. The argument given recalls Dewey's earlier position relating number theory to measurement or counting off into groups. He argues that number is not simply a matter of analyticity: "That definition, as put forth by Frege and Russell, makes mathematical number neither a property of physical things nor yet mere mental subjective things." This leaves number as a sort of fish out of water, for unless it has extensional reference to the operation of mathematical inference itself, its relation to any application remains a mystery. On the basis of the Frege–Russell definition, Dewey says, sets can only name generalized possibilities of collections of instances. But on this basis it is clear that not all sets have extensional reference apart from the process by which they have been constructed. The argument pursued by Dewey is designed to counter Russell's claim that every set must determine a possible being. Dewey's last point elaborates this same argument with respect to the circularity of Russell's theory of classes. He says that Russell starts out by replacing the common property of a given set by a "symmetrical transitive relation," which he regards as a purely formal relation, and then proceeds to define this formal symmetry as reducible to the defining property of the class. The conclusion "that seems to stare one in the face," Dewey says, is that "class and common (or defining) property are notions which describe things *within* the event of controlled inquiry; it is with respect to inference that things fall into sets, and that either they or the class possess common or defining properties" (*MW*10:96).[18]

What Dewey is seeking is a more explicit theory of classes than he had been able to articulate in the *Studies in Logical Theory*. He made progress in this effort by taking the metaphysical implications of the Frege–Russell theory seriously and finding a way to reject them. In doing so, he came to a better understanding of the implications of his own theory, and this launched him on the project of connecting the logic of experience with the metaphysics of existence.

In working out the account of inference as an event, he had provided the link between the ontology that was barely there in the background of the *Studies* and the theory of generic traits that he would elaborate in *Experience and Nature*. Inference in the classical logic of the syllogism presupposes a first philosophy of essences and subsistences. Russell and Frege treat these entities as logical objects in the realm of possible being—a realm to which they ascribe a logical necessity that has nothing to do with the existential realm of actual instances or classes. Dewey, by contrast, proposes to treat them as generic features of actual classes or kinds of existence.

Thus, while Russell finds himself in the awkward position of trying to derive a proof of the external world from the character of the implications that obtain with respect to his logical objects, Dewey is in the happy position of working from the other end of the problem. Instead of trying to ground inference in implication, he grounds implication in inference. Because successful inference is a temporal event with temporal consequences involving the use of evidence, the reference of Dewey's logical objects is to that use. And that use shows that the logical objects are none other than the lost souls of classical metaphysics, here rediscovered by means of experimental method. They are the empirical characteristics of individual things that allow them to be grouped together as a class. They are what Dewey calls the "generic traits" that provide the evidence from which inference can proceed. It is in the use of such evidence that intelligent behavior consists. Meanings are its means, and the truth of meanings what warrants their success.

It is important to recognize that Dewey had been groping toward this theory of classes ever since his discovery that logical necessity has existential force only in the context of purposeful behavior, in the temporal context of the problem-solving behavior that Peirce had described in his doubt–belief theory of inquiry. Dewey realized from the outset, as I have tried to show, that he was on a very different path in logic from Peirce. It was this difference, or one very much like it, that Dewey now saw as separating him from Russell. Indeed, it now seemed that the arguments that Dewey had developed against Peirce's conception of realism applied, *mutatis mutandis*, to the analytic realism of Russell. For the arguments of the paper on "Logical Objects" were already implicit in the *Studies in Logical Theory*, arguments that he had been trying to make explicit ever since. Now, in his opposition to Russell, they became clear. Through his attempt to work out the logic of classes, Dewey found himself able to articulate his own brand of realism. He now saw how to distinguish that realism from the brands of his fellow realists at Columbia, as well as those of Peirce and Russell, from the "Platform of Six Realists," as well as from James and Schiller. He saw too that his divergent path in logic was all one with his very divergent path in metaphysics.

The first steps down that path in metaphysics had already been taken in the *Studies*. But several further steps had been taken since then. For, beginning with "The Postulate of Immediate Empiricism," Dewey had turned again and again to a defense of the particular kind of realist theory that he knew would be required by a theory of inquiry. As it was not yet clear just what form that theory would take—perhaps even to Dewey himself—he appears to have adopted the strategy that the best defense is an attack. In the end he gathered together a number of these defenses from several different journals and reissued them, together with his original contributions to the *Studies in Logical Theory*, under the new title *Essays in Experimental Logic*, in 1916. In a lengthy new introduction Dewey tried to set forth the character of the metaphysical background which his theory of inquiry requires. If he succeeds in this at all, it is in spite of the fact that he devotes most of his effort to developing negative arguments against other realists.

In a prefatory note Dewey points out that, with one exception, all the

material included in the *Essays* dates from either 1903, the date of publication of the *Studies,* or later. The exception is his 1900 essay entitled "Some
Stages in Logical Thought." Although it was not the first essay in which
Dewey gave an account of the three stages through which logical theory
has passed, it seems clear that its inclusion is intended to show that this
early account is still applicable. Its three ways of treating logical entities are
identical with those that he delineates in his attack on Russell in "Logical
Objects," and both papers suggest that what we really need in order to
develop a wholly new logic is a radically new metaphysics to take the place
of the old metaphysics of fixed essences that has survived through all three
stages of logic, from Aristotle to transcendentalism to empiricism. Moreover, the 1900 essay clearly points the way in which this wholly new logic
must develop if it is to succeed, if it is to discover something real enough to
take the place of the old order of reality as fixed or transcendental, as 'being'
itself or Absolute Mind, as pure thought, reason, or independent 'being.'
Here is how the essay concludes:

> The practical procedure and practical assumptions of modern experi-
> mental science, since they make thinking essentially and not merely
> accidentally a process of discovery, seem irreconcilable with both the
> empirical and transcendental interpretations. At all events, there is
> here sufficient discrepancy to give occasion for further search: Does
> not an account of thinking, basing itself on modern scientific pro-
> cedure, demand a statement in which all the distinctions and terms of
> thought—judgment, concept, inference, subject, predicate and cop-
> ula of judgment, etc., *ad infinitum*—shall be interpreted simply and
> entirely as distinctive functions or divisions of labor within the doubt
> inquiry process? [*MW*1:174]

The new introduction reiterates this demand and begins to spell out the
way in which it can be met. One has to accept, Dewey argues, that the kind
of logic set forth in the *Studies* is a logic of discovery, not of proof in the
traditional sense. It is an account of what takes place in inquiry, of how
thinking occurs in a temporal context. It is an account that is frankly
realistic, that treats knowing as literally something that we do. And in an
"Added Note as to the 'Practical'," he reminds us that this is a behaviorist
theory, and that it was such even before the term became fashionable.

Yet the whole thrust of the new introduction is that thinking is not just a
peculiar kind of behavior that occurs at random, but rather an occurrence
having specific occasions and characteristics. He wants to show that the
objects of thought are not constituted by thought itself but are encoun-

tered in terms of existential factors and materials, that they are not just conjured up at random from the storehouse of experience or the inventive imagination, but that they arise from the experience of some things as signs of other things, as occasions of meaningful behavior. They are anticipations of results, and their use in anticipatory response is what inference is. On such occasions the real is relational. Things that serve as signs are thus suggestions as to how to act. In specific situations, they point to explanations of what has occurred; but in problematic situations they may indicate possible resolutions. "*Suggestions thus treated*," Dewey says with emphasis, "*are precisely what constitute meanings, subsistences, essences, etc.*" He continues: "Without such development and handling of what is suggested, the process of analyzing the situation to get at the hard facts, and especially to get at just those which have a right to determine inference, is haphazard— ineffectively done" (*MW*10:350). These "meanings, subsistences, essences are expressed as terms that signify that certain absent existences are indicated by certain given existences, in respect that they are abstracted and fixed for intellectual use by some physically convenient means, such as a sound or a muscular contraction of the vocal organs." And these terms are not mere words, but get put into sentences and propositions that have meaning and reference in use.[19]

There are three interwoven theses in the new introduction that reflect the criticism of Russell's analytic realism set forth in the unpublished paper on "Logical Objects." The first is the thesis that Dewey had originally advanced against Peirce in "The Superstition of Necessity," which claims that the concept of necessity is not a priori in origin or analytic as constitutive thought. It is a discovery of use in inquiry and has its genesis there; it is teleological in the context of the doubt–belief process, and *only* there. In other words, it is not a general feature of all existence but a generic feature of a class of instances of existence—that is, of existences as a provisionally homogeneous collection. It is this thesis that discloses the character of Dewey's pragmatism, which insists on the relativity of ontological commitments.

The second thesis emerges in direct opposition to the Russell–Moore–Frege theory of intension. It is that meanings emerge from action in the process of inquiry in which relations are found to be real. Dewey puts it in terms that suggest that the flaw in empiricism is the narrowness of the conception of experience insisted on by both Mill and the logical atomists. It is the fallacy of attempting to reduce intension to a logical construction of terms that have extension only in reference to immediate experience. It is the fallacy of limiting extension to atomic sense data.

Intensional events, Dewey argues, have a much broader context of reference and a much greater amplitude of extension. "The objection to analytic realism as a metaphysics of existence," Dewey says, "is not so much to an undue formalism as to its affront to the common-sense world of action, appreciation, and affection." If terms are to be reified at all, whether into commonsense objects or knowledge, why not objects of the sort denoted by "action, appreciation, and affection"? "There are questions at issue, but they concern not matters of logic but matters of fact. They are questions of the *existential* setting of certain logical distinctions and relations" (*MW*10:357).

The third thesis welds the first two together. It is the thesis of continuity which embraces both and which shows that the thesis of extension and that of intension are continuously related in inquiry as a temporal process involving ongoing action. Terms with possible intensional meaning acquire extensional meaning in the context of action, in practice. They are behavioral characteristics and traits that issue in judgments that are either more or less true. Intensional meanings are thus relative to extensional—or empirical and existential—evidence. Dewey refers to the relation of intension and extension as one of coexistence: "The results of abstraction and analysis (reached in judgment) are perfectly real; but they are real, like everything else, *where* they are real: that is to say, in some *particular* *co*existence in the situation where they originate and operate" (*MW*10:343).

The thesis of the continuity of inquiry is intended to show that "reflection is an actual occurrence as much so as a thunderstorm or a growing plant, and as an actual existence it is characterized by specific existential traits uniquely belonging to it: the entities of simple data as such. It is in control of the evidential function that irreducible and independent simples exist" (*MW*10:343). Nor is there any reason to think that they exist elsewhere.[20] The lost souls are not out there in some transcendental realm, independently existing and awaiting discovery, but are the givens of commonsense objects picked apart and employed as "expeditious and unambiguous signs" of other things. Generic traits are expressed as the terms of the conclusions drawn, in propositions that have projectibility, but in practice they have both extensional and intensional meaning: they are the temporal and existential evidence of valid inference.

It is primarily in connection with this third thesis that Dewey is most readily either understood or misunderstood. By seeming to locate all objects of knowledge where they are real, Dewey appears to be locating them within experience. It is thus possible to read his thesis of continuity as simply a new version of idealism, as denying that it is possible to have knowledge of independently real objects in an independently real world. According to this reading, Dewey is claiming that our knowledge of existences is restricted to those that present themselves in experience—a version of presentative realism, or even an objective idealism similar to that implied by Peirce's conception of synechism. It is a reading that clearly supports the conclusion that, for Dewey, the subject-matter of metaphysics must be experience itself. Moreover, additional support for such a reading can readily be found in Dewey's frequently repeated contention that thought is existential and not separate from the activity of inquiry. Finally, it could be maintained that, since Dewey argues consistently that knowing always begins with apprehension and proceeds by *means* of apprehension, its objects are always tainted, so to speak, by the apprehending mind—which is another way of saying that Dewey has failed to free himself from the idealism with which he began. On this reading, synthesis would be simply experiential for Dewey; it would be merely an updated version of Hegel's synthesis, but set in the context of experimental method rather than the dialectic of world process. Dewey's insistence that the object of knowledge is changed during the process of inquiry and that change is real can only mean that experience is changed, that the object of inquiry is changed by means of inquiry to the end of ever greater fulfillment of its intrinsic reality.

But if Dewey's realism is understood in this way, then there is almost no difference between his theory of continuity and Peirce's principle of synechism. Yet it is clear that Dewey was not merely offering an alternative version of synechism, but rather a genuine alternative to it. In fact, Dewey never attempted to devise a metaphysics of categories on anything like Peirce's model. Whereas Peirce intended his categorical scheme, with synechism at its apex, to serve as a first philosophy and a foundation to his whole system, Dewey did not view his own conception of continuity as a category at all.[21] Nor was it to function as a foundation on which to build a system. It is clear that Dewey views continuity as merely a feature of specific situations and circumstances, a feature that certain other situations and circumstances lack. Neither *existence* nor *experience* are terms denoting anything thought to be uniformly continuous in anything like Peirce's synechistic sense. They are terms as often associated with discontinuous events as with those continuous events that stand out, by virtue of their brilliance and focus, as having meaning. Indeed, it is part of Dewey's conception of inference as an event with temporal meaning that it cannot occur everywhere and always. For inference occurs only where and when reference to a continuous relation is possible because that relation is actual. And it is only possible occasionally, because only occasionally is it justified by the evidence. Dewey's metaphysics of existence focuses on those possible occasions as problematic situations amenable to resolution. The logic of experience is an account of such resolutions as have been achieved, for its focus is on success in judgment and on the means by which that success was achieved. The process of inference is indeed characterized as being a continuous event, but the continuity referred to is not categorical at all, but rather, piecemeal and situational. This is not transcendental realism, but transactional realism, for knowing is here regarded as a transaction that takes place between an organism and its environment, and its occurrence denotes changes in relationships as existential events, actual changes in the real world.

I have been arguing that Dewey's project of reconstruction, not only of pragmatism but of philosophy overall, drove him almost inexorably further and further into the thickets of metaphysics and ontology. It is apparent that Dewey was offended by the frequency with which his logic of experience was taken as little more than an exercise in psychology. But, to show that this was a misunderstanding, he wrote about the background theory of his account of experience as if it began with the naive realism of common sense, and as if all that is required in the way of an adequate metaphysics is simply an improved version of that initial and immediate commitment to the objects of common sense as reals. He was as disturbed as Peirce by the direction taken by James in "The Will to Believe" and became increasingly sensitive to the charge of subjectivism brought against pragmatism generally, but, unlike Peirce, Dewey did not respond to James by reaffirming an alliance with absolute idealism; he turned instead to Aristotle.

Dewey had heard much about the virtues of Aristotelian metaphysics from his colleagues at Columbia, particularly F. J. E. Woodbridge, who had pressed his own "functional Aristotelianism" on Dewey as the needed foundation for an instrumentalist theory of knowledge. But Dewey was not looking for foundations at all; he was looking for a vehicle to carry forward the process of knowing. To use Hook's phrase, he was searching for a "metaphysics of the instrument." He discovered it in his own reconstruction of the Aristotelian *Organon*, which allowed him to place the practical dimension of pragmatism in a metaphysical perspective. And he worked it out in a brief essay which he included in the *Essays in Experimental Logic:* "An Added Note as to the 'Practical'" (*MW*10:366–9).

He begins by considering the "legend" and misconception as to the justification of the pragmatic attitude. It is not, he says, that knowledge is "merely a means to a practical end, or to the satisfaction of practical needs." He admits that Peirce had pointed to the consequences of inquiry as "would exact of us different modes of behavior," but he goes on to point out that "it is not that consequences are themselves practical, but that practical consequences from them may at times be appealed to in order to decide the specific question of whether two proposed meanings differ save in words." And he adds that "Mr. James says expressly that what is important is that the consequences should be specific, not that they should be active. When he said that general notions must 'cash in,' he meant that they must be translatable into verifiable specific things. But the words 'cash in' were enough for some of his critics, who pride themselves upon a logical rigor unattainable by mere pragmatists" (*MW*10:367).

Against this, Dewey maintains that *pragmatic* means only a general rule of logic which applies without regard to the nature of the consequences—whether they are aesthetic, moral, or religious in quality—and is not limited to either the commonplace or the scientific domain. The concern of such a rule of logic, he argues, is not with the nature of consequences at all, but with the nature of knowing. Moreover, he continues, it means a logic of behavior.

> To use a term which is now more fashionable (and surely to some extent in consequence of pragmatism) than it was earlier, instrumentalism means a behaviorist theory of thinking and knowing. It means that knowing is literally something which we do; that analysis is ultimately physical and active; that meanings in their logical quality are standpoints, attitudes, and methods of behaving toward fact, and that active experimentation is essential to verification. [*MW*10:367]

He makes it clear that the situation that results from this logic of knowing may or may not be satisfying, as the case may be, for the fact that it is reached through instrumental thinking has no bearing on its intrinsic nature or on any consequences that may follow from it. The point is simply that the situation which results from the application of this rule of thinking is more significant and more controlled than the one from which it emerged.

It is in this context that Dewey allies himself with Aristotle:

> There is nothing novel nor heterodox in the notion that thinking is instrumental. The very word is redolent of an *Organum*, whether *novum* or *veterum*. The term "instrumentality," applied to thinking,

raises at once, however, the question whether thinking as a tool falls within or without the subject-matter which it shapes into knowledge. The answer of formal logic (adopted moreover by Kant and followed in some way by all neo-Kantian logics) is unambiguous. To call logic "formal" means precisely that mind or thought supplies forms foreign to the original subject-matter, but yet required in order that it should have the appropriate form of knowledge. In this regard it deviates from the Aristotelian *Organon* which it professes to follow. [*MW*10:367]

Dewey wants his own organon to follow, as far as possible, the Aristotelian model. He cannot, of course, accept the notion that essences are the extraorganic forms of eternal species, and in that respect a very different sort of organon is required. An object of knowledge that is not fixed in nature or antecedently determined is required: "not something with which thinking sets out, but something with which it ends." What he calls, in *Experience and Nature,* the eventual object of knowledge, would require a reconstruction of the Aristotelian doctrine of essences in terms of the generic traits of existences and an organon that is thoroughly empirical and existential, as well as an extensional ontology of the sort he later presents in *Logic: The Theory of Inquiry.*

Dewey's Aristotelian turn was anticipated in an essay of 1915 directed against the form of transcendental metaphysics involved in both mechanistic and vitalistic reductions of the world process to its ultimate origins. Such reductions, he argues in "The Subject-Matter of Metaphysical Inquiry" (*MW*8:1–13), are the result of a confusion between questions appropriate to experimental science and those with which metaphysics should be concerned. Dewey maintains that science is indeed concerned with origins—even ultimate ones—provided such origins are understood as temporal and not as referring to some nontemporal or transcendent source. But metaphysics should not be concerned with origins in this sense at all. Its concern should be with the ultimate traits of the world.

Much the same argument is used with respect to ultimate causes. Insofar as these are construed as temporal, they are appropriate questions for science; as nontemporal they are meaningless. So the ultimate traits are not to be thought of as either original antecedent causes or ultimate final causes, which precludes not only the older teleological systems of metaphysics, but also those modern ones based on the principles of Newtonian mechanics and those that presuppose that the science of evolution means that all change is evolutionary in character. Mechanical change is one kind of change, evolutionary change another. There is no one kind of change that is universal in the sense of being an ultimate trait of the world, though change in the temporal sense may be. "The question is, how one set of specific existences gradually passed into another." Some changes take place through mechanical processes, some through biological means, and some in diverse ways that are neither mechanical nor biological. This suggests that change may be an ultimate trait in the proper metaphysical sense, as long as it is not considered to be reducible to some specific kind of change applicable to some existences and not to others. If it is found to be reducible in this sense, it belongs to science rather than metaphysics.

But if change is synonymous with temporality and all temporal questions are referred to science, what is left for metaphysics? Dewey considers the positivist answer to this question—namely, that metaphysics is a pseudo-science. According to this view, all legitimate questions about existences belong to science, and ontology is thus displaced by the philosophy of science. The problem of determining which questions are legitimate is assigned to epistemology, which thus displaces metaphysics. In response, Dewey points out that the sciences all have their special subject-matters and that the philosophy of science is properly concerned with those sciences and their various ways of proceeding, rather than with any generic traits that their existential subject-matters may have in common. This implies that the subject-matter of metaphysics may still be legitimate insofar as it consists of inquiry into traits that cut across existences of all kinds. Such traits, he suggests, are not what either the philosophy of science or epistemology is concerned with, and yet they may help to explain both why science is possible and why it hangs together despite its divergent subject-matters and methods. Moreover, such traits may help to explain why science has become such a necessity. Thus metaphysics may legitimately be concerned with features of existences that are displayed with regard not to specific time or place, but to such characteristics as "diversity, specificality, change," understood as the "irreducible traits *of* the irreducible traits" disclosed by the special sciences. Construed in this way, he notes, "the name at least has the sanction of the historical designation given to Aristotle's considerations of existence as existence" (*MW*8:6, n.2).

The essay concludes with Dewey's caveat to the effect that he has "not (been) concerned to develop a metaphysics; but simply to indicate one way of conceiving the problem of metaphysical inquiry as distinct from that of the special sciences, a way which settles upon the more ultimate traits of the world as defining its subject-matter, but which frees these traits from confusion with ultimate origins and ultimate ends—that is, from questions of creation and eschatology." All the same, and despite the caveat, he has argued forcefully against the Aristotelian doctrine of predetermined, fixed essences, against the doctrine of determinate potentialities that is part and parcel of classical realism, and in favor of a conception of nature as changing through the interaction of existences. And he closes with the cautious admission that at least *one* metaphysical conclusion may be indicated. It is an inference reached from ubiquitous evidence, the judgment that although metaphysics properly takes the world "irrespective of any particular time, yet time itself, or genuine change in a specific direction, is itself one of the ultimate traits of the world irrespective of date" (*MW*8:13).

As Joseph Ratner has pointed out, Dewey was learning that "the only way of getting rid of bad metaphysics is to develop good metaphysics."[22]

Dewey's turn in the direction of a reconstructed Aristotelian realism, distinctly naturalistic and worked out in a context of controversy concerning the very legitimacy of metaphysics as such, is not just a response to the charges of subjectivism and psychologism leveled against his theory of logic. It is not just his way of showing the connections and contrasts between his reconstruction of pragmatism and both classical and contemporary conceptions of the foundations of knowledge and philosophy. And it is only in part a response to the challenges of analytic philosophy, logical atomism, and positivism. For, in addition, it is a reflection of his own earliest convictions that philosophy itself must be conceived as a force for change in the world, for reconciling the conflicts between science and theology, for mediating the conflicting interests and concerns of a culture increasingly divided against itself. It is a reflection of Dewey's long-standing concern with experience as "pedagogical," with communication and community, with the school as a social institution. It is a consequence of his concern with all social institutions, with the state and the nation, and with the breakdown of these institutions in a world wracked by war, famine, and disease.

Moreover, Dewey's metaphysical turn was not just an attempt to set his logic on the secure path of science in the spirit of Kant's metaphysics of experience. He was not concerned with metaphysics as either first philosophy or foundational in the accepted Aristotelian sense. Indeed, he had already directed a very large part of his work on logic against the view that thinking either has or needs foundations of the sort traditionally provided by metaphysics as first philosophy, whether classical or Scholastic realism, Cartesian rationalism, or neo-Kantian idealism. He had also rejected epistemology as first philosophy, both Mill's conception of epistemology as foundational to science and the empiricist logics which insisted that to be meaningful, propositions must be logical constructions founded on the stimulations of immediate experience. Moreover, if my reading of Dewey's reconstruction of pragmatism is on the right track, he had long since abandoned his own early conviction that it is psychology that provides the foundations and first philosophy on which the sciences are built. He had already rejected the Jamesian notion of the sameness of things as mere external "denkmittel" that carry thought forward in "seven league boots."[23] He had long since reconstructed these denkmittel as internal to the existential world of things, as existential generic traits of specific things and their relations, and had transformed the cognitive psychology of James into an ontological logic of experience. He had already deepened the realism that he recognized in James so that it no longer teetered on the brink of conventionalism, but reached down into the depths of the natural process of change. His was a thoroughgoing naturalism that avoids even a hint of the eschatological vision that remains a luminous possibility, however faint, in both Peirce and James. He had already closed the door on *super*naturalism.

According to this reading, the metaphysical turn taken in the later works is simply an extension of the early trajectory. It makes good on all the promissory notes that Dewey had scattered along the way. In the end, even the turn to Aristotle can be seen as consistent with the very earliest works, and even with the Oil City experience and the subsequent turn to Hegelian logic as the completed method of philosophy. For it is all one with Dewey's 1884 judgment, reached while a student at Johns Hopkins, that "it ought now to be evident that any philosophy which can pretend to be a method of truth must show Reason as both analytic *and* synthetic. If History can demonstrate anything, it has demonstrated this, both by its successes and its failures" (*EW*1:44). By 1915 Dewey was able to see even Aristotle's organon in this favorable light. For, once the notion of static essences is put aside, Aristotle's theory of inquiry can be seen to be rooted in Greek common sense and the cultural institutions that gave meaning and coherence to the lives of those dependent on them. Once the classical habit of construing nature as a fixed order of causal relations had been disposed of, it became possible to see the Aristotelian theory of inquiry as a way of knowing that sprang from the Greek experience. For the Greeks, Dewey now began to argue, it served the same sociocultural ends that he had earlier seen Hegel's logic as serving; it was an organon by means of which man's experiences of nature in all its diversity and evident discontinuity could be made intelligible, a means of unifying man with the world of nature of which he is a part.

Just as it was "logic in the Hegelian use," as he put it in 1885, that attracted Dewey's admiration and respect, so now it was Aristotle's use of the organon of inquiry, of logic as intelligent behavior and judgment. Just as he had earlier praised Hegel's logic for being "an account of conceptions or categories of Reason which constitute experience, internal and external, subjective and objective, and an account of them as a system, an organic unity in which each has its own place fixed," Dewey now praises Aristotle's logic for its conception of the natural unity of subject and object in *Phusis* ("nature"), identified with growth and change. Just as he had once admired Hegel for having healed the breach between the analytic and the synthetic by grounding his logic in the historical process, Dewey now commends Aristotle for suggesting a theory of inquiry that brings together the problems of science and the problems of men, that unifies the subjective experience of the precariousness of existence carried over from the age of Homer and Hesiod and the objective experience consequent on the establishment of a social order with a measure of permanence and stability in the Golden Age of Pericles and his successors. Thus: "The distinction and relation of the permanent, the fixed, from and to the variable and changing, was the ultimate problem of science and philosophy. The philosophy of Aristotle is a systematic exposition and organized solution of this problem carried through all subjects with which inquiry was then concerned" (*Logic,* p. 83).

It is the application of the organon to all subjects that impresses Dewey and excites his admiration for both Hegelian and Aristotelian logic. For it is clear that once logic is conceived as the method of intelligent behavior, as the logic of experience, it must be applicable to all dimensions of experience. It must provide human intelligence with access to nature in all its manifest diversity, oppositions, and contrasts, as well as its connections and relations. It must serve equally the understanding of all the diversity of cultures and individuals, of politics and art, of morals and medicine. The method is the medium of control developed from inside the culture, thereby freeing it from external control. It is the means of liberation from the tyranny of the gods, of release from the bonds of destiny. It does not exclude tragedy, of course, or guarantee happiness, and Dewey is quick to remind us of the bearing of his own metaphysical caveat on all this: "The more adequate that (Aristotle's) logic was in its own day, the less fitted is it to form the framework of present logical theory" (*Logic,* p. 82).

The great difficulty experienced by Dewey's critics in trying to understand a logic that comprises both an Aristotelian connection and a metaphysical turn arises from the simple fact that Dewey's conception of logic does not involve anything that would traditionally have been considered as either logic or ontology. Just as Russell critically appraised the *Essays in Experimental Logic* as not being part of logic at all, at least two generations of critics have seen Dewey's attempt to establish a metaphysics of existence in *Experience and Nature* as achieving merely a kind of philosophical anthropology and not serving the role traditionally assigned to metaphysics as first philosophy and foundation of knowledge. And at least two generations of logicians have looked on Dewey's *Logic: The Theory of Inquiry* as a strangely named book, since it does not concern logic at all in the received sense of the word, and have dismissed it as an exercise of Dewey's old age, long after the currents of mainstream logic had left the channels in which Dewey's thinking was still moving.[24]

I have tried to show that such criticism is rooted in a misapprehension of Dewey's conception of philosophy overall, and of his conceptions of logic and metaphysics in particular. I have been arguing all along that Dewey's project involved a total reconstruction of philosophy, one that initially took the form of a reconstruction of idealism and then moved on to a reconstruction of the pragmatism of Peirce and James, ending up with a kind of wholesale reconstruction of both logic and metaphysics. From this perspective it is clear that Dewey's conception of logic is not part of logic in the traditional sense, but is rather a conception of intelligent behavior in which traditional logical concepts play a role but are not the whole story. It was Russell's judgment that Dewey's logic of experience belongs to psychology, but it was Dewey's judgment that psychology belongs to the logic of experience. Psychology is part of logic once logic is conceived as a theory of inquiry. But then, so are physics and chemistry, ethics and aesthetics. It was Santayana's judgment that Dewey's metaphysics was just an account of the foreground of human life, a kind of sociology of experience and knowledge that fails utterly to reach the depths of nature traditionally explored by metaphysics. It was Dewey's judgment, however, that the sociology of experience and knowledge is part of nature, one that must be mapped in relation to nature's other parts, and that metaphysics reaches the depths of nature only when it succeeds in providing a background theory of existence that illuminates intelligent behavior and criticism.[25]

Perhaps the plainest statement of what Dewey intended in the way of a reconstruction of logic and metaphysics is found in his 1917 essay on "The Need for A Recovery in Philosophy." It is the essay that formed the basis of his lectures in Japan and China in 1919–21 and of *Reconstruction in Philosophy* in 1920. It is a kind of preface to all his later works, for it shows how radically Dewey intended to depart from traditional ways of conceiving the role of philosophy and the subject-matter of logic and metaphysics. In it Dewey makes plain his aim to recover the role of philosophy as a cultural force by emancipating it from "too intimate and exclusive attachment to traditional problems." He thus cuts himself off from both the problems and the methods of traditional philosophy—from the traditional subject-matter of both logic and metaphysics and from all methods of philosophy that are not "caught up in the actual course of events." The recovery of philosophy, he says, depends on a qualitative change in both the problems it tackles and its procedures:

> Until it frees itself from identification with problems which are supposed to depend upon Reality as such, or its distinction from a world of Appearance, or its relation to a Knower as such, the hands of philosophy are tied. Having no chance to link its fortunes with a responsible career by suggesting things to be tried, it cannot identify itself with questions which actually arise in the vicissitudes of life. Philosophy recovers itself when it ceases to be a device for dealing with the problems of philosophers and becomes a method, cultivated by philosophers, for dealing with the problems of men. [*MW*10:46]

It is just such a method that Dewey has devised in his logic of inquiry. And it is those problems of men, the kind that arise in the vicissitudes of life, that comprise the subject-matter of his metaphysics of existence.

I have represented Dewey's work in this chapter as if his main interest after the move to Columbia centered on problems of logic and metaphysics. In fact, of course, these problems were largely a background concern, while problems of ethics and social and political philosophy increasingly came to occupy the foreground of Dewey's attention. The twelve volumes of the *Middle Works* covering the period from 1903 to 1920 are ample evidence that his Aristotelian turn, as I have called it, was far from being simply an effort at the reconstruction of the Organon. What Dewey was engaged in amounts to a wholesale reconstruction of the entire corpus of Aristotle's work; he was attempting to build a philosophy of culture that would serve for the modern world the function that Aristotle's work had served for antiquity.

During these years Dewey became increasingly engaged in matters of public policy and wrote with growing frequency for the popular journals. He took an active role in opposition to the isolationist posture of the country prior to the First World War and advocated participation in the war after Sarajevo, but opposed entry into the League of Nations after Versailles. After the war he traveled to Japan, spent two years lecturing in

China, and visited post-revolutionary Russia, Mexico, and Turkey. His reports from these vantage points and his analyses of the meanings of the rapid changes in the world political scene gained widespread attention. He was well on the way to becoming the country's "national philosopher," though that title was bestowed on him only posthumously.[26]

Both before and after the war Dewey supported the cause of labor, advocating strong unions as necessary to counter the enormous power of well-organized financial and industrial interests. He was a founder of the American Association of University Professors and served as its first president. He was an active participant in the formation of the New York Teachers Guild and of the American Federation of Teachers. As the country moved closer to the depression in the late twenties Dewey commented on public affairs as a regular contributor to *The New Republic* and the *Bulletin* of the People's Lobby. He commented frequently on legislation pending before Congress and on decisions of the Supreme Court and consistently supported the rights of women and minorities, even leading a parade down Fifth Avenue in support of the women's suffrage movement. Although much of his political writing was considered to be radical in his time—he voted for Norman Thomas three times and worked for the establishment of a legitimate third party to represent the interests of the common man—Dewey consistently opposed the Marxist conception of philosophy that had become increasingly popular among his colleagues. His condemnation of Marxism for its dogmatic conclusion that the only hope for the oppressed masses lies in revolution earned him the bitter opposition of many on the left, but allowed Henry Steele Commager to appraise him as "the guide, the mentor, the conscience of the American people . . . for a generation no major issue was clarified until Dewey had spoken."[27]

What Dewey's critics have almost universally failed to realize is the dependence of all this activity and concern on the reconstruction of philosophy—in metaphysics and logic—that comprises the deep structure of Dewey's philosophy of culture. In the chapters that follow I shall try to show how it all hangs together in a comprehensively reconstructed theory of intelligent behavior and a cultural philosophy of meliorism.

CRITICAL BIBLIOGRAPHY

The account of the first meeting between Dewey and Russell used here is from Sidney Hook's introduction to volume 8 of the *Middle Works* (p. xx). See also the *Autobiography of Bertrand Russell*, 3 vols. (London: Allen and

Unwin, 1967–9). I have followed Russell's own account of the development of his thought in *My Philosophical Development* (London: Allen and
Unwin, 1959). The relationship between Russell and Moore is described
by Stephen Toulmin in Allan Janik and Toulmin, *Wittgenstein's Vienna*
(New York: Simon and Schuster, 1973), in terms that suggest a parallel
with the Dewey–Morris relationship. Russell remained committed to
Moore's conception of logical entities much longer than Dewey remained
loyal to Morris's idealism, of course; but Toulmin suggests that both
Russell and Wittgenstein were induced by Moore to think that ethics
relates more to mysticism than to science. While Russell and Wittgenstein
did share a mystical sensibility, Russell's seems to have been generated by
his reverence for the purity of mathematics, Wittgenstein's to have been
more akin to Kierkegaard's. It seems strange that Moore should have had a
role with respect to such different forms of mystical propensity.

It is also noteworthy that both Dewey and Russell wrote their respective
books on Leibniz while they were still under the influence of idealism.
Dewey's followed his 1887 *Psychology* and was written at the very time
when he was beginning to shake loose from idealism of the neo-Kantian
form but was still praising Hegelian logic for its unity of the analytic-
synthetic character of experience. Although the book, *Leibniz's New Essays
Concerning the Human Understanding* (*EW*1:253–435) was intended to
be purely expository, Dewey criticizes the rigidity of Leibniz's logic, which
sticks too closely to the formalist tradition descended from Aristotle. He
praises Leibniz for viewing the world as a dynamic process but blames him
for trying to fit that process into mathematical logic: "The unity of the
content of his philosophy, the conception of organism or harmony, is a
unity which essentially involves difference. The unity of his method is a
formal identity which excludes it. The unity whose discovery constitutes
Leibniz's great glory as a philosopher, is a unity of activity, a dynamic
process. The unity of formal logic is exclusive of any mediation or process,
and is essentially rigid and lifeless" (*EW*1:415).

Russell's book, *A Critical Exposition of the Philosophy of Leibniz* (Cambridge: Cambridge University Press, 1900), praises what Dewey blames.
Russell thinks that all Leibniz's philosophy follows from his doctrine of
propositions. He recognizes that Leibniz breaks away from syllogistic
Aristotelian logic and grounds inference in a new theory of formal relations, and in his 1903 *Principles* Russell credits him with already pointing
the way to mathematical logic: "It is from the recognition of asyllogistic
inferences that modern Symbolic Logic, from Leibniz onward, has derived
the motive to progress" (p. 10). The contrast between the two young
philosophers' responses to Leibniz is thus total.

There is a vast and growing literature on Frege, but I shall not cite it here, since the *Encyclopedia of Philosophy* article by Michael Dummett will suffice nicely. Dummett brings out the fact that Frege's later work moved him in the direction of Wittgenstein's *Investigations* and the use theory of meaning. In his essay on "Russell's Ontological Development," in *Theories and Things* (Cambridge, Mass.: Harvard University Press, 1981), W. V. Quine points out that Russell never seems to have seen the value of Frege's "three way distinction between the expression, what it means, and what if anything it refers to" (p. 79). It is for this reason, Quine thinks, that Russell continued to confuse meaninglessness with failure of reference. Dewey articulates the same complaint, of course, in his criticism of Russell's subsistent entities. But by then Dewey had long since adopted a use theory of meaning and an ontology that placed inference squarely in the midst of practice. With such an ontology in place, Russell's lost souls could be viewed as empirical traits and characteristics without the assistance of atomized bits of sense data, just as long as inference is successful—issues in successful judgments, that is. Meanings in such uses have reference; otherwise they have only a possible use and a possible reference. Even those bald-headed kings of France that Russell mentions as present objects have possible reference and meaning. Nor does the fact that they have no actual reference at present mean that Russell's mention of them is meaningless due to failure of reference. Dewey thinks that inference is temporal (see his discussion of the null class in *Logic*, p. 380, and his treatment of Russell's paradox of the barber who does and does not shave himself, of whom he says: "The contradiction alleged to exist arises only when the existential and the conceptual are confusedly identified" [*Logic*, p. 364]). The mention of the statement "The present king of France is bald" is not meaningless, since its intensional meaning may have had extension at some past moment or may even have extension at some time in the future. Dewey holds that statements *become* true or false depending on extension; he obviously does not hold that all intensional statements are reducible to their extensional meaning, since that would preclude meaningful hypotheticals.

It is Quine also who points out that the dazzling sequel to Russell's project in *Our Knowledge of the External World* (Chicago: Open Court, 1919) is Carnap's *Der Logische Aufbau der Welt* (1928). Despair at Carnap's failure, Quine says, is mitigated by the fact that we can see from it that "the worst obstacle seems to be that the assigning of sense qualities to public place-times has to be kept open to revision in the light of later experience, and so cannot be reduced to definition." Quine credits Burton Dreben with the observation that "the empiricist's regard for experience thus impedes the very program of reducing the world to experience"

(p. 85). Dewey, of course, would agree, which is why he constructs a metaphysics of existence rather than a metaphysics of experience (see the conclusion to his 1906 essay "Reality as Experience" [*MW*3:106]). It seems odd that Bernstein, among others, seems to have missed this point (*John Dewey* [cited in the bibliography of Chapter One] and "John Dewey's Metaphysics of Experience," *Journal of Philosophy*, 58 (5 Jan. 1961): 5–14).

Russell's neutral monism was influenced by Ralph Barton Perry and Edwin B. Holt and is expressed in his *Analysis of Mind* (London: Allen and Unwin, 1921) and *Analysis of Matter* (London: Kegan Paul, 1927). Russell comes closest to Dewey's naturalism in his *Human Knowledge* (London: Allen and Unwin, 1948), although it is clear in his *Logic and Knowledge* (London: Allen and Unwin, 1956) that he remains far from Dewey's naturalistic approach to logic. Even after Alonzo Church and Alan Turing had shown that one of the consequences of the work of Kurt Gödel was that elementary logic could not be completely mathematized, Russell stuck to the belief that mathematics should be considered primarily as an uninterpreted system. He never gave up the primacy of the analytic expressed in his early work *Mysticism and Logic, and Other Essays* (London: Longmans, Green, 1918). (See Quine, p. 154.) Dewey, of course, had taken it for granted that, since all knowledge begins with synthesis, mathematics begins with measurement and counting off. We begin, in other words, with an interpreted arithmetic and arrive at uninterpreted mathematical systems only by abstraction. He still held this view in his 1938 *Logic*.

That inference is existential and synthetic, rather than conceptual and analytic, that it is something that we do or make, is a key element in the unity of science and ethics as presented by Dewey in his lengthy essay on the "Logical Conditions of a Scientific Treatment of Morality," published in 1903 in the same University of Chicago Decennial Publications series as *Studies in Logical Theory*. As Rucker points out, "it received almost none of the attention paid to the logic volume" (*MW*3:xii). Dewey included it in his collection of essays issued in 1946, *Problems of Men* (Philosophical Library), together with material written in the 1930s. Moreover, it remains, as Rucker says, "of permanent importance in the corpus because it presents the most careful argument Dewey has worked out for his claim that ethics must become scientific." I shall return to this essay in Chapter Seven, but here it should be mentioned that it is in this essay that Dewey introduces both the phrase "the logic of conduct," in reference to the method of moral reasoning and judgment, and the "postulate of the continuity of experience" by means of which he wants to show the continuity of intellectual and moral judgment—the former being subsidiary to the latter (*MW*3:39). This postulate has sometimes been taken as applicable to Dewey's metaphysics, although it was advanced in the context of the logic of conduct and clearly refers to the continuity of judgment. Bernstein thinks that it is "undoubtedly the most fundamental principle in Dewey," but he understands it as a principle that has more of an "emotive or normative meaning than a descriptive, informative meaning" (*John Dewey*, p. 180). He assigns it to Dewey's naturalism, which, he thinks, is "never quite clear." But it is clear that *continuity* in the essay on "The Logical Conditions of a Scientific Treatment of Morality" is both a descriptive and an informative term, with specific reference to judgment, one that does not refer to either experience or nature, not being a category of either.

Dewey's extended lecture tour in China (May 1919–July 1921) is fully described by Ou Tsuin-Chen in the *Guide to the Works*, pp. 339–62, where a bibliography pertaining to Dewey's influence on Chinese education and culture is given. Ou's translations (or retranslations) of these lectures may not be authentic owing to the fact that Dewey lectured from notes which were supplied to his original Chinese translators (see John Dewey, *Lectures in China, 1919–1920*, translated and edited by Robert W. Clopton and Ou Tsuin-Chen [Honolulu: University Press of Hawaii, 1973]). It is quite clear, however, that Dewey lectured to his Chinese audiences on Plato and Aristotle as well as on his own educational theories. He evidently made many comparisons between the role of Confucius in Chinese cultural history and that of Aristotle in Western culture, pointing out that the influence of both restricted the growth of science and the assimilation of its methods in dealing with modern problems. (A complete listing of Dewey's Chinese lectures is given in *John Dewey: A Checklist of Translations, 1900–1967*, ed. Jo Ann Boydston [Carbondale, Illinois: Southern Illinois University Press, 1969], pp. 71–90.) There are several accounts of the encounter between Dewey and Russell in China, but I shall mention only John Hersey's delightful account in his recent novel, *The Call: An American Missionary in China* (New York: Knopf, 1985). Accounts of this and of Dewey's other travels are given by Dykhuizen along with appropriate bibliographies and references to Dewey's public defenses of Russell, Trotsky, and Maxim Gorki. (See also Dewey and Horace Kallen, ed., *The Bertrand Russell Case* [New York: Viking, 1941]; Dewey, *The Case of Leon Trotsky* [New York: Harper, 1937], and *Not Guilty* [New York: Harper, 1938].) William W. Brickman discusses these affairs among others in "*Dewey's Social and Political Commentary*," in *Guide to the Works*, pp. 218–56, where a full bibliography can be found.

5: *Existence as Problematic*

When Dewey wrote to Bentley in 1951 that he wanted to "write on *knowing* as the way of behaving in which linguistic artifacts transact business with physical artifacts," he was already engaged in writing an extensive "Re-Introduction" to *Experience and Nature*.[1] It was not that he had changed the perspective that he had tried to articulate there, for he still saw it as providing the necessary background theory of existence for his logic of experience and inquiry; it was just that he wanted to put that perspective in a different vocabulary. He was searching for words that would help his readers escape from the misunderstandings of the book's method and subject-matter. He had tried before, repeatedly. Now, perilously close to the end of his life, he would try once again.[2]

In the first edition of the book he had already tried to explain the essential fallacy involved in all empirical philosophies. He had begun his first chapter by pointing out the slipperiness of the word *experience*. When it "denotes whatever is experienced, whatever is undergone and tried, and also processes of experiencing," he had written, its meaning is lost in ambiguity. Quoting Ralph Barton Perry, he had called it a "weasel word." Citing William James's "double-barrelled" usage of the word to denote both the "how" and the "what" of experience, Dewey had written that it "denotes just this wide universe . . . everything without discrimination, so that experience ceases to have a meaning" (*LW*1:370–1). And he had gone on to point out that "the objection uncovers the exact meaning of a truly empirical method. For it reveals the fact that experience for philosophy is method, not distinctive subject-matter" (*LW*1:371). But his point had been ignored, and he now proposed abandoning the "weasel word" altogether. *Culture* would serve instead. Dewey was, in fact, projecting a wholly new book.[3]

But the new book, to be called "Culture and Nature," was never written.

All we have are a few pages of notes in which Dewey explains why the term *experience* must be abandoned.[4] It was not that it had ever been employed by Dewey to denote the subject-matter of metaphysics and that he was now trying to work out a metaphysics of culture; it was just that it no longer carried the meaning that would allow it to denote the distinctive method employed in Dewey's philosophy:

> The historical obstacles are now so conspicuous that I can at times but wonder how they came to be overlooked. There was a period in modern philosophy when the appeal to "experience" was a thoroughly wholesome appeal to liberate philosophy from dessicated abstractions. But I failed to appreciate the fact that subsequent developments inside and outside of philosophy had corrupted and destroyed the wholesomeness of the appeal—that "experience" had become effectively identified with experiencing in the sense of the psychological, and the psychological had become established as that which is intrinsically psychical, mental, private. My insistence that "experience" also designates *what* is experienced was a mere ideological thundering in the Index for it ignored the ironical twist which made this use of "experience" strange and incomprehensible. [*LW*1:362]

As he wrote to Bentley, he would try once again to clarify the character of inquiry as a transactional process by showing that the relationship between linguistic and physical artifacts is transformational. In the new vocabulary it would become clear that culture proceeds by radically transforming nature to serve its own ends, by naming "artifacts which rank as 'material' and operations upon and with material things" (*LW*1:363), operations from which ideals emerge. Dewey would return to the centrality of communication again and to language as the link between experience and existence.[5]

It is possible, of course, that the projected book, if it had been completed, might have articulated a very different metaphysics, or none at all, from that set forth in the earlier one. In support of this speculation, Rorty points out that Dewey had not only relinquished the term *experience* in favor of *culture*, but had also given up on *metaphysics* as well.[6] It had never been easy, Rorty says, to see how *Experience and Nature* fitted into the genre "which includes the central books of Aristotle's *Metaphysics*, Spinoza's *Ethics* and Josiah Royce's *The World and the Individual,* and similar paradigms." In the end, Rorty concludes that "it is easier to think of the book as an explanation of why nobody needs a metaphysics, rather than as itself a metaphysical system."[7] But the plausibility of such speculation vanishes when we realize that Dewey was giving up merely a vocabulary, not what the words of that vocabulary had stood for.

In the brief notes for the projected book, Dewey says that the term *culture* can "fully and freely carry my philosophy of experience" (*LW*1:361). And in vowing never to use the term *metaphysics* again, Dewey was explicitly responding to the misreading of his use of the term by his critics. There is no suggestion at all that Dewey was prepared to give up the project that the term "names and stands for."[8] Indeed, he says that the original text of *Experience and Nature* "makes it clear that I was proposing a use of the words so different from the traditional one as to be incompatible with it." Rorty's failure to grasp Dewey's radical reassignment of the task of metaphysics is all of a piece with his similar failure to grasp the fact that the subject-matter of that metaphysics is not experience—or culture—but the generic traits of existence as existence that make experience and culture both possible and necessary.[9] It is not that *Experience and Nature* cannot be read as a significant contribution to the history of ideas; it is just that in interpreting the book as an explanation of why nobody needs a metaphysics, Rorty has failed to see that what Dewey is in fact explaining is why nobody needs a metaphysical system of the traditional (foundational) kind. What Rorty has missed is Dewey's proposal of a new use for the term *metaphysics* and the antifoundational meaning and denotation implicit in such a use. But what is most surprising about all this is that Rorty has failed to recognize the new role that Dewey assigns to metaphysics in the very context in which Dewey argues most forcefully for his thesis of meaning as use.

To my way of thinking, there was no need for Dewey to abandon the terms *experience* and *metaphysics*. The *Studies in Logical Theory* had already made it unmistakably plain that he was treating experience as the subject-matter of his philosophical logic. By republishing that material in *Essays in Experimental Logic* together with further material articulating his criticism of all ontological logics of the kind that he had encountered in his skirmish with Russell, Dewey had reaffirmed his earlier view. In the meantime he had been struggling to work out a theory of the proper subject-matter and method of metaphysical inquiry that would bring together the ontological implications of the specific theory of inquiry and his long-standing concern with the generic problems of cultural conflict. It was in the course of this struggle that he took his Aristotelian turn and assigned to metaphysics the task of analyzing the generic traits of existence as existence. *Experience and Nature* indeed belongs to the genre of which Aristotle's *Metaphysics*, Spinoza's *Ethics*, and Josiah Royce's *The World and the Individual* are paradigms, but it must also be seen as a protest against the foundational character of those paradigms. It totally reconstructs the role and function of metaphysics and offers a systematic alternative to the quest for "Being" and the categories of ultimate reality presupposed by traditional metaphysics. It is metaphysics that adopts an empirical and denotative method to construct a perspective from which to see how problematic situations arise and how they can be resolved by the means available.

The remainder of this chapter is given over to a presentation of the character of Dewey's metaphysical perspective. Because I see that perspective as a controlling feature of Dewey's conception of philosophy, one that has been in the process of refinement all along, not something that newly emerges in *Experience and Nature,* I shall be trying to show how Dewey's metaphysical perspective draws together the various parts of his philosophy into a system of sorts—a systematic alternative to foundational systems that works, not by overcoming tradition but by reconstructing it.

The contention that Dewey doesn't even have a metaphysics is easier to deal with, it seems to me, than the contention that most probably gave rise to it. I mean, of course, the contention that he has a metaphysics of experience.[10] For, once it is accepted that the true subject-matter of Dewey's metaphysics is experience itself, which allows Dewey's project to be assimilated to Kant's in the *Critique of Pure Reason,* it becomes almost impossible not to agree with Santayana's accusation that Dewey is half-hearted in his naturalism. If Dewey is read as confining his metaphysics to the foreground of nature, as he is by Santayana, it is clear that a genuine realism is beyond its reach, despite Dewey's claims to the contrary. For if the foreground of experience supplies both the method and the subject-matter of metaphysics, the foregone outcome is necessarily idealism, regardless of the name given to it. Hence, as Rorty concluded, the better course might well be to deny that Dewey had a metaphysics at all.[11]

But why accept Santayana's judgment regarding the subject-matter of Dewey's metaphysics in the first place, or the suggestion that Dewey's philosophy of experience precludes an experiential encounter with an independently and antecedently existing reality? Already in the *Studies in Logical Theory* Dewey made repeated reference to the limiting conditions imposed by reality on experience. And in the note added to the *Essays in Experimental Logic,* he pointed out the significance of his method as a "return to the Aristotelian tradition about logic," in which "knowledge is shaped out of the same subject-matter to which it is applied" (*MW*10:368). The new organon of discovery, he said, "is frankly realistic in acknowledging that certain brute existences, detected or laid bare by thinking but in no way constituted out of thought or any mental process, set every problem for reflection and hence serve to test its otherwise merely speculative results" (*MW*10:341). The trouble is that Dewey's emerging realism is not the foundational functional realism that his Aristotelian contemporaries had adopted. Nor is it the naturalism of Santayana's *Realms of Being*. Dewey's metaphysics was neither foundational nor concerned with "Being" at all. It was both antifoundational and concerned with existence—not the kind of metaphysics that his colleagues and critics either expected or cared about.

The traditional task of metaphysics had been to provide a cosmic context in which the vicissitudes of everyday existence could be seen in the broader perspective of a stable order of ultimate reality and truth, in which the precariousness of ordinary life could be mitigated by reference to a more secure order than is immediately apparent in the foreground of experience. Its function had been to reach beyond existence to essence, to realms of being and ideas that could be disclosed only by means of reason or dialectic, intellectual means far beyond the reach of immediate experience. In traditional realism no less than traditional idealism, in traditional rationalism no less than traditional empiricism, the role of metaphysics had been to disclose an order of reality hidden from ordinary experience. Special methods were required that were not available to the common man. By stating his intention to write a "metaphysics of the common man" Dewey was clearly committing an unforgivable sin against tradition.[12]

It was an offense made all the worse by Dewey's insistence that the method of this metaphysics would also be that of the common man. But Dewey had been insisting all along that scientific method is nothing but the doubt–inquiry method made explicit, that his genetic method was just the logic of experience, beginning with some specific predicament in which the would-be knower finds himself. It is also central to Dewey's thesis that the predicament from which the inquirer seeks extrication be existential, without regard to the domain in which it arises—whether mathematics or aesthetics, physics or economics, psychology or politics, the practice of parenting or the practice of philosophy. It is as a consequence of this thesis that Dewey accounts for the various twists and turns of philosophy through the ages as existential responses of philosophers to situations that have been variously encountered and variously conceived. Every philosophy worth considering, Dewey tells us, has been an existential response to an existential situation, and each, by the nature of the case, is distinct and different from every other, since no two situations are identical. It is the nature of the case, too, therefore, that no two solutions are identical. We are bogged down in a hopeless relativism, it seems, the search for the ultimate solution being frustrated by the very nature of the case.

The problem posed in *Experience and Nature* is thus the specific problem of the nature of the case. The problem is existential, since the nature of the case is existential. It is the specific problem of the nature of existence, or, to use Dewey's terminology, it is the problem of the subject-matter of metaphysics as the "ground-map of the province of criticism." The problem is thus the subject-matter itself: "existence as existence." What can be said about it to relieve us of all this relativism of knowings and knowns that clutters up the history of our human civilization with contradiction after contradiction and confrontation after confrontation? What kind of map of all this chaos is possible? How can philosophy extricate itself from its self-created problematic situation?

The fact that the problem *is* self-created has been one of Dewey's contentions all along. It is a major element in his criticism of Hegel, Leibniz, Peirce, Russell, and even James. It is central to his criticism of Mill's logic and Lotze's, empiricist logic and mathematical logic. He made it a central theme of "The Need for A Recovery of Philosophy" and *Reconstruction in Philosophy*. It would be reiterated in *The Quest for Certainty* and *Art as Experience* and is fundamental to *Democracy and Education, The Public and its Problems*, and both versions of the *Ethics*. It is displayed in its most practical form in *Human Nature and Conduct* and is the one feature of Peirce's doctrine of synechism with which Dewey agrees unreservedly. For, as Peirce put it in his letter to Dewey in 1905: "The first maxim of my 'Synechism' runs: 'Let us not precide our conclusions beyond what our premisses definitely warrant.'"

The subject-matter of metaphysics is existence, Dewey tells us, but he also tells us that we encounter it only in specific situations. We cannot encounter existence as a whole or the whole of existence. It is not even clear whether we can ever encounter existence as such. For every encounter is specific and individual, both temporally and spatially, and is thus different from every other encounter. We never encounter existence, he tells us, except as we encounter an existent. Metaphysics deals with existence as singular, as qualitatively individual, and every individual existent is therefore qualitatively different from every other. Each is unique, the genetic method tells us; and yet there may be sameness, as James suggested, for without sameness there cannot be difference. And without difference there can be no individuality, no existences at all. Relief from relativism emerges from this reflection, sameness is the means of extrication. It is a measure of stability in an otherwise precarious world of qualitatively different individuals.

Thus might run a dialectical reflection on existence. But Dewey wants to proceed by the method of the logic of experience; he wants his method to be empirical and denotative. He protests to Santayana that "the method differs no whit from that of any investigator who, by making certain observations and experiments, and by utilizing the existing body of ideas available for calculation and interpretation, concludes that he really succeeds in finding out something about some limited aspect of nature" (*LW*3:76). He protests that he is simply applying the theory of inquiry worked out in the *Studies* and the *Essays* to the "large and constant features of human sufferings, enjoyments, trials, failures and successes together with the institutions of art, science, technology, politics and religion which mark them, [and] communicate genuine features of the world within which man lives." He protests that there is no novelty at all in regarding these features as subject-matter for metaphysics. If there is novelty, he says, it "lies in the use made of the method to understand a group of special problems which have troubled philosophy" (*LW*3:76). And yet, in spite of these protests—or perhaps because of them—the suspicion remains that Dewey is once again being disingenuous, that what he is *really* doing is either philosophical anthropology or just "clearing away the dead wood of the philosophical tradition."[13]

But Dewey is not being disingenuous at all. He is not just doing philosophical anthropology, although much that is of value for that discipline can be found in *Experience and Nature;* nor is he just clearing away philosophical "dead wood" from the tradition, although that is certainly one of his aims. I shall argue that he knows what he is doing in applying the genetic method to the metaphysics of the common man. The conception of "the generic traits manifested by existences of all kinds" links Dewey's approach to metaphysics with his conception of logic, and the Jamesian conception of the sameness of natural kinds, which is central to Dewey's theory of logical inference, is also central to his theory of the generic traits of all kinds of existences, traits that comprise the baselines of his metaphysical ground-map. We can understand this linkage between logic and metaphysics in Dewey's conception of philosophy only if we are prepared to accept both his logic and his metaphysics as radical reconstructions of pragmatism as understood by Peirce or James. It is the conjugate relation of Dewey's conception of logic to his conception of metaphysics that is of central importance if we are to understand him without splitting him up again, for it is this conjugate and transactional relation that unites his theory of inquiry with his theory of existence and determines the character of his version of pragmatism.

Dewey began preparations for what was eventually to become *Experience and Nature* in 1922. The first version was delivered as a series of three lectures at a plenary session of the American Philosophical Association in late December of that year, as the first Carus Lectures, an honor for which Dewey had been selected by committees appointed from the divisions. The titles of the lectures were: "Existence as Stable and Precarious," "Existence, Ends and Appreciation," and "Existence, Means and Knowledge," but by the time of first publication these had grown into ten chapters, and only the title of the first lecture was retained, albeit with the order of the adjectives transposed, as the heading of the second chapter. The book opens with a chapter on "Experience and Philosophic Method," in which Dewey tries to sum up the results of his investigations in the field of logic. It is a brief sketch of the genetic method of the *Studies* and the *Essays* under a new name, one that does not suggest that it is a rigorously conceived logic at all or that it has any connection with Dewey's critique of Peirce's conception of logic or with James's conception of the denkmittel of thought. Neither Peirce nor pragmatism as such are referred to at all, and James appears only as the initiator of a confusing term used by Dewey in defining his own use of the word *experience*. The method is renamed simply "empirical method" and is loosely associated both with what men do and suffer and how they act and are acted on.

It was not long, however, before Dewey realized that his chapter on "Experience and Philosophic Method" was misleading his readers both as to his method and his subject-matter. He therefore reworked it for the 1929 edition, attempting to make clear the distinction between the method and its subject-matter, and succeeding in making it clear that experience is part of the subject-matter of his inquiry.[14] But it was still not at all clear what else might be included. For he wrote about objects of knowledge as he had all along, as if they could be construed as the only real objects, and *as if* the objects of immediate experience are not to be so construed. The net effect was that more than one reader was convinced that Dewey was indeed denying the reality of objects apart from experience. Even Woodbridge thought that he was denying the antecedently real, much as the idealists had been doing all along.

As Woodbridge stated the problem, in a 1929 essay called "Experience and Dialectic," it is not just that Dewey makes experience into an object of inquiry, or even his assertion that known objects are not identical with objects antecedent to knowledge.[15] It is rather that Dewey has drawn an unwarranted conclusion in his claim that only the eventual objects of inquiry are legitimately known to exist. To make matters worse, Woodbridge thought that Dewey had no support for this claim other than a specious and controversial dialectics. Indeed, he ended up arguing that Dewey's conception of experience was based on a "dialectic which determines what experience is like." In short, Dewey had failed to make his point about the distinction between method and content, had failed even to show that his empirical method was not just a controversial version of a long-discredited dialectic. According to Woodbridge, even the newly published book *The Quest for Certainty* was of no help, since we are forced to the conclusion, he argues, that Dewey has neither an empirical method nor a realist metaphysics.

It would be pleasant to be able to report that Dewey cleared up all these misreadings at once, but this is not the case. He did reply to Woodbridge, of course, and to some of his other critics as well. But far from clearing up matters, he only seemed to make them worse. In his response to Woodbridge's charge, for example, Dewey first admits: "Of course, I employ dialectic. I do not suppose that any one could write on philosophy without using it." But then he goes on to say that his argument does not *depend* on dialectic but only on empirical evidence:[16]

> The evidence which I have cited at considerable length, running, in fact through several chapters, is drawn from the experimental sciences. The argument may be stated in a simple way. The sciences of natural existence are not content to regard anything as an object of knowledge—in its emphatic differential sense—except when the object in question is reached by experimental methods. These experimental methods involve overt operations which re-dispose the existences antecedently had in experience. Q.E.D. [*LW*5:212–3]

Rather than making himself clear, Dewey has merely compounded the problem. He has his own theory of what goes on in the experimental sciences and scarcely acknowledges that it is hardly, at this point, what anyone else thinks. In order to see his Q.E.D. as having any force at all, one would need to have been privy to the full impact of his arguments with Peirce, Lotze, and Russell, to have understood the yet unwritten chapter entitled "Logic and Natural Science: Form and Matter" in *Logic: The Theory of Inquiry*.[17]

Or again, regarding Woodbridge's doubts about Dewey's realism and the sincerity of his commitment to the antecedently real character of objects, Dewey's response slides right past Woodbridge's concern:[18] "If the distinctions (upon which I have insisted at considerable length) between something *had* in experience and the object *known*, between this something and data knowledge, and between the data and the final object of knowledge, be noted, I do not understand why any one should think I was denying the existence of antecedent things or should suppose that the object of knowledge as I conceive it does away with antecedent existences" (*LW*5:211). But Woodbridge had not been reading Dewey as doing away with antecedent existences, only as assigning them a lower-grade reality tantamount to the old idealist distinction between appearance and reality. But Dewey blithely continues: "On the contrary, the object of knowledge is, according to my theory, a re-disposition *of* the antecedent existences. After quoting a statement of mine that 'only the conclusion of reflective inquiry is known' Mr. Woodbridge goes on to say, 'I conceive the object to exist prior to its being known.' I, too, conceive that things had in direct experience exist prior to being known" (*LW*5:211). But do they exist prior to being had in direct experience—that is, antecedently in Woodbridge's sense? Dewey continues: "I deny the identity of things had in direct experience with the object of knowledge *qua* object of knowledge. Things that are *had* in experience exist prior to reflection and its eventuation in an *object* of knowledge; but the latter, as such, is a deliberately effected re-disposition, by means of overt operations, of such antecedent existences" (*LW*5:212). Dewey still does not address Woodbridge's questions; he merely raises a whole new problem as to what these overt operations might be in the context of metaphysical inquiry. What experiments we might perform to aid us in drawing the baselines of our ground-map of the province of criticism Dewey does not say. He just goes on: "The difference between Mr. Woodbridge and myself, as I see it, is *not* that he believes in the existence of things antecedent to knowledge and I do not; we differ in our beliefs as to what the character of the antecedent existences with respect to knowledge is. While Mr. Woodbridge says 'the object exists prior to *its* being known,' I say that '*the* object' is the eventual product of reflection, the prior or antecedent existences being subject-matter *for* knowledge, not *the objects* of knowledge at all" (*LW*5:212). He thus seems unable to recognize that what bothers Woodbridge is the conclusion that he had reached through his conception of method and metaphysics—namely, that real objects are not merely antecedent to being known, but antecedent to being had in experience, antecedent to experience altogether. Dewey's response leaves the reader quite free to draw the conclusion that Dewey's conception of reality is limited to the contents of experience, that all objects are either had in noncognitive experience or known in cognitive experience.

That this was the conclusion reached by Woodbridge is not immediately apparent. But it is surely the conclusion reached by all those who have found Dewey's metaphysical subject-matter to be experience itself and have, accordingly, assigned Dewey's conception firmly to the tradition of idealist metaphysics, the "metaphysics of experience" as they call it. And if all they had to go on in drawing this conclusion were texts like these, texts like even the revised version of the first chapter of *Experience and Nature,* they could hardly be faulted.

But, of course, there are other texts, texts which show that all along Dewey was trying to work out a reconstruction of Hegel's logic, that all along he had been critical of the Kantian and neo-Kantian conception of the real as approachable only by means of a priori categories of experience. There are texts that show that he was bent on a reconstruction of all the traditional forms of realism as well, that he rejected Peirce's nostalgia for Scholastic realism as well as Russell's analytical realism, that he was working out his own reconstruction of the attenuated realism of James's pluralistic universe and was unhappy with James's failure to see the connection between his pragmatism and his radical empiricism. There are texts in which Dewey can be seen to be trying to work out an organon that would restore both facts and values to the legitimate subject-matter of inquiry, that would replace bad metaphysics with good metaphysics, as Joseph Ratner puts it. Indeed, he was trying to work out a metaphysics that would display the very connection between science and human values that James had despaired of ever being able to reach in philosophy, the need for which had driven even Peirce, in the end, to his "Neglected Argument for the Reality of God."[19]

The despair of Dewey toward the end of his life was not at all like that. He simply despaired of making himself clear. He still wanted what he had wanted all along, to communicate the connections of things in experience with things in existence. For, as he wrote in the original version of *Experience and Nature:* "Of all affairs, communication is the most wonderful. That things should be able to pass from the plane of external pushing and pulling to that of revealing themselves to man, and thereby to themselves; and that the fruit of communication should be participation, sharing, is a wonder by the side of which transubstantiation pales" (*LW*1:132).

Sometimes the boldest conjectures are also the simplest. The Copernican revolution in astronomy appealed to Dewey, as it did to Kant before him, as symbolic of how a simple change in perspective can change everything else. Kant had used it as a metaphor for his own change in perspective, and Dewey had used it in characterizing the impact of Francis Bacon's *Novum Organum*. It is the basic idea underlying Dewey's argument in "The Need for A Recovery of Philosophy" and *Reconstruction in Philosophy*. In *The Quest for Certainty* he makes an extended case for the simple change in perspective that results from recognizing the traditional 'quest for being' as hopeless, an exercise in futility. "The other course," he says, "is to invent arts and by their means turn the powers of nature to account; man constructs a fortress out of the very conditions and forces which threatened him."[20]

This other course is what *Experience and Nature* is all about. It is not just another attempt to set forth the categories of existence or of 'being' in the style of traditional metaphysical systems, to set forth the basic principles of reason, or to lay the foundations of knowledge in a first philosophy. It is a bold conjecture telling us that we already have all the categories that we need in order to turn the powers of nature to account, that we already have the means to control our destiny, those means having been invented by the homely art of communication. For it is communication that makes all things possible that *are* possible of human achievement. It is not merely the central problem in the subject-matter of philosophy, but its means and method as well. If anything is foundational about philosophy, it is communication, since everything else depends on it. It is this theme that Dewey had been working on from the outset, that had drawn him in the direction of logic and scientific method almost from the beginning, that had posed the problem he was trying to work out in his logic of experience. In *Experience and Nature* it is the focus of his central chapter "Nature, Communication and Meaning." The whole book is an attempt to work out a theory of how communication is possible, and why we need it. It is an attempt to discover the relationship of communication to nature, to disclose the traits of nature that support it as well as those that impede it. For communication may be the most wonderful of all things, as Dewey says, but it is certainly not the easiest to achieve, as he himself knew.

It is through this consideration, then, that I propose to move into a discussion of what I have insisted is Dewey's metaphysics of existence. Once it is seen that Dewey's attempt to give an account of the generic traits of existences of all kinds is part of an attempt at a general theory of communication and meaning, the connection between this account and his account of the logic of experience is already implied. For it is the thesis of both his logic and metaphysics that "when communication occurs, all natural events are subject to reconsideration and revision; they are re-adapted to meet the requirements of conversation, whether it be public discourse or that preliminary discourse termed thinking. Events turn into objects, things with a meaning. They may be referred to when they do not exist, and thus be operative among things distant in space and time, through vicarious presence in a new medium" (*LW*1:132). That Dewey's theory of communication is the necessary link between his logic and his metaphysics is sometimes obscured by the notion that experience is, after all, a more fundamental category than discourse. Or it may be obscured by the significance that Dewey himself attaches to science as the preferred form of communication, an emphasis prominently displayed in both *Experience and Nature* and *Logic: The Theory of Inquiry*. It may even be obscured by the reflection that Dewey's emphasis on communication simply anticipates the linguistic turn taken by mainstream philosophy under the pervasive influence of Wittgenstein and Austin.

But Dewey's account of communication as the means of intelligent behavior shows that discourse is the *condition* of experience in the sense in which that term is employed in Dewey's conception of philosophy. It is the sine qua non of experience in the logic of experience set forth in the *Studies* and *Essays* and in the philosophy of science laid out in the *Logic,* and it is the backbone of *Human Nature and Conduct.* It is central to his conception of experience as *pedagogical* and of *Art as Experience.* If anything should be regarded as Dewey's first philosophy, it is his genetic account of communication. It is here that Dewey's Aristotelian turn can be seen most clearly, for again and again in the development of his theory of communication, Dewey compares his own theory of the generic traits of existences with the classical account of essences in which the role of grammar is determinate.

On the basis of this comparison, Dewey maintains that the error in classical thought was that it derived its sense of the essences of things from the structure of its grammar. What Dewey contends, rather, is that the structures of discourse are derived from the structures, relations, and properties of *things,* and he goes on to show how the notion of fixed species, static conceptions of natural kinds, arises from the fixed and static character of grammatical forms. He argues that the fixed, static concept of the real that determines both Aristotle's logic and his conception of scientific method also determines his Platonistic conception of the ideal and gives rise to his ethical preference for the contemplative life, for intellectual over practical virtues. In arguing that it is the empirical generic traits of things that make discourse possible, Dewey wants to show how the forms of reasoning are generated from the practice of communication. He wants to show that conversation is the *art* on which all forms of knowledge depend, and that philosophers should have realized this all along—and could have, but for their systematic skepticism of the vagaries of everyday practical arts and commonsense knowings.

What Dewey is arguing for here is not, of course, linguistic analysis as we have come to understand it in the last two or three decades, nor ordinary language philosophy of the sort that grew up in response to the positivist venture into the construction of artificial languages, despite the evident similarities between Dewey's approach to communication, Wittgenstein's approach to meaning as use, and Austin's analysis of doing things with words. For from Dewey's perspective, these approaches are still beholden to the classical habit of thinking that grammar controls our way of knowing things, as opposed to seeing that it is our way of knowing things that ought to control our grammar.[21] Instead of deriving his ontology from the forms of discourse, Dewey derives his forms of discourse from his ontology.[22] It works this way:

> Gestures and cries are not primarily expressive and communicative. They are modes of organic behavior as much as are locomotion, seizing and crunching. Language, signs and significance, come into existence not by intent and mind but by overflow, by products, in gestures and sound. The story of language is the story of the *use* made of these occurrences; a use that is eventual, as well as eventful . . . they became language only when used within a context of mutual assistance and direction. The latter are alone of prime importance in considering the transformation of organic gestures and cries into names, things with significance, or the origin of language. [*LW*1:139]

Dewey's point is not merely that language is instrumental to action, a point of agreement between Lotze, the Kantian idealists, and the followers of Wittgenstein, but that the instrument is existential. These others treat language as expressing thought "as a pipe conducts water," but they miss the transforming function of the instrument "exhibited when a wine-press 'expresses' the juice of grapes," the transformational character of discourse that is recognized only when the signs of language are seen as works of a *social art* invented to turn the powers of nature to account (*LW*1:134). For if existence has generic traits that make discourse possible, it also has generic traits making it necessary. It is instrumental not merely to social existence, but to social survival. To say that the transformation of gestures and cries into names, things with significance, is the origin of language is to insist that all discourse is transformational. It is to insist on a transformational ontology on which meaningful discourse is contingent.

It is just such a transformational ontology as Dewey provides in *Experience and Nature* that shows how language hooks onto the world and provides the connection with his theory of inquiry. The logic of experience is thoroughly ontological and transformational. The boldness of Dewey's ontological conjecture lies in his regarding the object of knowledge as both real and as transformed through the very process by means of which it becomes such an object. The use of language in communication is the art of transformation. Words and sentences are the linguistic artifacts by means of which we transact business with the world, using them to invent those "physical artifacts, tools, implements, apparatus" employed in the process. Tools are indispensable for raising knowledge above the level of common sense, Dewey tells us, "but at every point appliances and application, utensils and uses, are bound up with directions, suggestions and records made possible by speech; what has been said about the role of tools is subject to a condition supplied by language, the tool of tools" (*LW*1:134).

In order to grasp the transformational character of Dewey's ontology it is necessary to recognize that instrumentality is not ascribed merely to linguistic and physical artifacts, but to the objects of knowledge as well. There is a sense in which Dewey's treatment of such objects is thoroughly instrumental—so much so that it is tempting to say that he views these objects as artifacts as well, as convenient fictions invented to aid in the process of discovery. But Dewey insists that invention stops short with the arts of discourse and tool-making. We cannot invent objects of knowledge to suit our purposes, although our purposes may sometimes be served by such objects. A genuine—that is to say existential—transaction is conducted when an object *for* knowledge is transformed into an object *of* knowledge. What we invent is a use for the object once it has been discovered. The *meaning* of the object carried in discourse is, accordingly, a matter of use. But its use is neither its validity in discourse or its truth. Truthful discourse, valid reasoning, is contingent on the existential reference—the *extensional* meaning—of the terms of discourse used therein. It is only the greater projectibility of the discourse reached by means of experimental inquiry that gives it any advantage over discourse that is merely anchored in common sense. But that greater projectibility is not wholly due to the greater sophistication of experimental technique in inquiry, it is also due to the transformational effect consequent on the application of more powerful means—both conceptual instruments and physical artifacts of a developed nature—for getting at the objective character of the object itself, its properties and relations. The transformations thus effected in the object of knowledge are disclosures of possible meanings and uses of the object. The nature of the object does not lie in its inner or intrinsic character, but in its extrinsic properties and relations. It is inquiry, Dewey contends, that intervenes between the taken-for-granted nature of the object and the eventual object that has been transformed by the process into an object having new uses as a result of the discovery of new properties and relations. That these *are* new is precisely because they are extrinsic and did not exist previously or independently. While the object itself endures throughout the process, its character undergoes a very considerable reconstruction.[23]

It is tempting to say that this account of ontological change that results from the process of knowledge is not properly ontological at all. For what changes, it might be said, is not the real object, the object per se, but the object as known. But it is not at all clear how such a real object could be known to remain unchanged. Indeed, it is not clear how such a real object could be known at all. Dewey sees Aristotle as simply postulating the existence of unchanging essences or as ascribing them vaguely to some sort of direct apprehension. But in Dewey's view, this move is totally unnecessary once we are willing to see our whole cognitive enterprise as a natural process that, instead of setting up knowledge as mimesis, views it in terms of co-operation with nature in the task of turning the latter's powers to account. Dewey does not wish to deny the intrinsic nature of things; he merely argues that such intrinsic natures can be known only by means of their extrinsic qualities.[24] And these are what are clearly not fixed in advance of inquiry, or independently.

The extrinsic qualities of a thing are disclosed only as it relates to other things; indeed, they *are* its relations to other things. What happens in the process of inquiry is that these relations change. The thing is not merely *seen* differently as a result of inquiry, nor is the difference merely the effect of causal factors present in the operations of inquiry, which intervene between the noncognitive object and the object as known. For the object, by being placed in wholly new relationships becomes a different object. The transaction that takes place in inquiry reconstructs the object by reconstructing its relations. It is, of course, the self-same object that undergoes this transformation, and it endures this change because it is a feature of existences of all kinds that they are extrinsically stable through change. The table of common sense is the same table that the physicist may describe as a complex electrochemical energy system. And both the commonsense description and the physicist's description are descriptions of extrinsic traits of the table, empirical traits. Moreover, it is not just because the physicist takes into account more of these traits than the common man that he is able to give a more complete description. It is that his explanation includes empirical characteristics—that is, relations—that had no antecedent existence. The original object—one is tempted to say the thing-in-itself, despite Dewey's ban of such terminology—is nevertheless the same qualitative individual object—still real, but really changed. What the table really is depends on who wants to know. For most of us the commonsense table will do very nicely. But that is no reason to deny the physicist's table. It is, rather, a reason to accept the continuity of common sense and science and of ontological change; ontology thus becomes a provisional and transactional affair.

There can be little doubt that, overall, the notion of the real as transformational derives from both Hegel and Darwin. But Dewey makes the genetic history of his ontology explicit, and that ontology is explicitly his own. He accepts neither Hegel's conception of change as dialectical nor Darwin's notion of adaptation to a relatively stable environment. All along he has been arguing that change occurs in the environment in all sorts of ways, and that the way of intelligent behavior is one of them. He saw Peirce's "Lamarckist" approach to evolution as fundamentally misguided, since there can be no destined truth, no ultimate synechism. He accepted that we cannot construct our metaphysical conceptions a priori, derive them from the logical principles of ordered discourse, or construct them from the innate ideas and forms of dialectics. He took the view that knowing is an extrinsically social activity, one that can be considerably enhanced by the formal institution of education, and that knowing of all kinds gets on best—even in the institutional setting of the schools and the democratic setting of the state—when it is reached experimentally. Moreover, he pointed out that experimental knowing is nothing new, that the logic of experience has been there all the time. It is just that the metaphysics of the common man has been ignored by philosophers. He has argued all along for the practical arts as the genetic forebears of both the fine arts and science. He now makes all this explicit:[25]

> That character of everyday experience which has been most systematically ignored by philosophy is the extent to which it is saturated with the results of social intercourse and communication. Because this factor has been denied, meanings have either been denied all objective validity, or have been treated as miraculous extra-natural intrusions.

If, however, language, for example, is recognized as the instrument of social cooperation and mutual participation, continuity is established between natural events (animal sound, cries, etc.) and the origin and development of meanings. Mind is seen to be a function of social interactions, and to be a genuine character of natural events when these attain the stage of widest and most complex interaction with one another. [*LW*1:7]

Language, he says, is the link that vitiates the alleged necessity of dividing up the world into the physical and the mental, the real and the ideal.

It remains, then, simply a matter of showing how this link is forged. Gestures and sounds, he has been saying, are not initially taken as signs and signals. But when they are so taken, are intentionally used as such, they take on an objective import. "Something is literally made common in at least two different centres of behavior. To understand is to anticipate together, it is to make cross-reference which, when acted upon, brings about a partaking in a common, inclusive, undertaking" (*LW*1:141). The link is forged in communication. Both success and failure in communication are existential facts, since linkage is not assured. "Human beings illustrate the same traits of both immediate uniqueness and connection, relationship, as do other things" (*LW*1:138). Communication is as perilous an undertaking as it is wonderful. Because it is existential, it illustrates the same generic traits as human beings and other things. Because it involves human beings in their immediate uniqueness and attempts to link such individuals in a common undertaking of cross-reference, success is elusive. The linkage of intentionality with the object of reference is not always or easily established. Yet it can occur, and once it has happened, Dewey tells us, the "story of language is the story of the *use* made of these occurrences; a use that is eventual, as well as eventful." The link is forged in action and judgment, in common action and common judgment. It is a linkage that is existential in character through and through. It is a common ontological commitment.[26]

I have been trying to portray the development of Dewey's metaphysics as an empirical inquiry into those characteristics of man and nature that make communication both possible and necessary. In taking this approach I have been working from the end of what I understand to be Dewey's ontology of existences in the direction of his metaphysics of existence. I have thus been suggesting that we had best understand Dewey in his own terms and by means of his own conception of the genetic method, the

method scorned by Peirce as intolerant, the one that even some sympathetic critics think that pragmatism can well do without. For we can ignore
Dewey's genetic approach only at the cost of misconstruing his whole
conception of philosophy.

The process of knowing the world begins with knowing things, those
objects or existences that Dewey says are "had" in casual situations as the
possessions of noncognitive experience. In immediate experience these
objects are qualitative, specific, and individual; they are not objects of
communication at all. We don't talk about them because we have no need
to talk about them. We don't understand them in terms of their relations
with other things because we don't understand them at all. And yet, as soon
as an occasion arises—what Dewey calls a "felt need"—the object has the
possibility of becoming an object *of* knowledge. Knowing is thus an
activity of "doing and making." And every doing is a redoing, and every
making a remaking, once it is recalled that early on Dewey rejected the copy
theory of knowing and the mimetic account of empiricist epistemology.
But, Dewey insists, these reconstructions of the givens and hads of casual
experience that comprise our eventual objects as knowns are reconstructions made possible by nature's own materials. They are remakings on
account of having been placed in new contexts and employed in new ways.
Gestures and cries take on extensional meaning as they acquire referring
uses and are interpreted. Intended uses do not always succeed, however, for
nature is not subservient to our every whim. The ontological commitments
of everyday discourse are contingent and necessary only as provisionally
required. What counts as real is precisely what makes discourse possible,
the relations of things that can be counted on. Dewey calls these relations
objective properties because of their characteristics *as* stable. They are the
empirical traits of the qualitatively individual existences that comprise the
extensional reference of the generic propositions that Dewey delineates in
his *Logic*. In *Experience and Nature* he refers explicitly to the extrinsic
stability of existences of all kinds as a generic trait that makes communication, knowing as a social affair, possible.

Dewey agrees with the Greeks that "the presence in things of generic
form renders them knowable" (*LW*1:163). But he disagrees that this is an
inherent and intrinsic possession of natural kinds and with their whole idea
of individuality as being a "failure of realization of objective forms on the
part of the indwelling family to impress itself adequately, owing to stubborn resisting material constitution." Once it is clear that there is no such
permanent and unchanging "indwelling family," it becomes equally clear
that individual things have no indwelling essences.[27] The posited perma-

nence of generic form, which constitutes the basis of Aristotelian logic and organon, turns out to have been a snare and a delusion. The Greeks may have been right in thinking of matter as the principle of individuality, but they were wrong in thinking of it as chaotic and formless, as incapable of generating forms of its own or admitting of existential transformation through inquiry. Dewey agrees with the Greeks that precariousness is a trait of all material things, but he disagrees with their seeing it as a trait of material objects only. It is a trait of forms as well, at least as far as forms are real objects in the real world. Generic form is indeed what makes knowing possible, but it is the very precariousness of such forms as we know them that makes continuing inquiry necessary. The real world is a changing world, a relational world, not one of fixed potentialities and permanent possibilities.

As Dewey said to Max Eastman apropos of his Oil City experience, "Everything that's here is here, and you can just lie back on it." In a more expanded articulation of what it is in our experience of nature we can "just lie back on," McDermott puts it this way:

> The setting is the interaction of the human organism with nature or with the environment. Nature has a life of its own, undergoing its own relatings, which in turn become what we experience. Our own trans-action with the affairs of nature cuts across the givenness of nature and our ways of relating. This is *how* we experience *what* we experience. Dewey was a realist in the sense that the world exists independent of our thought of it, but the meaning *of* the world is inseparable from our *meaning* the world.[28]

And in Dewey's own articulation of the same point, in the chapter on "Nature, Communication and Meaning" which McDermott presupposes, we read:

> Meaning, fixed as essence in a term of discourse, may be imaginatively administered and manipulated, experimented with. Just as we overtly manipulate things, making new separations and combinations, there-by introducing things into new contexts and environments, so we bring together logical universals in discourse, where they copulate and breed new meanings. There is nothing surprising in the fact that dialectic (or deduction, as it is termed by moderns) generates new objects; that, in Kantian language, it is "synthetic," instead of merely explicating what is already had. All discourse, oral or written, which is more than a routine unrolling of vocal habits, says things that surprise

the one that says them, often indeed more than they surprise any one
else.   [*LW*1:152]

In this way the precariousness of our meanings turns out to be to our
advantage. We need no fixed essences of rigid natural kinds, no permanent
ontological commitments to carry the conversation forward. But our
"meaning the world" is still inseparable from "the meaning *of* the world."

Peirce constructed his metaphysical schemes in terms of destiny, confident that everything would come out right in the end, that truth is what
we are fated to come up with if we can just get our meanings clear. Dewey
sees no metaphysical support for such confidence, for he cannot trust to
fate even in the form of the doctrine of the synechistic theory of the
continuity of inquiry. He maintains that nature is not that well organized,
contains no rational core such as Peirce presupposes. What it does possess,
however, are generic traits that offer piecemeal support, temporal generic
forms that allow provisional inference, and regional ontologies. The precariousness that Dewey describes as a generic trait is mitigated by the
opposing trait of stability. The generic trait of qualitative individuality, by
contrast, is not paired with anything like Peirce's overall scheme of con-
nectedness or continuity. No ultimate order of universal rationality is
needed to counterbalance the particularity and uniqueness of the individual existent, for every existent is already related to other existent particulars
in some way. But this relatedness, which Dewey points to in the predications of primitive discourse, is contingent or dependent on the particular
domain of discourse. And each such domain is extrinsically social in
character, and thus existentially related to and contingent on an environment that is extrasocial in character.[29]

In developing the conception of communication that issues both in
Experience and Nature and in his long-standing concern with logic as a
means of inquiry, Dewey had consistently maintained that acquired habits
of behavior are the extrinsic empirical traits necessary for the making of a
society or culture. He had maintained all along that we cannot simply
assume, as it had been traditionally assumed, that human beings have been
created by nature as intrinsically—that is, essentially, in the classical sense
of a rigidly designated set of potentialities—social. As far back as his
collaboration with Mead at Michigan, Dewey had been arguing that there
is nothing in physiological psychology that defines the destiny of man or
determines the specific character of a culture. He had convinced Mead that
mind is not a substance located in the brain, but simply the power of the
individual organism to manipulate signs and symbols in its quest for

survival. He had long ago persuaded him to concentrate on social psychology, rather than physiological psychology, in accounting for mind, self, and society. For Dewey had long since convinced himself that "emergent life changes the character of the world."[30]

I do not mean to argue that Mead's achievements were entirely due to Dewey's influence. For it is clear that the central chapter of *Experience and Nature* owes much to Mead's independent researches and to his conception of the "generalized other" made possible by means of discourse. Nor is it possible to argue that Dewey was not enormously influenced by Mead's contention that "the significant symbol is then the gesture, the sign, the word which is addressed to the self when it is addressed to another individual, and is addressed to another, in form to all other individuals, when it is addressed to the self."[31] What I do mean to suggest, however, is that Mead arrived at this theory of communication by means of the method set forth by Dewey in his *Studies in Logical Theory,* the method that Peirce suspected of intolerance for its exclusion of subject-matters that cannot be studied genetically, and that Dewey goes far beyond Mead in applying the genetic method to those subject-matters that Peirce thought were excluded. For Dewey applies it not merely to the science of society—including what is today called the sociology of science—but to the more inclusive subject-matter of nature and the generic traits of existences of all kinds. It can be argued that Dewey's debt to Mead is enormous, but it cannot be argued that Dewey's conception of philosophy—or of pragmatism—is due to Mead. For it was Dewey who made the connection between the social conception of communication, which he shared with Mead, and the subject-matter of logic and scientific method worked out in *Experience and Nature* and *Logic.*[32]

In Dewey's reconstruction of pragmatism Mead provides the needed counterbalance to Peirce, in Dewey's analysis of mind the needed counterbalance to James. But the background theory is Dewey's own.

This chapter will have to end inconclusively, not because I shall not attempt a summary of Dewey's conception of the generic traits of existences of all kinds, but because any such summary must inevitably fall short of the kind of closure that we have come to expect of a metaphysical system. If we take the history of such systems as *defining* the nature of metaphysics, inclusively and exclusively, Dewey's system is not a system at all. But why should we accept such a definition in the first place? Certainly analogous definitions of subject-matter and method in other domains of discourse and inquiry have long been suspect and largely abandoned. And Dewey himself has in part been responsible for showing us why such procedures ought to be abandoned. So why should we continue to demand of a metaphysics that it reach closure as a system of first principles all neatly packed and delivered? Why should we continue to think of metaphysics as a system of the foundational categories of 'being'—or even of existence as existence—at all? Why not give up the whole idea of first philosophy entirely?

This last question brings us back to reality, for we do need a basis for our norms and principles of judgment, for reaching closure with respect to our knowings and knowns. We have long searched for some grounding for our theories of the world that would help us to know what to do next. And it is here that the radical nature of Dewey's conception of philosophy stands out most clearly, for he tells us that there are no such foundations. It is not just that a particular system fails to reach closure; it cannot do so by the very nature of the case. It is not just that we are fallible, as Peirce said, or the consequence of what he called our four incapacities. Nor is it just that chance everywhere mitigates necessity in the natural order of things—that is, that tychism is a feature of existences of all kinds. For although it is true that all existence is precarious, it is also true that it is stable—and temporal. It is an unfinished universe, and because it does not itself reach closure, neither can metaphysics.

Reflection on this melancholy state of affairs, Dewey tells us, readily becomes refusal to acknowledge it; instead, we substitute a realm of transcendent forms and transcendental categories. The Platonic ideas may be repudiated, but only to be transformed into the innate ideas of the Cartesians or the Absolute Mind of the idealists. And even when the dualism of the mental and the physical is rejected explicitly, it creeps back in by the back door. Weary of his critics' attempt to read his metaphysics as a foundation for knowledge and science, Dewey attempted once again, in his ninetieth year, to set matters straight in a new introduction which was never completed:

> The dualism of matter and mind may no longer overtly supply cur-
> rently dominant philosophical problems with their *raison d'être*. The
> assumptions underlying the cosmic dichotomy have, however, not
> been eliminated; on the contrary, they are the abiding source of issues
> which command today the attention of the very philosophers who
> pride themselves upon having replaced the philosophical "thinking"
> of a bygone period with a mode of treatment as exact as the former
> discussions were sloppy. One striking example is found in the efforts

now put forth to provide "foundations" for science in both its physical and mathematical aspects. In formulated statement, this concern differs from that of how knowledge is possible anyway; no explicit reference is made to the chasm between the knowing subject as mental and "object to be known" as physical as the source of the problem. But what is not explicit is, in principle, implicit. It is assumed that science as a total enterprise is inherently non-self-supportive, that it is necessarily incapable of supplying itself with whatever "foundations" it may need and hence it is the task of the new type of rigoristic philosophers and their Logic to do for science what science cannot do for itself. [*LW*1:349–50]

As against this, Dewey proposes starting from the other end altogether, from the knowledge we already have, what we already know about existences of all kinds, the generic traits that are everywhere encountered in experience, not least experience itself.

A quarter of a century earlier he had stated all that can really be said about the task of metaphysics: "We live in a world which is an impressive and irresistible mixture of sufficiencies, tight completenesses, order, recurrences which make possible prediction and control, and singularities, ambiguities, uncertain possibilities, processes going on to consequences as yet indeterminate. They are mixed not mechanically but vitally like the wheat and tares of the parable" (*LW*1:47). The task is one of noting these features, for "they have rarely been frankly recognized as fundamentally significant for the formation of a naturalistic metaphysics." Once noted they form the baselines of the metaphysical ground-map. In a text both familiar and frequently misread:

If philosophy be criticism, what is to be said of the relation of philosophy to metaphysics? For metaphysics, as a statement of the generic traits manifested by existences of all kinds without regard to their differentiation into physical and mental, seems to have nothing to do with criticism and choice, with an effective love of wisdom. It begins and ends with analysis and definition. When it has revealed the traits and characters that are sure to turn up in every universe of discourse, its work is done. So at least an argument may run. But the very nature of the traits discovered in every theme of discourse, since they are ineluctable traits of natural existence, forbids such a conclusion. Qualitative individuality and constant relations, contingency and need, movement and arrest are common traits of all existence. This fact is source both of values and of their precariousness; both of immediate possession which is casual and reflection which is a precondition of secure attainment and appropriation. Any theory that detects and defines these traits is therefore but a ground-map of the province of criticism, establishing base lines to be employed in more intricate triangulations. [*LW*1:308–9]

What remains is merely to point out that these "traits" are what Dewey has been talking about all along. They are the empirical characteristics of "kinds" of existences that make inference possible, that are instrumental in the resolution of specific problems in the *Studies* of 1903. Here, of course, he is taking them in reference to *all* kinds of existences—that is, to the more inclusive kind denoted by the all-inclusive term *natural existence*. For here he is talking metaphysics, not logic. He is talking about the character of existence, not just that part of it called experience.[33]

CRITICAL BIBLIOGRAPHY

The reader is urged to consult the Carbondale edition of *Experience and Nature* (*LW*1) published in 1981. The appendixes and textual apparatus conveniently assemble the scholarly material needed for following the troubled history of the work. Reviews of both the 1925 and 1929 editions are cited, and the story of Dewey's attempt to put together a new introduction in his ninetieth year is told by Joseph Ratner who has brought together Dewey's manuscripts relating to that project. Assessments of either the method or the subject-matter of Dewey's metaphysics that do not take this material into account are necessarily incomplete, and one should bear this in mind when judging the early appraisals of Dewey's metaphysics made by Santayana and Woodbridge, which I have referred to in the text. Although I am convinced that both Santayana and Woodbridge misread Dewey, there is a sense in which they can hardly be blamed for doing so, for I think it is fair to say that Dewey did not make much progress in clarifying either his subject-matter or his method in his responses to his critics, or even in his revisions and prefaces, including the abortive 1949 versions. That is why I have put so much stress on the need to view *Experience and Nature* as intimately related with Dewey's work on method, his logic of experience as worked out in the *Studies* and the 1938 *Logic*. For it is only in this way that we can see how the subject-matter and method of Dewey's metaphysics hang together with the subject-matter of his conception of logic, art, ethics, politics, and human nature, and that it is a metaphysics at all and not just a critical survey of past systems and traditions.

It has been pointed out by Randall that Woodbridge learned a great deal from Dewey and that his conception of metaphysics underwent some fairly radical changes due to Dewey's influence (see John Hermann Randall's essay entitled "Dewey's Interpretation of the History of Philosophy" in the Schilpp volume). Randall's collection of essays called *Nature and Historical Experience* (New York: Columbia University Press, 1958) contains what is surely the best single treatment of Dewey's metaphysics extant: the essay called "The Nature of Metaphysics: Its Function, Criteria, and Method." Unfortunately Randall tends to conflate the views of Dewey and Woodbridge, which leads him to neglect their differences and to miss the radical nature of Dewey's emphasis on metaphysics as a background theory only. Randall appears to see Dewey as treating metaphysics as first philosophy, just as Woodbridge does. I have made plain my disagreement with Randall on this, although I have learned more about both metaphysics and Dewey from Randall than from any other source save Dewey's own writings. It is symptomatic of what seems to go wrong in Randall's reading of Dewey's method that he treats that method as an extension of Peirce's method of following out "leading principles" of science to see where they lead. But, in Dewey's view, it is not the leading principles of science that are the key to metaphysics but what science shows to be the generic traits of particular existents of all kinds.

Randall understands Dewey's references to "existence as existence" differently than I do. I take it that Dewey is referring to nothing other than the generic traits of existences, that his reference to existences of all kinds does not establish that kinds are permanent substances in the Aristotelian sense, in the naturalistic sense of Woodbridge, or in the sense of Randall's definition of *substance* as a "cooperation of processes" (see the title of chapter 6 in *Nature and Historical Experience:* "Substance as a Cooperation of Processes: A Metaphysical Analysis"). Rather, I see Dewey as rejecting outright the whole notion of substance, including the kind of reconstruction suggested by Randall. Substance cannot be one of Dewey's categories because he rejects all categories. Neither are Dewey's generic traits categorical in the sense of analytic, which makes me suspicious of what Randall calls metaphysical analysis.

I take it that what Dewey was undertaking in *Experience and Nature* is an empirical denotation of traits that are helpful to inquiries of the type pursued by Randall, but it is also clear that Dewey includes traits that are not helpful at all. He would place as much emphasis on noncooperation as on cooperation, it seems to me. In the end Randall seems to share Woodbridge's view that metaphysics "lays bare those generic traits and distinctions which terms can *formulate*" (p. 144). He calls this "functional realism" and ascribes it to Dewey as well as to Woodbridge. By contrast I take Dewey to say that structure is just as important an aspect of his realism as function. I take Dewey's conception of inquiry, his theory of logic and its subject-matter, as showing that he takes structure as a limiting condition of function, and thus of existences of all kinds. It seems to me that it is not the unique function of metaphysics, as Dewey conceives it, to "lay bare the generic traits and distinctions which terms can *formulate*," since that is the function of inquiries of all kinds. The function of metaphysics is much more modest; it is to note those empirical features of existences of all kinds that make the other kinds of inquiry both possible and necessary—a very limited task indeed in comparison with that envisaged by Randall. (It may also be noted that Randall tends to brush aside ontology and proceed directly to metaphysics, whereas Dewey approaches metaphysics through ontology—that is, by means of existences as qualitatively individual.)

Because I regard Hook's early book *The Metaphysics of Pragmatism* as a much more successful appraisal and interpretation of Dewey's instrumentalism than the later effort of White, I find it somewhat disappointing that Hook should offer support for the view of *Experience and Nature* as philosophical anthropology in his introduction to the Carbondale edition (*LW*1:xvi). While it is true that Dewey's book makes a significant and durable contribution to that field of inquiry, to emphasize that aspect of his achievement seems to make the mistake that Dewey himself called "taking the part for the whole" (see "The Superstition of Necessity," *EW*4:36). It is the mistake that underlies Bernstein's view that the subject-matter of Dewey's metaphysics is experience, and that helps support the contention of Rorty, in "Dewey's Metaphysics," that "two generations of commentators have been puzzled to say what method might produce 'a statement of the generic traits manifested by existences of all kinds without regard to their differentiation into mental and physical' while differing 'no whit' from that employed by the laboratory scientist" (reprinted in *Consequences* [cited in the bibliography of Chapter One], p. 73). In my view, Bernstein, Hook, and Rorty all fail to see how Dewey's metaphysics relates to the traditional conception of metaphysics, how radical a reconstruction of the traditional conception it is. They seem to think that because Dewey does not attempt to write his metaphysics in the way in which metaphysics has traditionally been written, then somehow he is not doing metaphysics at all. What I have tried to show, however, is that he has reconstructed the tradition by aiming at a different target and using a different method.

In 1939 Hook gave the following account of traditional metaphysics as he thought Dewey saw it: "Traditional metaphysics has always been a violent and logically impossible attempt to impose some parochial scheme of values upon the cosmos in order to justify or undermine a set of existing social institutions by a pretended deduction from the nature of Reality" (*John Dewey* [cited in the bibliography to Chapter One], p. 34). It is true that sometimes Dewey did view traditional metaphysics in this way, for the ideological uses of metaphysical systems cannot be denied (see Dewey's essay "Antinaturalism in Extremis," in *Naturalism and the Human Spirit,* ed. Y. H. Krikorian [New York: Columbia University Press, 1944]). But he also saw other uses for metaphysics. His very sympathetic reading of Plato and Aristotle shows that he saw metaphysics as serving a positive function in binding together the divergent and conflicting elements of a culture and in giving that culture some measure of coherence in its relation to the natural environment. Moreover, I take it that Dewey recognized the difference between a traditional metaphysics serving this positive end and one used for the sort of ideological ends noted by Hook—not that it is always easy to distinguish between the positive and negative uses of metaphysics. But it is one of the virtues of Dewey's conception of philosophy that it shows how to get at the grounds for making such a distinction, for making our cultural evaluations more objective. Neither Hook nor Rorty dismisses Dewey's achievement in this respect, for they laud his astute criticism of the relationship of philosophy to culture and agree regarding how completely Dewey is committed to the view of that relationship as reciprocal in character. But they want to ascribe that criticism to Dewey's philosophical anthropology, rather than his metaphysical perspective. (Morton White and George Geiger have a similar tendency, as I pointed out in my essay "Dewey's Metaphysical Perspective: A note on White, Geiger and the Problem of Obligation," *The Journal of Philosophy,* 57 (1960): 100–15.) Randall's essay on "The Nature of Metaphysics" makes the best case I know of for viewing traditional metaphysics in its positive aspects as well as in its negative impact on culture—aside from Dewey's own case, that is.

The only substantial treatment of Dewey's theory of criticism that takes Dewey's metaphysical perspective seriously enough to trace the connections between the subject-matter and method of Dewey's metaphysics and his general axiology is James Gouinlock's *John Dewey's Philosophy of Value* (cited in the bibliography to Chapter One). Its only weakness is the brevity of its treatment of the development of Dewey's logical theory and its bearing on Dewey's theory of generic traits.

6: The Language of Logic and Truth

hen A. J. Ayer published his *Language, Truth and Logic* in 1936, thereby capturing a title that could well have served for the volume that Dewey was working on at the time, the philosophical tide was running in his favor. Mainstream logic was preeminently the mathematical and symbolic logic descended from Frege and Russell, but shorn of its earlier metaphysical pretensions, and mainstream epistemology and philosophy of science were already under the influence of the logical empiricism evolved by the Vienna Circle from the nineteenth-century scientific positivism of Comte. Ayer's reformulation of Hume's famous division of all meaningful statements into the exclusive categories of the analytic and the synthetic, on the basis of his own principle of verification, had the effect of directing these two powerful mainstream currents into a mighty confluence that threatened to carry all philosophy with it.

By comparison with the attention accorded Ayer's book, Dewey's *Logic: The Theory of Inquiry,* published two years later, was virtually ignored. It was not just that Dewey's book was difficult to a degree verging on incomprehensibility, or that it appeared not to be about logic at all in the sense in which that term was currently used, or that hardly anyone noticed that it was a book about language and meaning, or even that Dewey insisted on using vaguely defined terms such as *warranted assertibility* in place of the crisper, more definite *truth.* It was also that even Dewey's most sympathetic critics seemed unable to grasp its relevance to the mainstream currents of the day. Dewey was running against the tide not only in philosophical logic and epistemology, but in the philosophy of language and ethics as well. By the time the tide turned, Dewey's philosophy of the language of logic and truth had been all but forgotten. Ironically, much that it contained would be painfully rediscovered in the undertow.

It seems clear that what counted most against the success of the *Logic* at the time was that Dewey had distanced himself from the prevailing rigorous formal techniques, abjuring even the commonplace methods of symbolic formulation consequent on the paradigm of *Principia Mathematica*. Even Dewey's most competent admirers seemed unable—or unwilling—to see that he had selected these very same rigorous formal techniques and systems of symbolic formulation as the central targets of attack in his critical reconstruction of logical theory. The trenchant critique of a priorism that the work contained was brushed aside as already outmoded and, as Nagel put it, "directed upon issues which dominated thinkers of the preceding century—problems which, though intelligible enough in terms of the scientific, religious, and social conceptions then current, have lost much of their meaning and relevance for the contemporary reader" (*Sovereign Reason* [cited in the bibliography to Chapter One], p. 136). Condemnation by faint praise has rarely been more effective. But what was missed was the attack advanced by Dewey on the categorical foundations of modern symbolic logic itself, for Dewey's target was the very dogma of empiricism descended from Hume that insisted on the categorical distinction between the analytic and the synthetic. Missed, too, was Dewey's effectiveness in undermining the very foundations on which the theories contained in Ayer's *Language, Truth and Logic* were built.[1]

Far from reflecting the aversion to the symbolic formulation of logic imputed by Nagel, the insistent theme of the *Logic* is that an adequate system of symbolization is contingent on both a better theory of language than was then available to philosophical logicians and a better theory of the materials to be symbolized. The categorical disjunction between matter and form that underlies the analytic-synthetic dichotomy of extant systems of logical symbolization is picked out by Dewey as the latest form of the philosophical fallacy. It is the form of dualism that comprises both the fatal flaw in the program envisaged by logical empiricism and the flaw that caused Frege's foundations of arithmetic to totter. His *Logic* is dedicated, Dewey says in the preface, to the conviction that the general principles of language which he will set forth "will enable a more complete and consistent set of symbolizations than now exists to be made." For what now exists is a philosophy of language in which matter and form are separated by the analytic-synthetic disjunction. In his own work, then, "the absence of symbolization is due, first, to a point mentioned in the text, the need for development of a general theory of language in which form and matter are not separated; and secondly, to the fact that an adequate set of symbols depends upon prior institution of valid ideas of the conceptions and relations that are symbolized" (*Logic*, p. iv). Dewey's argument in the *Logic* is thus directed against the very duality that he had been attacking all along, now transformed into a powerful criticism of the modern symbolic logic that Nagel and similar critics had unwittingly and regretfully assumed to have passed Dewey by.

The fact is that Dewey's 1938 *Logic* is not so much directed at themes that preoccupied the nineteenth century, as Nagel suggests, but toward themes and problems that have continued to occupy our own century. It is an attack on "The Superstition of Necessity" now as much as then, on modern intuitionist logics from Brouwer to Michael Dummett as much as Venn, on modern modal logics from Lewis to Carnap and Kripke as much as Russell and Frege. In *Experience and Nature* he had identified the fallacy of converting the logic of reflection into the rationality of being and existence and had called attention to the fact that the consequences of the fallacy range far beyond the limits of logical theory itself:

> Selective emphasis, choice, is inevitable whenever reflection occurs. This is not an evil. Deception comes only when the presence and operation of choice is concealed, disguised, denied. Empirical method finds and points to the operation of choice as it does to any other event. Thus it protects us from conversion of an eventual function into antecedent existence: a conversion that may be said to be *the* philo- sophical fallacy, whether it be performed in behalf of mathematical subsistences, esthetic essences, the purely physical order of nature, or God. The present writer does not profess any greater candor of intent than animates fellow philosophers. But the pursuance of an empirical method, is, he submits, the only way to secure execution of candid intent. Whatever enters into choice, determining its need and giving it guidance, an empirical method frankly points out with equal open- ness. [*LW*1:34]

What Dewey sets out to accomplish in the *Logic* is an empirical theory of language, logic, and truth that will locate these subject-matters on the ground-map of the province of criticism. It is an essay on the logic of experience that carries it to full realization by means of an inquiry into the generic traits of existences that comprise what he calls the ultimate subject-matter of logic. It is, accordingly, a theory that provides logic with an ontology reached by empirical means, an ontology in keeping with the denotative method and empirical metaphysics already sketched in the background theory of *Experience and Nature*, that is linked with the reconstruction of logical theory by means of the transformational theory of language set forth in the central chapter of that volume. He wanted to work out the details of the operations of the linguistic artifacts that transform events into objects in the shared experience of communication, and to develop the social theory of language that he had been working on in conjunction with Mead to the point where it could be applied to the language and logic of scientific inquiry and to scientific truth. This ontology would, in short, be in keeping with the precariousness of existence identified in his metaphysics, one that would capitalize on whatever stability individually qualitative existents could provide by means of their own generic traits. It would be a provisional ontology of emergent natural kinds.

In *Experience and Nature* Dewey attempted to demonstrate the fallacy of constructing metaphysics on a foundation of first principles assumed to be self-evident truths. Such a procedure, he argued, is the root cause of the dualisms that litter the trail of Western thought from Plato to positivism, driving conceptual wedges between matter and form, body and mind, fact and value. His portrayal of form as matter's product, mind as body's evolved consequence, value as fact's eventual meaning, was framed as a radical reconstruction of Peirce's doubt–belief theory of inquiry combined with James's theory of behavioral response to the pluralistic universe. He transformed James's conception of the role of the sameness of things in providing cognitive access to the "blooming, buzzing confusion" of the world as experienced into a metaphysical theory of the generic traits of existences of all kinds. He outlined the idea of a metaphysical perspective formulated as a background theory rather than a foundational first philosophy. He argued, against classical conceptions of metaphysics, that we evolve our first philosophy from the logic of experience, from the analysis of existential problems and their means of resolution, rather than from the contemplation of eternal truths dimly perceived as somehow transcending and governing the confusing world of the live creature. He had set forth a conception of metaphysics as a ground-map of empirical generic traits, rather than a system of categories of reason or "Being."

In *The Quest for Certainty* Dewey broadened his attack on "*the* philosophic fallacy" to cover the whole range of philosophic subject-matters. No branch of inquiry, he argued, is free from the danger of mistaking the part for the whole, of assuming a necessity where none is present, of postulating a reality beyond the reach of experience as foundational to inquiry. He attacked even science as in imminent danger of succumbing to the temptation of regarding itself as a sanctuary the findings of which enjoy "a privileged relation to the real" (*LW*4:176). He argued for the naturalization of intelligence and for the subservience of methods of inquiry to the conditions of nature. He argued that all knowing is an art, that science evolves from the practices of the craftsman and artisan, rather than springing fully formed from either the brow of Zeus or the minds of scientists. He portrayed the intimate relationship of art and science in the construction of the Good and in building the fortress of culture as a defense against the peril of existence and of nature (*LW*4:3). He returned to this theme and developed it in his 1931 Harvard lectures, which were published in 1934 as *Art as Experience*. It is a theme that is central to the systematic and massive revisions that Dewey made in the 1932 edition of the *Ethics,* one that had been fundamental to his argument in the 1927 essay on the meaning of democracy in *The Public and its Problems,* where it comprises the focus of his concluding chapter, "The Problem of Method."

He had been arguing the central theme of *Logic: The Theory of Inquiry* all along, the theme that knowing is an experimental art of behavior directed at survival and growth by means of intelligence and culture. He had been maintaining all along that methodology cannot be subservient to a transcendental logic any more than to a disembodied Absolute Mind or Pure Reason, that form cannot be divorced from matter or language from existential reality. And he had long ago argued the folly of taking logical necessity as anything more than a provisional tool of analysis, of converting it into an ontological category of antecedent reality. He had been arguing against the separation of logic and scientific method ever since his attack on "The Superstition of Necessity" in 1893, and had opposed the duality of the analytic-synthetic distinction ever since his attack on Venn's logic in his 1890 essay "Is Logic a Dualistic Science?" In *The Quest for Certainty* he put the logician's fallacy succinctly in the following terms: "We take out of our logical package what we have put into it, and then convert what we draw out to be a literal description of the actual world" (*LW*4:197). We mistake the eventual object known by means of inquiry for the antecedently real object and ascribe to it a kind of a priori existence, as Mill and Peirce do when they accord to the antecedent object the status of being the "permanent possibility of sensation." The reality of all such unactualized possibles as objects of modal logics must be ruled out from the outset, Dewey argues in the *Logic.* This is the methodological intolerance against which Peirce protested in his letter of 1905, the feature of the 1903 *Studies in Logical Theory* that marked the fundamental divergence between Peirce's route to reference and Dewey's.

In Dewey's account the "interpretant" of a "sign" is not just another "sign" but a *known object*. Moreover qualities are signs that lead back to the objects of which they are qualities. They are natural signs of a causal connection between sign and object and not, as Peirce would have it, indexical signs already embedded in a linguistic and conceptual semiotic. Linguistic practice, Dewey argues, follows the existential practice that governs behavior of all organisms by means of the sign–signified relation, the causal, existential connection of the quality with the thing as qualitatively individual. What Dewey is arguing is that we get our semiotic from our semantics, not our semantics from our semiotic. He is arguing that theory derives from practice, language from action. The symbols and symbol-relations of language and logic reach the ontological domain only indirectly, Dewey says, through their functions in inquiry (*Logic,* p. 390). Thus, "existence in general must be such as to be *capable* of taking on logical form, and existences in particular must be capable of taking on *differential* logical forms. But the operations which constitute controlled inquiry are necessary in order to give actuality to these capacities or potentialities" (*Logic,* p. 389). Dewey's metaphysics deals with the generic traits of existences of all kinds, whereas the *Logic* deals with the traits of different kinds of existences and the differential forms of logic instituted for expressing them. The *Logic* is thus, in a very clear and tolerant sense, a study of the ontology of kinds and of the relevant language. It is an inquiry into the ways in which the forms of discourse and of logic express the existential relations that comprise the warrants for our cognitive claims and provide the provisional projectability of those claims as judgments of practice and evaluations.

Dewey's aim in the *Logic* is the same as it was in "The Superstition of Necessity." He wants to show how the relation between logic and existence can be demystified. He sets out to do this by reconstructing logical theory in such a way that the usual order of logical procedure is reversed. Where Russell began with the rules of implication, for instance, Dewey begins with the practice of inference. Where Russell took the implicatory relation to be self-evident, Dewey takes it to be an abstraction from the existential relation of "involvement." Where Russell believed in implication and trusted it as a guide to the psychology of inference, Dewey believes in inference and trusts it as a guide to the construction of hypotheses. Where Russell took the norms of logical theory as the controlling principles of scientific inquiry, Dewey takes the controlling principles of scientific inquiry as the sole justification of the norms of logical theory. Thus Dewey's *Logic* is also an attempt to unify logic and scientific method, to overcome the dogmas that separate epistemology and logic and divide the analytic from the synthetic in an intractable duality.

In the early chapters I tried to show that Dewey was already engaged in this project of reconstruction when he took up the position, in opposition to Peirce, that logical necessity arises from practice, is needed, and that it was the trajectory of this project that increasingly involved him in problems of metaphysics and ontology. Just as he found that the only way to get rid of bad metaphysics was by means of good metaphysics, so he found that the way to get rid of bad logic is not merely to criticize it, but rather to reconstruct it. I wanted to show that the melioristic concern from which Dewey started propelled him to undertake a major overhaul of the pragmatisms of Peirce and James, one that would avoid idealism on the one hand and psychologism on the other. I wanted to show that Dewey's logic of experience was an attempt to pull together all the various aspects of his philosophy in an integrated network or system. I now want to suggest that in the *Logic* that goal is achieved to a considerable extent.

Integrated into the *Logic* are Peirce's doubt–belief theory of inquiry, a reconstruction of the logic of relatives, a modified semiotic of signs and relations, and a provisional version of synechism. The doubt–belief theory is reformulated as a theory of the problematic situation which accounts for the origins of inquiry and its context. Signs are removed from their purely linguistic context and are seen as referring to the existential qualities of existent things, to generic traits or empirical characteristics, features of objects that lead to those objects, rather than just to other signs. Dewey makes the eventual object of knowledge that which is signified by a sign, thereby modifying Peirce's intentionalist view and equipping it with an extensionalist perspective. Synechism is stripped of its cosmic reference altogether; as the principle of continuity, it is applied solely to the pattern of inquiry and not at all to its content. Peirce's community of inquirers is relativized to actual occasions and specific instances, from which any suggestion that social habit has a cosmic foundation has been eliminated. While Dewey works out a piecemeal version of Peirce's realism, he rejects unequivocally Peirce's pragmaticism and objective idealism.

Less surprisingly, what Dewey takes from James is almost entirely limited to what he could extract from the *Principles* in the way of an account of experience, the inherently experimental pattern of inquiry that he had already elaborated in his 1903 *Studies in Logical Theory*. Dewey rejects James's view of conventional denkmittel, and all remnants of the method of tenacity. In the end Dewey rejects the famous pragmatic test of truth, holding instead that what must justify our cognitive claims is what inquiry discloses and not what disclosure may lead to in the way of consequences. In the *Logic* Dewey attempts to rid his theory of inquiry of all traces of James's residual subjectivism, or psychologism, with respect to what comprises the content of knowledge. Objects of knowledge, he wants to show, may be instrumental to satisfaction, but their warrant does not consist in that instrumentality. Dewey takes great pains to demonstrate that "warranted assertions" are the reliable means of obtaining desired results, that they function in controlled action designed to resolve problematic situations and produce valued consequences. But he also takes pains to demonstrate that those valued consequences are reliable only when the means employed to obtain them are causally related to objective reality. He wants to show not merely that matters of fact *have* value as instrumental to satisfaction, but that they *are* values. He wants to demonstrate not only that there is no conceptually valid basis for the disjunction between factual judgment and value judgment, but that there is no basis for an ontological disjunction either. He seeks to attain by means of an objective realism and a logic of scientific method what James despaired of achieving except by the method of tenacity, and what Peirce thought could be reached only through objective idealism.

The argument of the *Logic*, which is intended to accomplish all this, is cast in the form of a theory in which the formal character of reasoning is explained as derivative, as an emergent product (or consequent) of the animal organism associated by means of language into social systems, or communities. What Dewey very consciously postulates is the claim that inference is the sine qua non of associative behavior, that it is common inference that allows one individual to understand the behavior of another, to communicate. It is on this postulate that the whole reconstruction of logical theory depends, and Dewey is up front in presenting that reconstruction as a postulate system and nothing more. He views logic as a needed system of orderly discourse, not as a system of self-evident truths characterized by logical necessity. All along his approach to logic has been based on the conviction that the analytic nature of logical necessity arises from the synthetic necessity of inference, that logical necessity is the formal expression of the existential connection experienced materially. "Whenever this, then that" is simply the derived form of material connections of events that are causally related. Dewey puts it this way in the *Logic:*

> The theory, in summary form, is that all logical forms (with their characteristic properties) arise within the operation of inquiry and are concerned with control of inquiry so that it may yield warranted

assertions. This conception implies much more than that logical forms are disclosed or come to light when we reflect upon processes of inquiry that are in use. Of course it means that; but it also means that the forms *originate* in operations of inquiry. To employ a convenient expression, it means that while inquiry into inquiry is the *causa cognoscendi* of logical forms, primary inquiry is itself *causa essendi* of the forms which inquiry into inquiry discloses. [*Logic,* p. 4]

Dewey gives us a causal theory of language and logic, of meaning and truth, one that is based on objective realism and is thoroughly ontological. Inference as the route to reference leads to the object of knowledge.[2]

Dewey's argument in the *Logic* begins with a careful analysis of the organic bases on which any theory of knowledge claiming to be empirical must depend. He wants to explain how language as a cultural phenomenon is existentially connected with biological behavior, how social communication is contingent on material traits and characteristics already present in the natural organism and its environment. He wants to show that the human organism shares with all organisms a behavioral trait that is fundamental to all forms of communication, and that language is simply an evolved form of a behavioral process generically common to all natural organisms. That process is what inference, as an existential action or behavioral response, is all about. It is the stimulus–response pattern reconstructed, not as an arc but a circuit. Dewey makes repeated use of his earlier thesis of the reflex arc essay, now viewed in terms of the active involvement of the organism in its environment. He now wants to argue that the behavioral circuit of the organism involves a pattern of interaction in which the physical stimulus operates causally to effect a response that transforms the existential situation in which the organism exists. The organism's involvement with its environment is described as a relation of reciprocal causation or interaction. It is this relation for which Dewey adopted the term *transaction* in his later years, in order to emphasize its reciprocal causality aspect and to direct attention to its transformational effect on both the organism and the environment.

The world of the living creature, Dewey argues, is a complex of various involvements with the individual organism at its center. The survival of the organism is contingent on the manner in which it responds to the environment, its adaptation to its situation and its capacity for making changes in its environment as required. The needs of the organism are causally efficacious in determining behavior that changes the environment, just as changes in the environment are causally efficacious in determining alterations in the behavior of the organism. The interaction is thus reciprocally causal, or transactional, a circuit, not an arc. It is the ontology of this relation as existentially transformational that grounds Dewey's conception of logic as a theory of inquiry.

Dewey argues that the material relations of involvement are the primordial forms on which a theory of logical forms must be based. The argument moves from existence to disclosure, from the existential relations of involvement to the ordered forms of language, and thence to the formal structures of logical relations. Inference is fundamental, and social discourse, language as a means of communication, depends on it. It is the needed connection between existence and language and between language and logic. Dewey works it out by taking the relation of involvement as a causal relation between signs and things signified. Inference is the taking of a sign as evidence of the thing signified. It is as much a trait of the behavior of organisms of a lower order as it is of human behavior. It is fundamental to the relation of an organism with its environment that the behavior of the organism is contingent on stimuli received from the environment. This stimulated behavior, Dewey argues, is caused by the presence of the sign–signified relation as a natural fact of the "involvement" relation and is a feature of what he calls the biological matrix of inquiry. He takes it that the sign–signified relation as an existential causal connection is what every inference aims at, and what it discloses when the signified object is reached. The implicatory relation of logical necessity is posited by abstraction, by conceptualization of the formal character of the sign–signified relation. As conceptual material, the forms of logical relations are not existential; rather, they are symbol-relations that stand for possible existential connections or causal relations and are reached through the formalization of inferences expressed in everyday social discourse. The development of formal logic, Dewey argues, presupposes the successful development of social discourse as the verbal symbolization of the sign–signified relation— *conversation*, to use the term employed by Dewey in the central chapter of *Experience and Nature*. In the *Logic*, social discourse, or language, is called the "cultural matrix" of inquiry. But, already in the account of communication in *Experience and Nature*, the connection between natural signs and verbal symbols had been made explicit. It is the transformational art of communication that makes that connection: "When communication occurs, all natural events are subject to reconsideration and revision; they are re-adapted to meet the requirements of conversation, whether it be public discourse or that preliminary discourse called thinking. Events turn into objects, things with a meaning" (*LW*1:132).

In the preceding sketch of Dewey's line of argument in the *Logic*, I have condensed material that Dewey spreads over nearly three hundred pages. I have risked this condensation in order to bring out the basic steps in the argument and to emphasize at each step the empirical grounds that Dewey invokes to justify proceeding to the next step of his argument. For it is clear that Dewey's conception of the genetic method as an empirical process of explanation, whether of logical forms or anything else, is a conception rooted in causal connections or relations. I have wanted to demonstrate how the causal ontology on which Dewey's conception of the genetic method is based made it necessary for him to reconstruct the pragmatism of Peirce and James. For it can be shown that Dewey's theory takes the object of knowledge as the extensional material object, reached by means of causal analysis of empirical traits and characteristics of existences of different kinds. Dewey's naturalism must be understood as comprising not merely an empirical theory of knowledge, but a theory of the causal origins of the empirical logic of experience. It is a theory, I now want to show, that is rooted in a reconstruction of realism, in a reconstruction of the traditional realist doctrine of natural kinds.

In traditional realism, including the version appropriated by Peirce as Scotistic, the logic of predication is based on the idea that the essence of a thing determines what it is. A properly drawn predicate ascribes to the subject of a proposition a generic feature of that subject—that is, a feature of the thing referred to that is an essential property of the thing. The traditional realist notion of natural kinds arises from the fact that proper predicates, or "essential predications," provide a basis for generalization in the form of universal propositions. The subject term of such propositions can be seen as standing for a natural kind, or class, of entities which, because they share a common essence, share common essential properties. Predications made of such entities are thus taken as capable of being projected across all members of the class, or kind. That such projectible predications are guaranteed by real essences is the fundamental thesis defended by classical realists against nominalism. The doctrine of natural kinds is thus one with the classical notion of fixed essences. Hence, once it is *denied* that there are any fixed essences, the whole notion of natural kinds is in trouble. The classical basis for generalization, the projectible predicate that is true of all those, and only those, members of a natural kind, disappears, reappearing now as the problem of induction, now as the question of the status of the universal.[3]

Scattered throughout the *Logic* are a number of attempts to clarify the connection between two different kinds of universals and to show why the two are often either confused or conflated. The two kinds, which Dewey wants both to distinguish and to connect, are expressed by means of what he calls generic propositions on the one hand and abstract propositions on the other. Generic propositions are universals that express the existential causal relations of involvement and refer empirically to the connections between existing entities that warrant generalization. These propositions are reached by a process that involves two other kinds of propositions, which Dewey identifies as "particular" and "singular." A particular proposition refers to some quality of an individual object. Recalling Dewey's claim in *Experience and Nature* that qualitative individuality is among the generic traits manifested by existence of all kinds, it is clear that Dewey is here talking about the qualities of some particular individual existent. Such qualities are identified by an empirical process, or "operation performed by means of a sense organ—for example" (*Logic*, p. 289). The important point is that the operation by means of which the identification is made is a case of involvement, in which causal interaction takes place, or would take place if performed. Thus:

> "This is sour" means either that the actual performance of an operation of tasting has produced that quality in immediately experienced existence, or that it is predicted that if a certain operation is performed it will produce a sour quality. "This is soft" means that *it* yields easily to pressure and will not cause most other things to yield when applied to them. When it is said of *this* "It is bright," an actual consequence of physical interaction with light is indicated. In short, the proposition is particular not because it applies to a singular but because the qualification is of *something taking place at a definite here and now*, or is of an immediate change. In the particular proposition there is no ground for intimating that the *this* in question will remain sour, sticky, red, bright or whatever. "Is" is a verb of the strictly temporal present tense; or, if it is an anticipation of what will happen, it refers to an equally transitory local time in the future. [*Logic*, pp. 289–90]

Here Dewey tries to bring out the fact that the usual treatment of propositions of this sort—Russell's atomic propositions for instance—results in "confusion of the causal conditions under which the particular quality occurs with the logical form of the quality" (p. 290). What he wants to show is that the logical import of the particular is strictly limited to the actual occasion, "the local and temporal occurrence of the quality in question," and that predicates of particular propositions are not projectible as they stand.

Because of this, a further set of operations has to be performed, by means of which the particular is transformed in such a way as to afford the information needed for generalization. These subsequent operations are not accomplished by any *formal* means whatsoever, but by further observation and experiment. Membership of an existential kind must be conferred on the particular, and this involves a more thorough examination of the conditions under which the change denoted by the particular proposition occurred, or in which the designated event took place. As a result of such thoroughgoing inquiry the particular, as the subject-content of the propositional form of the particular proposition, is no longer immediately present. Other, similar particulars are substituted; other, similar existent objects replace *this* object. We move from "*This* object is red" to "*These* objects are red." By attending to the conditions under which the perception of red occurs, both with respect to the similarity of the object and similarity of the perceptual conditions, it is possible to reach a dispositional predicate concerning red objects as a class. Now the perception of red is a sign indicating a generic trait of these objects as a class. The immediate quality of the particular instance is now projectible as a trans-temporal trait of these objects, each one of which exhibits or will exhibit it as a characteristic. The empirically instituted class is what Dewey calls a kind, and propositions identifying particulars as instances of a kind are "singular propositions."

Two features of Dewey's analysis of how singular propositions are instituted are worth noting. First, the process of classification that results in the institution of a kind is strictly empirical and causal; it is one in which verbal representation is contingently related to what is being represented. The change that takes place in the physical act of perception is causally produced. The act of perception involves the perceiver in a causal interaction with the object perceived such that the quality of the object is the emergent consequence of the act. The move from the experienced relation expressed in a particular proposition to that expressed in a singular proposition is a contingent move. It is the emergent consequence of repeated perceptual experiences in which perceptions of a particular quality are produced in such a way that a regular pattern can be recognized. The regularity of the pattern is itself causally produced; it is a causal consequence of recurrent events. But Dewey insists that it is not that the same event happens over and over again: each event, or existence—Dewey uses these terms interchangeably—is qualitatively both similar and different from each other event. So what recurs is not the same event, but the same *kind* of event. It is in this sense that kinds, like particular objects, are contingently experienced. Dewey reconstructs the notion of natural kinds by showing that the notion of kind emerges from the perceptual transaction as an empirical consequence, rather than from an antecedent a priori determination. Not all classes or sets are kinds in Dewey's treatment.

A second feature of this way of constructing singular propositions designating a particular object as one of a kind is that it results in a causally constituted basis for inference. Because membership in a class is not assigned arbitrarily, but is the causally generated consequence of a pattern of events characterized by regularly recurrent changes (or perceptual interactions), each object becomes a member of the class by virtue of its qualities. For it is those qualities that objectively determine the perceptual outcome in each instance. Thus each particular that can be designated as one of a kind can be taken as a case of a general fact. The idea of class membership is superseded by the idea that belonging to a kind renders each member a representative instance, or specimen, of the designated kind, and it is this representative feature of particulars belonging to a kind that grounds projectibility. Moreover, because each kind is causally instituted, owing to the causal dependence of the perceptual experience on the qualitative object, even kinds are extensional objects.

Dewey is arguing that kinds exist, that they are existentially real. He has worked out an empirical argument against nominalism. At the same time, he is quick to acknowledge that kinds instituted in this way are temporal. They are neither the eternal objects that philosophers sometimes invoke nor objects having necessary existence. Not modal, they are contingently real objects. That they are not *permanently* real in Dewey's ontology is not merely a consequence of the fact that they are temporally instituted as the consequent objects of cognitive inquiry; it is also the result of their being causally contingent on conditions the permanence of which cannot be taken for granted. Dewey puts the matter this way: "The specific nature of these conditions is usually 'understood' or taken for granted. Even in scientific inquiry and inference they are never completely stated. For a complete statement is impossible since it would have to exhaust practically everything. *Standardized* conditions are postulated, and are explicitly stated because, and as far as, they have *differential* effect" (*Logic*, p. 293).

Once he has established kinds as existential objects, Dewey can make his move to universal propositions with extensional meaning and reference. The move is to the extensional relationships of kinds expressed in "generic propositions". Universal propositions of this sort extend the range of reference, and thus the grounds of inference, by applying the basic relation of involvement to the relationship of kinds. The discovery of inclusion of one kind in another is fundamental. "The membership of a kind in another kind not only extends enormously the number of characteristics that are inferable, but, what is even more important, it orders observed and inferred traits in a system" (*Logic,* p. 294). Indeed, it is just this systematization of inclusive and exclusive kinds, Dewey argues, that marks the difference between common sense and science, between inference on a purely intuitive basis and inference based on a careful determination of empirical traits and characteristics demarcating the limits of both the including and included kinds. It is an important part of what Dewey wants to show that while ordinary language may, as a system of ordered discourse, have given rise to the formal character of logical relations, it allows only a rough approximation of actual kinds and their relationships.

Commonsense kinds are always giving way to more accurately determined kinds, to scientific kinds that eventually come to displace them by themselves becoming part of the commonsense way of looking at the world. Dewey clearly wants something more reliable in the way of known objects than his 1903 *Studies* was able to provide by drawing on the notion of the sameness of kinds in James's *Principles of Psychology.* He wants something that will explain the rough-and-ready notion of inference that he had employed in his attack on Russell in the *Essays on Experimental Logic.* He wants to show that inference is not just guesswork guided by the self-evident laws of deduction, but rather, that there are empirical grounds for inference, as he had shown in his 1916 paper on "Logical Objects." He wants to show that valid inference is not based on trial and error or some sort of intuition or habit of thought, but rather on real objects and their relations, extensional objects and the existential relations among them.

At the same time it is equally clear that Dewey's move to a reconstruction of natural kinds continues and extends his early devotion to behavioral semantics. But this does not lead him down the path to ordinary language philosophy that Wittgenstein was to follow in the 1940s. Dewey was already following the path of behavioral semantics of the *scientific* community in the 1930s. He was already thinking of generic traits as indices of causally efficacious and transitive relations, rather than as family resemblances. He was thinking in terms of the shared meanings of language systems in use in the sciences, while Wittgenstein was still en route to the use theory of meanings and the discovery of the forms of life. In 1925 Wittgenstein still held his copy theory of language, whereas Dewey, in the central chapters of *Experience and Nature* had already shown how to do things with words. And while Carnap in *Der Logische Aufbau der Welt* of 1928 was trying to account for the existence of the external world by means of a logical construction of sense data, Dewey was already arguing for a naturalized epistemology utilizing the resources of natural science, which was the next step in mainstream philosophy of knowledge. By the time Russell had come around to recognizing the virtue of the pragmatic solution to the problem of induction in his 1948 *Human Knowledge: Its Scope and Limits,* Dewey's realist solution in the *Logic* was already ten years old, and he had gone beyond "pragmatics."

It is important to recognize, however, that Dewey had been looking for a realist solution only because realism offered an escape from idealism. What he was doing when he set out was defending Course 5, the course whose outline began: "Section 1.—Philosophy (science) is the conscious inquiry into experience. It is the attempt of experience to attain to its own validity and fullness; the realization of the meaning of experience" (*EW*3:211). That he had been working on logic was only because he had been attempting to synthesize scientific method and ethics. That he had worked out a synthesis of formal logic and the methodology of inquiry was only because he had been concerned to avoid the duality of both empiricist and transcendental logics. Likewise, his metaphysics of naturalism had evolved only as an attempt to show that value and fact are not two distinct ontological orders. He was searching for ways to demonstrate that grounds for valuation are every bit as good as the grounds for judgment in any of the sciences. But once he saw that it was possible to generate even the central forms of pure logic from the experienced relations and causal connections obtaining among the generic traits and characteristics of things, everything seemed to come together. He found that he could extend the reach of the logic of experience to a theory of inquiry that would pull together the various strands of his project of reconstruction. This is why a critical understanding of kinds and their relations is a must if the character of Dewey's pragmatism is to be fully appreciated.

Dewey thought he could show, by analysis of the process through which kinds are instituted, that our concepts are causally linked with their objects—not always, of course, perhaps not even very often, but often enough to have given rise to the idea of logical necessity. In time, and under appropriate cultural conditions of linguistic development, logical necessity becomes joined with other well-known principles, among which are the stock-in-trade items of classical logic, the relational principles of identity, contradiction, and excluded middle. Dewey saw the history of logic, its astonishing record of success and failure, as demonstrating the fallacy of basing inquiry on apart thought, the systematically mistaken assumption of rationality as the character of the real, of taking for granted the antecedently coherent character of objects of knowledge. In critical commentaries on the history of philosophy and culture, he had argued that the inherent duality of logic and methodology and its consequence in the superstition of necessity had been a disaster, driving wedges between mind and body, value and fact, the real and the ideal. He had argued for a resolution of all these dualities in a logic of experience and metaphysics of existence.

In the end his argument comes down to the discovery of the analytic in the context of the synthetic. He argues that we can understand the theoretical uses and applications of logical necessity, of the implicatory relation, only if we are willing to take seriously that it is an abstract construction of the material relation of involvement. Implication is simply the abstract form of the causal relation that turns up when signs are found to be significant, that is, when a causal relation between sign and object is suggested. The inference that smoke is a sign of fire is valid only when it turns out that there is a causal connection between fire as the signified object and smoke as a trait that signifies it. The proposition "Where there is smoke there is fire" may be either an abstract universal, the meaning of which may be simply a matter of how the words are defined, or in effect a hypothesis to be tested, and confusion is avoided by understanding which is intended. In pure deductive inference, antecedent definition of terms is not only permitted but required, whereas in hypothetical inference it is prohibited. If a fire is by definition smoky, then no smokeless fires will ever be found. If "all ravens are black" by definition, no "non-black ravens" *can* turn up. Valid inference depends on our ability to form our propositional calculus in terms that are open both to inferential testing and to closed propositions, to hypothetical propositions as well as to those closed propositions whose immunity to empirical disconfirmation is relatively assured by prior definition. That this assurance is relative is a matter that Dewey insists on, for even antecedent definition is not beyond the challenge of variant interpretation. It is clear that precariousness is a generic trait even of such abstract entities as those presumed by analyticity, for they too are members of an instituted kind.

Dewey's contention that serviceable kinds are instituted, rather than given, must be dealt with carefully. For it had long been a conviction of realist ontology that kinds are antecedently real. This belief became a bone of contention between Dewey and Woodbridge on the basis of the view outlined by Dewey in the first chapter of *Experience and Nature*. The idea that real objects are instituted rankles. It is an idea that has no place among the planks of the platform of the Six Realists, one that Montague selects as a principal target of attack in his own version of presentative realism. If there are real kinds at all, they must be "out there," Montague held, waiting to be discovered and to present themselves to our representations of them. Dewey could hardly be a genuine, card-carrying realist if he was going to insist on "eventual objects of knowledge" and "instituted kinds." The best that could be hoped for would be membership in the conventionalist camp, or so went the judgment of his peers. In fact, Dewey showed little interest in the honor denied but cared much about the stigma of subjectivism entailed in that denial. For if at times he seemed indifferent about claiming realism, he was never indifferent about claiming objectivism. Moreover, he was always irked by the suggestion that his claim to objectivism was vitiated by a covert current of carefully concealed idealism. On one occasion, when Charles W. Morris was attempting to interpret his theory of mind, he even acquiesced to being construed as an emergent realist along with Mead. Perhaps he found the qualifying term suggestive of where he wanted to take his stand. It is at least consistent with the objectivism insisted on in the *Logic*.[4]

Indeed, in the *Logic*, he chose the case of emergent kinds to illustrate what instituted kinds are all about. The emergent kinds of evolutionary biology, he pointed out, are not merely given to inquiry; they are instituted by means of inquiry. The text is instructive:

> The consideration that propositions of one of a kind and of a relation of kinds are related to inference is equivalent to a surrender of the old system of rigid taxonomy; i.e. "classificatory" systems. As long as kinds were supposed to be ontological species marked off in nature, rigid taxonomic classification was inevitable. The substitution for such schemes of flexible relational kingdoms, orders, families, species, varieties, etc., in zoology and biology, was equivalent to determination of the relation of kinds on the ground of relationship to systematic inference. The immediate effect of the destruction of the idea of fixed natural species was, however, logically disintegrative. For it led to the idea, which still obtains in traditional empiricistic logical theory, that all division into related kinds is *merely* a matter of practical convenience without intrinsic logical meaning. However, the discovery of progressive derivation, through differentiation under environ-

ing conditions, from a common ancestry, institutes an objective basis. In comparison with the theory of fixed species it marks restoration of an objective status of classification but on a different basis. Externally, the difference is marked by the substitution of belief in "the origin of the species" for the assumption of fixed natural kinds. [*Logic,* p. 295]

It is in texts like this, which deserve, but scarcely inspire, careful and contextual reading, that Dewey makes the connections that show how his theory of inquiry hangs together; here, too, he exhibits most clearly his conception of the unity of scientific methods and formal logics. He starts out by reminding us of the rigid hold of the classical notion of essences on empirical science, of the domination of fixed ideas from Aristotle to Kant and beyond. He reminds us of the ontological species presupposed by the petrified tree of Porphyry, the properly proportional system of reasoning that Cajetan found implicit in Aquinas, of Cartesian innate ideas, and Kant's "perfected form of the syllogism." He alludes to Hume's reduction of causal inference to habit, as well as to the disclosure of the causally objective basis of the origin of species in the last century. He makes explicit reference to the disintegrative effect on logic of that disclosure, to the dogmas of empiricism that drove the wedge between the chance variations of empirical materials and the logical necessity of conceptual forms, the duality of logics that drove Hume to backgammon to take his mind off the problem and led Carnap to *Der Logische Aufbau der Welt.*

It is in tangled texts like this, which show how tortuously Dewey wended his way between rigid designators and practical convenience, that the ontology of eventual objects of knowledge is delineated. An ontology of natural kinds emerges, but one not restricted to the subject-matter of biology. For, as the text shows, it was not the uniquely biological character of the subject-matter that led to the reconstruction of procedures, but the discovery of progressive derivation through all sorts of causal relations of all sorts of classifications and kinds across the board. Dewey's argument is not that of Bergson, despite his admiration for the latter's theory of creative evolution, for he is not suggesting that biological transformation is paradigmatic of all material change. For Dewey, organic evolution is but one kind of change, which, like others, is explicable only in terms of causal involvements of qualitative existents. The paradigmatic case is not the transactional pattern of the organism interacting with the environment, but the pattern of transactional involvement as such, the reciprocal causal relationships that obtain among all kinds of existences. Dewey is not trying to reduce the subject-matter of mathematical physics to the patterns of biological change, or vice versa. He is not a reductionist at all. There are all kinds of change out there, and capturing them for conceptual use and control is no easy matter.

Dewey characterizes the process of instituting kinds as "arduous," one that involves a degree of attention to detail and an operational ingenuity rarely achieved by commonsense methods, as this text shows:

> If sound generalizations could be formed by placing, mentally, a number of singulars in a row and then throwing out unlike qualities until a number of "common" qualities remains, institution of kinds and general conceptions would be an ultra-mechanical and easy operation. One has only to consider the traits that describe a kind in scientific inquiry to note that their institution is an arduous process, and does not proceed in the way here criticized. For scientific kinds, say that of *metals,* are instituted by operations that disclose traits that are not present to ordinary observation, but are produced by operations of experimentation, as a manifestation of *interactions* that are taking place. For only qualities that are capable of being treated as signs of definite interactions facilitate control and inference. [*Logic,* p. 270]

Not only is the process an arduous one; it also takes time. Dewey takes time seriously, as a mark of the ontology of existences of all kinds and one that helps to explain why the institution of kinds is both possible and useful. For our observation sentences are all of existences of times past, recounting not what *is* out there, but what *was* out there on the occasion mentioned. We deal in knowledge of events that have already taken place, not only in history and paleography, but across the board. Observing a star, we cannot rightfully say that it is out there without the warrant obtained by knowing that it is the kind of thing that it is, a kind that has among its generic traits the required stability. That this particular star has it is a contingent matter, a probable inference based on an instituted kind. The stimulus–response pattern of observation and report is a circuit mediated by the ordered discourse of language, in which it is taken for granted that mention of a particular relates it to a kind.

Familiarity with this taken-for-granted feature of common discourse, Dewey points out, breeds contempt and is therefore ignored. The desired projectibility of "disposition predicates" is sought elsewhere, in logics that proceed from self-evident principles and so-called laws of thought. But no such conceptual apparatus can do more than reach the transitive relations with which it began. No warrant for existential disposition predicates is obtained by means of transitivity exclusively grounded in conceptual involvements. Existential involvements are required. Thus:

> The relation of transitivity is also exemplified in terms denoting *kinds* when, and only when, an extensive or inclusive *kind* has been determined with respect to included kinds in an order of progression. To take a simple example: When whales have been determined to be mammals and mammals vertebrates, there is warranted transitivity from whales to vertebrates. This transition is logically possible only when the set of conjoined characteristics that describes each kind has been previously inclusively-exclusively determined by the functions of affirmation and negation. Scientific natural inquiry is notoriously concerned to establish related kinds. This concern is not final, its purpose being to institute terms that satisfy the condition of transitivity, so that systematic inference is promoted and controlled. [*Logic,* p. 332]

Here, as elsewhere, Dewey is unconcerned with the status of the universal as antecedently real. What concerns him is the legitimacy of descent—that is, the procedures that objectively determine a kind.

Closure is reached when hypothetical universals direct inquiry to the specific operations and experimental conditions needed to reveal kinds and their relations. Thus, warranted assertions are obtained only when the symbols and symbol-relations of our verbal hypotheses lead us to the object through existential operations that succeed in disclosing it. Dewey is not denigrating the deductive function in inquiry; he is simply trying to locate it on the ground-map of the province of criticism. In Dewey's reconstruction of logical theory, Peirce's leading principles are redirected. Signs lead not only to other signs, as Peirce claimed, but also back to the objects, to particular existents, kinds, and relations. Warrants for assertion are such objects and are reached when deductive processing of information previously obtained suggests procedures of observation that lead to the acquisition of new information. Dewey's hypothetical universals are leading principles aimed at generic propositions expressing the sign–signified relation of involvement. It is the causally efficacious involvement relation that is the eventual object of knowledge. Closure on the eventual object is reached only through what Dewey calls the "conjugate" union of universals denoting existential kinds with universals of the if–then type, a union that he clearly views less as a correlation than as an existential connection. For it is plain that a union that can be termed "conjugate" is itself a causal relation of involvement. It is causally efficacious in generating and structuring the forms that knowledge takes. It is this consummated relation that resolves problematic situations, transforming conjectural materials into existential warrants and evidence. As involvement, the conjugate relation is the *causa essendi* of knowledge.[5]

In the end, of course, as Dewey reminds us, all such closures and consummations are themselves events. The objects reached by means of inquiry are at best transitory and replaceable, despite their extensional properties and existential attributes. Even kinds are superseded in the continuum of inquiry and become superfluous. Every problematic situation is particular and unique, its resolution specific. Offsetting this intolerably piecemeal character of inquiry, however, is the fact that some inquiries reach objects of kinds that are generally recurrent, objects that turn up with such frequency that we are led to speak of "laws of nature" and of "causal laws." These "figures of speech" or "cases of metonymy," as Dewey calls them, are useful means of referring to "the existential temporal-spatial orders of sequence-coexistence, which are constituted by their operational application" (*Logic*, p. 445). But as constituents of *natura naturans* they have no standing. Like logical necessity, causation is a category of inquiry only; there are no fixed causal laws or eternal objects. There are only specific connections and involvements, existential and relational; qualitative individuals and instituted kinds. Deprived of ontological status, however, causation acquires an ontological function. Denied direct standing, it takes on a reference in use, the indirect standing of all logical forms. As a category of inquiry it remains indispensable: "Recognition of the value of the causal category as a leading principle of existential inquiry is in fact confirmed, and the theory of causation is brought into consonance with scientific practice. The institution of qualitative individual situations consisting of ordered sequences and coexistences is the goal of all existential inquiry. 'Causation' is a category that directs the operations by which this goal is reached in the case of problematic situations" (*Logic*, p. 462). It is a category of inquiry arising from the involvements of existences and kinds, an a posteriori category arising from synthesis and empirically instituted evidence, never from apart thought supervening upon existences as an a priori form of intuition.[6]

I have left until last, as Dewey does, the treatment of mathematics in the *Logic*. Here Dewey develops the position that he had earlier maintained in the company of McLellan and had reiterated in his exchange with Fine. It is, in short, that like all genuine inquiry—and in contrast with the accrual of common sense—the development of mathematics is a serial process. By this he does not mean that it is cumulative, but that it develops in piecemeal fashion, moving from specific problem to specific problem. What begins with interpreted systems in arithmetic and geometry, counting and measurement, moves to uninterpreted systems and abstractions as a matter of course. Just as inferences in the world of practice lead to implications in abstract discourse, thereby suggesting hypotheses for empirical testing that direct subsequent investigative operations, so numeration and measurement give rise to mathematical abstractions. This move to uninterpreted systems does not relieve mathematics of all relation to eventual application, however. In a pair of texts Dewey suggests first why it might *seem* so, then why it does not:

> [In the *Logic*] we have been concerned with the relation of meanings and propositions in discourse where discourse is conducted in reference to some final existential applicability. In discourse of this type application is suspended or held in abeyance but relationship to application is not eliminated in respect to content of the conceptions. When, however, discourse is conducted exclusively with reference to satisfaction of its *own* logical conditions, or, as we say, for its own sake, the subject-matter is not only non-existential in immediate reference but is itself formed on the ground of freedom from existential reference of even the most indirect, delayed and ulterior kind. It is then mathematical. The subject-matter is completely abstract and formal because of its complete freedom from the conditions imposed upon conceptual material which is framed with reference to final existential application. Complete freedom and complete abstraction are here synonymous terms. [*Logic*, p. 396]

Now comes the connecting link with language, not through application but through continuity with the general pattern of inquiry. The role of transformation is critical:

> Change in the *context* of inquiry effects a change in its intent and contents. Physical conceptions differ from those of common sense. For their context is not that of use-enjoyment but is that of institution of conditions of systematic extensive inference. A further new context is provided when all reference to existential applicability is eliminated. The result is not simply a higher degree of abstractness, but a new order of abstractions, one that is instituted and controlled only by the category of abstract relationship. The necessity of transformation of meanings in discourse in order to determine warranted existential

propositions provides, nevertheless, the connecting link of mathematics with the general pattern of inquiry. [*Logic,* p. 396]

Dewey's point is that mathematical operations are conducted on the same
pattern as existential operations of experimental procedure, that in trying
to solve mathematical problems, we postulate possible ways of arranging
our conceptual materials in just the same way that we deal with conceptual
materials in the natural sciences. Dewey is intent on showing that in
mathematics we experiment with various arrangements of the concepts
comprising its subject-matter until we reach those generic traits or characters that lead us to the solutions we seek. He is trying to illustrate that
mathematical processes are, *mutatis mutandis,* the familiar procedures of
controlled inquiry designed to resolve problematic situations.

Dewey wants to do this in order to give substance to his thesis that
mathematical forms accrue to a subject-matter in the process of inquiry and
are thus serially, but not ontologically, linked to existential material. By
insisting that mathematical forms are not ontologically meaningful, even
remotely, Dewey is carrying through his criticism of all ontological logics.
He is explicitly denying, once again, Russell's realm of possibilities (*Logic,*
p. 401). Moreover, he is trying to illuminate an important, but neglected,
feature of the history of mathematics, the progressive liberation of mathematics from existential reference. He wants to show that the normative
function of symbolic logic and mathematics has to do solely with the
method of reasoning and inquiry, and not with existential content. Here, it
seems, Dewey is anticipating a view later expressed by Wittgenstein:
"Mathematics teaches us to operate with concepts in a new way. And hence
it can be said to change the way we work with concepts. But only a
mathematical proposition that has been proved or that is assumed as a
postulate does this, not a problematic proposition."[7]

This seems to express Dewey's view in a nutshell. For, by calling the
relation between the operations of mathematics—that is, transformations
of meanings—and those of existential inquiry—that is, experimentation—
a connecting link, Dewey, like Wittgenstein, intended to renounce all
remnants of direct correspondence. Moreover, like Wittgenstein, Dewey is
not rejecting what can be learned from the isomorphism, or operational
correspondence, between the procedures of pure mathematics and those of
the natural sciences. Indeed, what both Wittgenstein and Dewey are after is
a clearer conception of the relation between purely symbolic uninterpreted
systems of reasoning and the interpreted systems of the experimental
sciences. It was precisely for this reason that Dewey insisted in the preface

to the *Logic* that we need a general theory of language before we can expect to develop an adequate symbolic logic (*Logic*, p. iv). It was for this reason that Wittgenstein turned to language in use in the *Investigations* once it became clear that the copy theory of the *Tractatus* had collapsed.

Dewey stated the problem succinctly on the first page of the *Logic:* "No one doubts that the relations expressed by such words as *is, is-not, if-then, only (none but), and, or, some-all,* belong to the subject-matter of logic in a way so distinctive as to mark off a special field." These relations, he says, are the proximate subject-matter of logic, about which there is not only general agreement but confident advance in development. As to the "ultimate subject-matter" of logic, however, there is little agreement about what these relations stand for, how or why they have come to comprise the content of logic, and how or why they are relevant to the language and operations of scientific inquiry. These are questions about which controversy is rife. What we need in order to resolve this controversy is a more carefully constructed theory of language. For an adequate system of symbolization depends on an adequate understanding of the conceptions and relations thereby symbolized. "Without fulfillment of this condition, formal symbolization will (as so often happens at present) merely perpetuate existing mistakes while strengthening them by seeming to give them scientific standing" (*Logic*, p. iv). Wittgenstein's formulation of the problem is even more specific: "'Mathematical logic' has completely deformed the thinking of mathematicians and of philosophers, by setting up a superficial interpretation of the forms of our everyday language as an analysis of the structure of facts. Of course in this it has only continued to build on the Aristotelian logic" (*Remarks*, p. 300). Like Dewey, Wittgenstein had come to the realization that common sense and forms of agreement in everyday language are not enough. If they were, there would be no need to proceed beyond Aristotelian logic, no need for a reconstruction of realism and a logic of inquiry.

It is Dewey's contention that once our theory of language avails itself of the resources of both scientific and mathematical discourse, the various transformational operations that provide the subject-matter linking the various chapters of the *Logic* as a generic account of inquiry, it puts us in a better position to say what we are talking about. We are put in that better position by the realization that all discourse is transformational, that it is by means of the transformational process of language formation that immediate experience leads to objects of knowledge and meanings to action. The central thesis of the argument is the continuity of this transformational character of language, which arises from the prelinguistic behavioral responses in sign–signified situations and extends to the everyday language of common sense which transforms the involvements of immediate stimulation into known relations and ordered discourse. It extends from the cultural matrix of everyday language to the generation of improved discourse consequent on improved methods of inquiry and involves the transformation of commonsense kinds of objects into scientific kinds.

It is this central contention of the continuity of inquiry as transformational that Dewey puts forward in his treatment of mathematical inquiry. He wants to show that mathematics, like all inquiry, is engaged in a transformational process of instituting new kinds of objects from old kinds, that its mathematical operations are the abstract counterparts of the experimental procedures of the natural sciences. But he is also trying to show that we should not fall into the fallacy of thinking that our abstract objects, whether of pure mathematics or mathematical logic, share in the ontology of spatiotemporal existences. He wants to show, once again, the fallacy of assuming that logical necessity is a generic trait of existence. By pointing out that it is not logical necessity that comprises the connecting link between the subject-matter of mathematics and that of the empirical sciences, Dewey confirms Peirce's pragmatic argument against cosmological determinism. But by pointing out that the principle of continuity in inquiry is restricted to the continuity of *method,* Dewey offers an alternative to the continuity presupposed by Peirce's objective idealism. It is ontological realism, but on a piecemeal basis. For it is not the ontology of "Being" that links the doubt–belief theory with the semiosis of pure mathematics, but the activity of doing and making involved in inquiry. Peirce's thirdness—the category of thought—is reconstructed in terms of the theory of inquiry as intelligent behavior.

I suggested at the outset of this chapter that Dewey's *Logic* can be read as an essay in ontology as well as an essay on the history of logic. That it can be read in this way has not gone unnoticed. In an early symposium on the *Logic,* Evander Bradley McGilvary acknowledged that, among other virtues of the work, Dewey had recognized that "a logical theory without an ontology as its identical twin is not even an adequate *logical* theory." And he rightly noted Dewey's reluctance to adopt the language of ontology then in use. But he put the matter this way: "Again, Mr. Dewey recognizes and has brought others to recognize that logic is all of a piece with ontology. I know that this word is to him as a red rag to a bull: he uses it as such in challenging *other* bulls. But this is perhaps because it has never occurred to him that the word can ever be used except in a malicious sense.

Only those who have 'perverse' views of what it is 'to be' are for him 'ontological'."[8] But to say that logic is all of a piece with ontology is a misstatement. For it is not Dewey's *ontology* that links the various branches of inquiry together, but the *method*. It is not *being* that is continuous, but *inquiry*. As I have been suggesting, the ontology that Dewey connects with inquiry is piecemeal rather than continuous. Rather than his logic and ontology being all of a piece, their relations are provisional and contingent as I see it. It is time to make these implied reservations more explicit.

Dewey's theory of inquiry, of which logic in its more formal character is an integral part, is based on the proposition that existential relations among individual entities are disclosed by the means employed in inquiry. Among such means Dewey is quick to identify the act of inference, for it is only by actually making inferences that the two most fundamental forms of existential relations are discovered. These two relations are involvement and that between the sign and what is signified. Both are relations of causal interaction involving individual existences and the existential conditions of the situation in which these interactions take place (*Logic*, p. 278). The act of inference is an operational involvement of an organism in a situation in which the causal relation—what Dewey sometimes loosely calls a "connection"—between the sign and what it signifies takes the form of a behavioral response. If the situation of the organism responding is one that Dewey calls, indifferently, "problematic" or "indeterminate," the behavioral response may or may not transform the situation by resolving it or, what amounts to the same thing, by converting "the elements of the original situation into a unified whole." The sign–signified relation is a potential case of involvement that is actualized by inference. In other words, it becomes existential by means of the act of inference as a causal intervention, and it is this causal intervention that institutes the sign–signified relation as a stimulus of behavioral response. In other words, it is inference that makes the connection between a sign and what that sign signifies or leads to. In its most primitive form, the object indicated by the sign is what Dewey means by the eventual object of knowledge. The transformation of the situation, again in its most primitive form, is accomplished by the action of inference which institutes the evidence as stimulus to an appropriate behavior. The whole thing may be nothing more complex than what occurs "when an animal flees when it scents the hunter."[9]

The institution of language introduces another dimension. The sign–signified relation, which rests on the existential (causal) connections between an existence and its qualities, can now be expressed by symbol-relations, through formal implication. The formation of abstract universal propositions of the counterfactual or if–then type allows a fourth type of relation to be instituted. Dewey calls this relation "reference," and it is instituted when symbol-relations are brought into conjugate relation with the sign–signified relation. Institution of reference is accomplished when the symbol-meanings of the abstract universal proposition are disclosed to be the meanings of propositions reached by means of inquiry into the existential sign–signified relation. Such propositions are termed by Dewey "generic universals," and the process by which they are instituted, through the operations of experimental procedures designed to produce the necessary and sufficient evidence of their validity, comprises what Dewey calls the "pattern of inquiry." By using the term *conjugate* to describe the relation of reference achieved when the meanings of abstract universals as hypotheses are confirmed by the empirical generalizations that he calls "generic propositions," Dewey intends a stronger sense of reference than would be conveyed by terms such as *correlation* or *correspondence*. By calling his empirical generalizations generic propositions, he intends not merely this stronger sense of reference, but also that reference be to the generic relations between traits and existences. The stronger sense of reference also suggests that it is the ontology of the object that is Dewey's ultimate ground of reference.

Thus we can read Dewey's theory of logic as involving a theory of ontology, or at least a theory of what are sometimes called the ontological commitments of existential propositions. For it is clear that Dewey's ontology is not the identical twin of his logic, as McGilvary put it. Nor can it be described as all of a piece. It is an ontology of existent objects of knowledge, of the relations of those objects, and of the kinds that are instituted by means of those relations, an ontology that is pluralistic and relativistic, of course, since Dewey accepts no eternal objects or permanent kinds.

CRITICAL BIBLIOGRAPHY

Critical analysis and appraisal of Dewey's *Logic: The Theory of Inquiry* is thin and undistinguished. Early reviews were almost unanimous in commending Dewey for his long struggle with problems of knowledge and for his effort to heal the breach between methods of scientific inquiry and the process by means of which value judgments are reached, but few critics thought that he had achieved anything new in the *Logic*, either in bringing his own project any nearer to fulfillment or in contributing to philosophical logic per se. Typical of the response is a symposium of reviews organized by the editors of *The Journal of Philosophy* and published in vol. 36, no. 21 (12 October 1939), and reprinted in *Dewey and His Critics* (cited in the bibliography to Chapter One), pp. 545–6. Advertised as part of the celebration of Dewey's eightieth birthday, these reviews celebrate the *Logic* more as an exercise in gerontology than ontology. And the one exception, that by McGilvary that I have discussed in the text, seems to get the ontology wrong. For McGilvary fails to note that Dewey's treatment of logical forms involves a reconstruction of traditional realism, thereby suggesting that there is no reason not to think that, after all, such forms as Dewey assigns to logic are "actually the forms of the subject-matter under investigation" (p. 549).

In this same symposium, G. Watts Cunningham argues that Dewey's conception of logic is consonant with the idealist tradition in logical theory, a tradition that Cunningham both admires and defends. He thinks that Dewey's failure to acknowledge this is due to his fear of being criticized as a subjectivist. Cunningham regards Dewey's rejection of epistemology as foundational as a serious mistake. Logic must not pretend that it does not presuppose epistemology, or that it can take the place of epistemology, as Dewey argues. He accepts Dewey's account of the relationship between the problem of knowledge and logic but concludes that Dewey is confused about how that relationship should be understood. He recognizes that Dewey wants to explain the relationship from a genetic perspective but argues that he in fact presupposes an antecedently given subject-matter (p. 554). He concludes that Dewey's *Logic* is a "serviceable" contribution to the idealistic tradition in logical theory once this confusion is cleared up (p. 555).

C. I. Lewis, obviously unaware of what Cunningham was planning to contribute to the symposium, argues that Dewey's central point in the genetic approach is both correct and important (p. 556), and he singles out Dewey's theory that all knowing proceeds from action as the central point. But he persists in thinking that Dewey allows meaning to be determined by reference to action in the predictive sense, that he sees meaning as consisting in predictable eventualities (p. 559). He seems to allow his own conceptual version of pragmatism to influence his reading of Dewey's *Logic,* a reading that ends up closer to Peirce's pragmaticism than to the reconstructed realism allowed by Dewey's theory of the object of knowledge. He fails to see that Dewey connects meaning with reference in the sense of warranted assertibility concerning objects known by means of inquiry already completed, predictions already made and operationally confirmed as warrants for action, rather than in terms of some eventual consequences. This very Peirce-like reading of the *Logic,* although very differently argued, tends to confirm the idealistic reading of Cunningham. It agrees with Peirce's notion of truth as what is destined as the eventual outcome of the synechistic continuity of thought, and would thus turn Dewey into an objective idealist.

Nagel, the fourth contributor to the symposium and the only one to have actually worked with Dewey is completely free of any need to see Dewey as a closet idealist. He takes seriously Dewey's effort to show how logical theory goes wrong when it starts from a priori or self-evident principles. He is the only one of the four reviewers to see the *Logic* as making a contribution to the philosophy of science, to understand the radical nature of Dewey's project of reconstruction, his naturalistic philosophy, and his criticism of logics that take for granted that logical forms are intrinsically real. He thus recognizes that Dewey's ontology is not all of a piece with his logic, as McGilvary held, or its identical twin. Unlike McGilvary, he does not try to make Dewey into an unreconstructed realist, or a realist of any kind. Rather than making him out to be a closet idealist, however, Nagel simply denies him *any* ontology by neglecting to refer to Dewey's theory of existential relations, his involvements, or the connections that are open to an ontological reading. Accordingly, he does not connect the *Logic* with *Experience and Nature* at all, thereby neglecting the link between the generic traits of Dewey's metaphysics and the generic propositions that are central to the *Logic*. He ends up seeing Dewey's distinction between generic propositions and hypothetical universals as just a puzzle that Dewey ought to resolve by restating the matter "with greater clarity and fullness" (p. 564). He makes no attempt to follow the statements in the *Logic* that might have clarified the issue, for he makes no reference to the reconstructed theory of natural kinds or to the sign–signified relation. By neglecting Dewey's ontology, he entirely misses Dewey's theory of reference, as well as his conception of truth and meaning.

It would be going too far to suggest that this early review of Nagel's set the tone for most subsequent criticism, but it was certainly the most influential of the four reviews comprising the symposium. In 1939 Nagel was still in the process of abandoning his early commitment to a version of ontological logic that he had put forth jointly with Morris Cohen in their influential text *An Introduction to Logic and Scientific Method* (New York: Harcourt, Brace, 1934). That text had adopted a view of the relation between logical principles and being which is but a slight modification of the Aristotelian view. Thus, "as principles of being, logical principles are universally applicable. As principles of inference, they must be accepted by all, on pain of stultifying all thought. . . . (We must mention in passing that this view of the nature of logic is not accepted by all thinkers.)" (p. 186). The priority of logic with respect to scientific method was also forthrightly asserted by Cohen and Nagel: "It has also been supposed that we can prove logical principles to be necessarily true by showing that they are involved in every reflective inquiry. This also is an error, if by proof is meant what is ordinarily understood by proof. . . . The priority of logic lies simply in its expression of the utmost generality possible" (p. 187).

Dewey had attacked both these views directly in the *Logic* (p. 375). In view of this, it is curious that Nagel makes no mention of the matter in his review nor in his subsequent essays on Dewey's work conveniently gathered in *Sovereign Reason* (cited in the bibliography to Chapter One). By 1944, of course, Nagel had put all ontological logic behind him and was ready to claim an alliance with positivism in which non-ontological logic would provide the link with American naturalism (see his influential essay, "Logic Without Ontology," in *Naturalism and the Human Spirit* [cited in the bibliography to Chapter Five]; note also Dewey's contribution to this volume). By 1956 Nagel had extended his rejection to metaphysics, and the essay "Logic Without Ontology" was reprinted as a central paper in Nagel's volume on logical topics, *Logic Without Metaphysics* (Glencoe, Ill.: Free Press, 1956).

Dewey and Nagel had been exchanging views on the relation between logic and existence since at least 1929. Nagel had responded to Dewey's 1928 article "Meaning and Existence" in *The Journal of Philosophy* with an essay of 1929 entitled "Intuition, Consistency, and the Excluded Middle." In the same year Dewey attacked Nagel's ontological presuppositions in "The Sphere of Application of the Excluded Middle." Nagel responded, still in 1929, with "Can Logic Be Divorced from Ontology?" in which his own answer to the question was clearly negative. Dewey responded in 1930 with "The Applicability of Logic to Existence," in which he set forth a view of applicability substantially in accord with that elaborated in the *Logic*. There was then a lull in the exchange until the 1939 symposium, to which Dewey did not respond directly, although his response to Russell's criticism in *An Inquiry into Meaning and Truth* (London: Allen and Unwin, 1940), in "Propositions, Warranted Assertibility, and Truth," comprises a general response to the reviews as well. In this response (in which, incidentally, Dewey transposes Russell's title as *"An Inquiry into Truth and Meaning"*) Dewey congratulates Russell on clearing up most of the misunderstandings concerning the causal relation between an event and a proposition; it thus stands as indirect evidence for the interpretation of the relation of generic propositions to existences offered in my text. In retrospect, the whole series of exchanges between Nagel and Dewey and between Russell and Dewey provides the clearest route available to an understanding of Dewey's final position on the ontology of logic as inquiry. (All the essays mentioned are conveniently brought together in *Dewey and His Critics,* which has turned out to be the best single source for approaching the *Logic!*)

To my knowledge there are no commentators on the *Logic* who share my conviction that Dewey there completes his project of demonstrating the thesis of "The Superstition of Necessity" and Course 5. There is, however, a directly antithetical critique that attempts to demonstrate that Dewey's project ends him up in rationalism. While I have argued that Dewey was trying to show that the assumed disjunction between the analytic and the synthetic was not to be tolerated, Morton White argues that Dewey takes the disjunction for granted in the *Logic.* The essay designed to show this was widely published in several versions, and the final version can be found in White's collection *Pragmatism and the American Mind* (cited in the bibliography to Chapter One), in which the previous incarnations are listed. White's view, expressed also in the earlier *The Origin of Dewey's Instrumentalism* (cited in the bibliography to Chapter Two), seems to me to be a serious distortion of Dewey's project. White seriously misconstrues Dewey's concept of the abstract relation of necessity in the *Logic* by neglecting Dewey's explicit denial that this necessity has any direct relation to the subject-matter of inquiry (*Logic,* pp. 389–91). White's contention that Dewey views all natural science as consisting of analytic a posteriori statements (pp. 152–3) is clearly insupportable. White sees Dewey as treating the empirical sciences and mathematics as identical (p. 154), thus confusing Dewey's theory of the origins of mathematics with its eventual development. But I am unaware of any published refutation of White's view of this matter.

By contrast, White's view of Dewey's ethics in "Value and Obligation in Dewey and Lewis," which is included in the collection cited, has been criticized: by Sidney Hook in "The Desirable and Emotive in John Dewey's Ethics" (in *John Dewey: Philosopher of Science and Freedom,* [cited in the bibliography for Chapter One], pp. 194–216) and by myself in "Dewey's Metaphysical Perspective" (*The Journal of Philosophy,* 57 [1960]: 100–15).

H. S. Thayer, in *The Logic of Pragmatism: An Examination of Dewey's Logic* (New York: Humanities Press, 1952), has contributed the only book-length study of the *Logic*. The critical portions echo Nagel's criticism for the most part, but are substantially revised in his subsequent *Meaning in Action* (cited in the bibliography for Chapter One); see especially the Appendix on the analytic-synthetic. Thayer's earlier criticism is refuted by Gail Kennedy, in what is possibly the best single essay on the *Logic*, in his contribution to the *Guide to the Works;* this should also be consulted as to the importance of Dewey's fourfold theory of relations. Regarding Dewey's theory of knowledge, Kennedy's essay is perhaps less valuable than Joseph Margolis's contribution to *New Studies in the Philosophy of John Dewey,* edited by S. M. Cahn (Hanover, N.H.: University Press of New England, 1977). Richard Rorty's contribution to the same volume on "Dewey's Metaphysics" is wide of the mark, however, in discussing what he takes to be Dewey's view of metaphysics without consideration of the *Logic* at all. But Rorty's treatment is not nearly as peculiar as that accorded Dewey by May Brodbeck in her essay "The Philosophy of John Dewey," originally prepared for publication in the *Indian Journal of Philosophy* and reprinted in *Essays in Ontology* (Iowa Publications in Philosophy [The Hague: Nijhoff, 1963]). But see also her essay on "The New Rationalism: Dewey's Theory of Induction" (*The Journal of Philosophy,* 46 [1949]: 781–91) for a positivist critique developed largely from the perspective of Gustave Bergmann.

Dewey acknowledges his debt to Peirce several times in the *Logic,* but he does not indicate to the reader that he is engaged in a radical reconstruction of several of Peirce's doctrines, among them his theory of leading principles, the principle of synechism, the principle of logical necessity, and the theory of signs. That Dewey knew what he was doing at the time seems clear to me, but Max Fisch has advanced evidence that Dewey came to realize the extent to which he was reconstructing Peirce only after the publication of Peirce's *Collected Papers,* the first six volumes of which were completed in 1935. It is almost certain, however, that Dewey was familiar with Nagel's fairly detailed studies of Peirce's theory of signs that appeared in the *Journal of Philosophy* between 1933 and 1936 (see n. 1 for this chapter). That Dewey explicitly accepts Peirce's theory that the "interpretant of a sign is another sign" as but a *part* of his own theory of signs in the *Logic* seems to be deliberate. There can be no question of his disagreement with Charles W. Morris and Thomas A. Goudge over how Peirce should be understood. He argued against the view that Morris formulated in his *Foundations of the Theory of Signs,* International Encyclopedia of Unified Science, vol. 1, no. 2 (Chicago: University of Chicago Press, 1938) and against Goudge's article on "The Views of Charles Peirce on the Given in

Experience" which appeared in the *Journal of Philosophy* in 1935 (see Dewey's "Peirce's Theory of Quality," *Journal of Philosophy*, 32 [1935]: 701–8). His disagreement with Morris surfaced after C. L. Stevenson, in *Ethics and Language* (New Haven: Yale University Press, 1944), took it for granted that Peirce and Dewey both held that the interpretant of a sign was always some human interpreter, citing Morris's book as his authority for doing so. Dewey made it clear, in "Peirce's Theory of Linguistic Signs, Thought, and Meaning," that Peirce always meant the interpretant of a sign to be another sign, thus denying the psychological interpretation accepted by both Morris and Stevenson (see also the discussion in the critical bibliography to Chapter Seven). He argued that Peirce was depending on his doctrine of synechism to guarantee objectivity for the concatenated sign system, and he chastised Stevenson for relying on Morris's "extraordinary interpretation of Peirce's theory of signs and meanings." (The last quotation is from Dewey's "Ethical Subject-Matter and Language," *Journal of Philosophy*, 42 [1945]: 708n.; reprinted in *Dewey and His Critics*, pp. 676–87, where the note on Morris's extraordinary view of Peirce's theory of signs appears on p. 683. Dewey's "Peirce's Theory of Linguistic Signs" appeared shortly after in the *Journal of Philosophy*, 43 [1946]: 85–95, but, unfortunately, was not reprinted in *Dewey and His Critics*.) I have relied upon Fisch's account of this matter in the *Guide to the Works*, pp. 329ff. Note that Fisch thinks that Dewey had interpreted Peirce correctly, citing Peirce's letter to Lady Welby, given in *Charles S. Peirce: Selected Writings*, edited by P. Wiener (New York: Dover, 1966), p. 404, as evidence. Peirce wrote: "I define a sign as anything which is so determined by something else, called its Object, and so determines an effect upon a person, which I call its Interpretant, that the latter is thereby mediately determined by the former. My insertion of 'upon a person' is a sop to Cerberus, because I despair of making my own broader conception understood" (*Guide to the Works*, p. 332).

I take it that Dewey was correct not only about Peirce's theory of signs, in his own reconstruction of Peirce's theory, which omits the synechistic guarantee of eventual objectivity, but in making the reference to the object that Peirce says determines the sign the eventual object of knowledge. It is the object of reference that warrants assertions and that stimulates consequent behavior. In other words, it is not consequent behavior that provides the warrant, but the object reached by means of inquiry—that is, the object of reference as Dewey uses that term. (See also Dewey's discussion of this whole problem in the Dewey–Bentley correspondence, pp. 52, 152, and 324.)

7: *The Theory of Intelligent Behavior*

*I*t is a conventionally neglected and paradoxical fact that Dewey's project in the reconstruction of pragmatism and the Vienna Circle's project in the reconstruction of positivism converged at a moment in time and upon a point of critical importance for both projects. That moment came almost immediately after the completion and publication of Dewey's *Logic* in 1938, just when the Vienna Circle was forced to disband, on the eve of the Second World War, when its original project was reconstructed in terms of the "unity of science" and relocated from Austria to the United States. It was among the consequences of that reconstruction and relocation that the organ of the unity of science movement, *The International Encyclopedia of Unified Science*, began publication in America in 1938, Dewey's essay on the *Theory of Valuation* being among the earliest contributions.[1]

The editor-in-chief of the new encyclopedia was Otto Neurath, and the story of his effort to obtain Dewey's contribution tells us much about both Dewey's stance and the direction in which the movement was being pressed by Neurath. As told by Nagel the immediate circumstances were these:

> I remember one memorable occasion when the late Otto Neurath sought to interest Dewey in the Unity of Science movement, by having him contribute a monograph to the *Encyclopedia of Unified Science* which Neurath was then planning. I accompanied Sidney Hook when they called on Dewey at his home; and Neurath was having obvious difficulty in obtaining Dewey's participation in the *Encyclopedia* venture. Dewey had one objection—there may have been others, but this is the only one I recall—to Neurath's invitation. The objection was that since the Logical Positivists subscribe to the belief

in atomic facts or atomic propositions, and since Dewey did not think that there are such things, he could not readily contribute to the *Encyclopedia*.

Now at the time Neurath spoke only broken English, and his attempts at explaining his version of Logical Positivism were not very successful. Those of us who knew Neurath well will remember his elephantine sort of physique. When he realized that his efforts at explanation were getting him nowhere, he got up, raised his right hand as if he were taking an oath in a court of law (thereby almost filling Dewey's living room), and solemnly declared, "I *swear* we don't believe in atomic propositions." This pronouncement won the day for Neurath. Dewey agreed to write the monograph, and ended by saying, "Well, we ought to celebrate," and brought out the liquor and mixed a drink.[2]

That monograph, as might have been anticipated, was an all-out attack on the views of noncognitivism in ethics—the ethical emotivism—that Moritz Schlick, of the Vienna Circle, had developed and that A. J. Ayer had embraced in his 1936 *Language, Truth and Logic*.[3] It was a polemical critique of the reductionist program of the whole unity of science movement and of the conception of the logic of science on which that program was predicated. Dewey's 1939 *Theory of Valuation* simply articulated in plain language the theory of the logic of science that he had worked out in *Logic: The Theory of Inquiry*. It was an application of that theory to the problems of valuation and moral practice which fitted the context of the *Encyclopedia* like a square peg in a round hole. The moment of "convergence" between Dewey's *own* program in the unity of science and that of the *Encyclopedia* was transformed by Dewey into a moment of explicit *divergence*.

Ever since he had inaugurated Course 5 at the University of Michigan back in 1892, Dewey had been working out his own unity of science program. It was a central feature of that program that it would include the subject-matter of ethics and aesthetics along with the subject-matter of the natural sciences in a theory of inquiry that could be applied across the board. He had not been following the reductionist path of trying to make everything scientific that he was sometimes accused of, and now—in the 1938 *Logic* and the 1939 *Theory of Valuation*—it was just that reductionist program that he singled out to attack.[4] In both works the foundationalist program that sought to discover the unity of science by means of the logical syntax of the language of science, the program that had resulted in Russell's ill-fated "Logical Objects" and Carnap's *Aufbau* and that was now proclaiming the *Foundations of Logic and Mathematics* (Carnap), the *Foundations of the Social Sciences* (Neurath), and the *Foundations of the Theory of Signs* (Morris), was repudiated. Science, including the social sciences and ethics, Dewey argued, needs no foundations of the type that would be envisaged in the twenty monographs that were to comprise the first two volumes of the *Encyclopedia,* which were to bear the collective title *Foundations of the Unity of Science.* Dewey had been trying to block that path from the beginning. By the cunning of history his own subversive monograph was among the twenty selected by Neurath, Carnap, and Morris.[5]

Dewey's *Theory of Valuation* argues the thesis of Course 5 in the vocabulary of the genetic theory of inquiry that he had been developing in the *Studies* and *Essays* and had put together in systematic form in the *Logic.* It argues in terms of the continuity of inquiry, the thesis that he had called in the syllabus for Course 5 the "unity of judgment" in the "three philosophic sciences, corresponding to three ways in which the individual, or organized action may be regarded . . . [that is] Logic, Aesthetic and Ethic" (*EW*3:230). Once again it is the theory of judgment, with primary emphasis on the necessity of inference, that Dewey uses to explain the cognitivity of valuation. It is what he had in mind when he argued for the closing of the reflex circuit and for the thesis that "the separation of science and philosophy has reference to the incompleteness of knowledge" (*EW*3:211). In *The Theory of Valuation* he contends again that judgment unites the analytic and the synthetic by an "act which connects the various conditions stated in the judgment" (*EW*3:232). He now states in the vocabulary of valuation what he had stated in the vocabulary of Course 5 under "Ethic." Judgment unites the subject-matter of science with the "ideal side" that aims to "discover the method of expression which shall secure the best organization of action; the fullest or freest movement" (*EW*3:234). Ethic, in Course 5, was aimed at uniting "the two sides distinguished in logic and aesthetic. It deals with the practical situation; the organized action" (*EW*3:235). It deals with what I shall be calling in this chapter "the theory of intelligent behavior."[6]

I have introduced this omnibus chapter dealing with Dewey's approach to the problems of ethics, aesthetics, and the social sciences as I have because I want to emphasize how different Dewey's projects in metaphysics and logic were from those of his contemporaries. I want to bring out the fact that Dewey was not at all tempted by the unity of science movement that attracted Nagel and Morris, and that promised to rid philosophy of the so-called pseudo-problems of metaphysics. Dewey had long been opposed to the program directed at the construction of the foundations of science that had been envisaged by Frege's successors, the program that Carnap had articulated in his announcement that "The Logic of Science is the Syntax of the Language of Science," in 1934.[7] He had long since been opposed to the "Two Dogmas of Empiricism" that Quine was to identify in 1950 as the ill-founded factors that had controlled the development of modern empiricism in large part, and that were integral to the unity of science program stemming from Ernst Mach and the Wittgenstein of the *Tractatus*, which was carried forward in the 1930s by Carnap and in the 1940s by Nagel and Carl Hempel.[8] I have wanted to show Dewey's direct opposition to the noncognitivist line in ethics taken by C. L. Stevenson, which was predicated on the very dogmas that Quine attacked and that Herbert Feigl and Wilfred Sellars defended in the 1950s and later.[9] I have been trying to suggest the similarity between the path that Dewey was following and that which Wittgenstein took after his break with Brouwer and the Vienna Circle and his repudiation of the program of the *Tractatus*. But I have also suggested that it would be a great mistake to view Dewey's project as an attempt to make everything scientific, for that is to confuse the aim of Dewey's undertaking with the foundationalist aims of his younger contemporaries.

In Quine's essay on the "Two Dogmas of Empiricism," which he identifies as the belief in "some fundamental cleavage between truths which are *analytic* . . . and truths which are *synthetic*" and the reduction of meaningful statement to "some logical construct upon terms which refer to immediate experience," it is easy to recognize the theme that Dewey had been articulating ever since his response to Peirce in "The Superstition of Necessity." And it comes as no surprise when Quine suggests that the effect of abandoning these two dogmas should be "a blurring of the supposed boundary between speculative metaphysics and natural science," or that "another effect is a shift toward pragmatism."[10] For that is what Dewey had been arguing all along. As Quine points out, even such foundationalists as Carnap and C. I. Lewis were compelled to take a pragmatic stand when choosing between alternative conceptual schemes, but that their version of "pragmatism leaves off at the imagined boundary between the analytic and the synthetic." Because Dewey had never imagined such a boundary to exist, he had long since made the more thorough pragmatism espoused by Quine his own. It was, in fact, the more thorough quality that distinguished Dewey's version of pragmatism from that of his predecessors that now came to distinguish his position from that of his contemporaries in the foundational project of the unity of science movement.

But the Hegelian deposit that remained in Dewey's conception of philosophy had an even more thoroughgoing consequence than that which followed simply from the relinquishment of the imagined boundary between the analytic and the synthetic. From the outset, the Hegelian conception of philosophy as transformational rather than foundational had led Dewey to applications scarcely envisaged by the more thorough pragmatism espoused by Quine in the 1950s (or, for that matter, the insouciant pragmatism embraced by Rorty in the 1970s). All along Dewey had been trying to work out the transformational consequences of the rise of science and technology for culture, and it was this project that had led him to attempt a redefinition of both *philosophy* and *science* in the syllabus for Course 5. He was already launched on the project of working out the transactional relations in the mutual involvement of science and culture that were to occupy him for the rest of his life, and it was in this context that Dewey put to his students the problem: "Consider how the old question of sensationalism *vs.* rationalism stands when each element is considered from the whole action, or reflex arc; when, that is, sensation is considered as itself an act, and the ideal element, or relation, as the active adjustment of that act" (*EW*3:214). And it was then that Dewey suggested that the solution is to be found in the integration of the backward look of logic and science with the forward look of art. It was then that he first began to argue the emergence of theory from practice, of science from art, and to repudiate the isolation of the fine arts from the practical arts of everyday life. It was then that he put the consequence of his more thoroughgoing pragmatism this way:

> That is, if a statue at a given date is regarded as essentially artistic, and a locomotive as merely useful, it is because owing to the narrow relations of the former the whole has attained expression in it, while the whole (the function in the service of the organized action of man) has only partially subdued the latter. The limitation in the artistic character of the locomotive, in other words, is the extent to which it functions in the interest of a part or class, instead of in the interest of the whole, so that its full meaning and energy are not freed or realized in consciousness. The development of the arts is thus a political phenomenon, since the whole which is seeking to embody itself in every particular is nothing less than the organized action of man. So far as the whole moves freely through any part, that part is artistic. [*EW*3:234–5]

This taking of the locomotive as a sign of a cultural problem by virtue of its limitation as an artistic object is itself a sign of the deeper engagement of philosophy in culture in which Dewey believed, a belief that distinguishes his conception of pragmatism from that of his successors.

It is this transformational role of philosophy as criticism that surfaces again, not only in the 1903 *Studies in Logical Theory,* but in the companion essay published in the same year on the "Logical Conditions of a Scientific Treatment of Morality" (*MW*3:3–39). In both these accounts of the logic of experience, Dewey was trying to overcome the "familiar notion that science is a body of systematized knowledge," a dominant presupposition of the epistemological tradition from Kant to Mill that conceives of the task of philosophy as the construction of foundations on which that body may rest securely. He argued that science must be construed, rather, as consisting of those "activities of observing, describing, comparing, inferring, experimenting, and testing, which are necessary in obtaining facts and in putting them in coherent form" (*MW*3:3). He offered a reconstruction of the notion of science in which the distinctively normative character of judgment is as integral to the methodology as the descriptive function. The point of view advocated, Dewey says, "expressly disclaims any effort to reduce matters of conduct to forms comparable with those of physical science. But it also expressly proclaims an identity of procedure in the two cases" (*MW*3:5). It is this same assertion of the identity of procedure that is claimed in the central chapters of the *Logic* and spelled out in the *Theory of Valuation.*

In the 1903 essays Dewey held that the preconceptions of logic divide facts from values in such a way that the cognitive procedures applicable to the first are irrelevant to the methods of the second. The result is a duality of logics consisting of those applicable to scientific method and those applicable to human conduct, there being "such an inherent disparity between moral judgments and physical judgments that there is no ground in the control of judging activity in one case for inferring the possibility of like control in the other" (*MW*3:5). Moreover, the assertion of this logical disparity leads to the assumption of an ontological disparity, thereby widening the gap between the real and the ideal and lending credibility to the view that judgments of what ought to be cannot be inferred from what is the case. This same disparity has led ethical theorists to claim on the one hand that value judgments are immediate and intuitive, on the other that they rest on higher-order laws of nature or reason that are irreducible to the contingencies of the natural order of physical reality.[11]

From the side of scientific theory, Dewey pointed out, it is this same logical disparity that gives credibility to the view that scientific judgments depend on the principle of causation so interpreted as to carry with it the notion of necessity implicit in determinism, whereas ethics implies free will and the pursuit of ideal ends and final causes. This makes scientific judg-ment appear to deal in "sequences in time and . . . co-existences in space," moral judgment in "actions which are still to be performed." For this reason, Dewey argued, it is thought that moral judgment must transcend anything found in past experience and that it cannot be subjected to the control of judgments based on matters of fact. In the end, he concluded, the antinomies created by the assumed logical disparity finally reduce them-selves to one. Thus:

> Scientific statements refer to *generic conditions* and relations, which are therefore capable of complete and objective statement; ethical judg-ments refer to an *individual act* which by its very nature transcends objective statement. The ground of separation is that scientific judg-ment is universal, hence only hypothetical, and hence incapable of relating to acts, while moral judgment is categorical, and thus individ-ualized, and hence refers to acts. The scientific judgment states that where some condition or set of conditions is found, there also is found a specified other condition or set of conditions. The moral judgment states that a certain end has categorical value, and is thus to be realized without any reference whatsoever to antecedent conditions or facts. The scientific judgment states a connection of conditions; the moral judgment states the unconditioned claim of an idea to be made real. [*MW*3:7]

Put this way, it is clear what must be done to get rid of the disparity of method and the ground of separation. It must be shown that scientific judgments refer to individual acts, and that ethical judgments refer to generic conditions.

By making judgment the central issue in scientific method, Dewey is already moving to an emphasis on the act of inference as the key to reference and to the warranted assertion as that on which meaning must be based if it is to be reliable. Here he argues that scientific method can control the formation of judgments only when it is able to abstract certain elements in the experience to be judged that can justify the projectibility of its generic propositions as general facts, or universals. These propositions will therefore comprise statements of the connections of conditions as causal relations, that is, as objects, or universals. But all such generic propositions rest ultimately upon the identification and reidentification of particulars, judgments which are individualized acts.[12]

Already in this 1903 essay Dewey was prepared to argue that the universals that take the form of hypotheticals are but the instruments of science, not science itself. But he had not yet made the critical distinction between universals as generic propositions and universals as counter-factuals, a distinction that is crucial to the logic of propositions developed in 1938. His 1903 text already suggests the later distinction, however, as well as the strong sense of reference carried by the conjunction between the hypothetical (if–then) form of the universal and its generic form that he would later call a "conjugate relation." As he puts it there, "Science has its life in judgments of identification, and it is for their sake that generic propositions (or universals or laws) are constructed and tested or verified. . . . Such judgments of concrete identification are individualized, and are also acts" (*MW* 3:37). Dewey stressed that the presence of action as a logical element can be shown by the selection of the subject term of the prospective proposition, by active search for the appropriate predicate, and in the "copula"—which he describes as the "entire process of the reciprocal forming and testing of tentative subjects and predicates." Here he was anticipating his later stress on the importance of operations and the transformational consequences of cognitive intervention in the given materials of immediate experience in the institution of evidence. But he points out that all this activity is generally ignored or presupposed in judgments of the intellectual type, for it is assumed that this mediating activity and intervention is "impartial in its influence upon the quality of the content judged." On the other hand, in judgments of the moral type, all this mediating activity and intervention is a critical matter, for the activity and intervention itself "becomes an object of judgment whose determination is a prerequisite for further successful judgments" (*MW* 3:38).

Dewey is here pointing out the continuity of the kind of inquiry designed to provide guidance for judgmental discrimination between a good experiment and a bad experiment, between an instance of research that cooks its data and one that does not. It is plain that if we can have an inquiry that supplies us with such guidance in science, then there is no reason to suppose that we cannot have an inquiry that will supply us with like guidance with regard to moral judgments. Indeed, Dewey clearly thinks that one and the same kind of inquiry suffices to give guidance in both domains, for what he is already making use of is the kind of inquiry that he was working out in the *Studies* and that would culminate in the 1938 *Logic* and the 1939 *Theory of Valuation*. He points out that what is taken for granted in scientific inquiry as not affecting the outcome of judgment is of critical import in judgments of valuation, where the object of reference is the very determination of activity and content that is taken to be impartial in the case of "normal" science. What he says is that "control of moral judgment requires ability to constitute the reciprocal determination of activity and content into an object"—the very process that we have come to accept as the sociology of knowledge, of cognitive psychology, semantic inquiry. For the object to which Dewey refers is clearly not the given or antecedent object, but the eventual object of knowledge. He refers to the need to develop an inquiry into the behavioral sciences and the logic of conduct, into the science of psychology and sociological science as prerequisites. He sums it all up in this fashion:

> The whole discussion implies that the determination of objects, even when involving no conscious reference whatever to conduct, is, after all, for the sake of the development of further experience. This further development is change, transformation of existing experience, and thus is *active*. So far as this development is intentionally directed through the construction of objects as objects, there is not only active experience, but *regulated activity*, i.e., conduct, behavior, practice. Therefore, all determination of objects as objects (including the sciences which construct physical objects) has reference to change of experience, or experience as activity; and when this reference passes from abstraction to application (from negative to positive), has reference to conscious control of the nature of the change (i.e., conscious change), and thereby gets ethical significance. This principle may be termed *the postulate of the continuity of experience*. This principle on the one hand protects the integrity of the moral judgment, revealing its supremacy and the corresponding instrumental or auxiliary character of the intellectual judgment (whether physical, psychological, or social); and, upon the other, protects the moral judgment from isolation (i.e., from transcendentalism), bringing it into working relations of reciprocal assistance with all judgments about the subject-matter of experience, even those of the most markedly mechanical and physiological sort. [*MW*3:38–9]

It is plain that what Dewey is saying is not that scientific inquiry is value-free, but that we can take its impartiality for granted only insofar as it is self-reflexively critical of its own methods and presuppositions. Dewey was already making it plain that scientific method is not immune to criticism, but also that we have only that very same method by which to criticize it.

He was showing that all the characteristics of behavior that have been regularly assigned to morals, including all those propensities that go by such names as "motives," "preferences," and "feelings," and even "biases" and "predispositions" rooted in "culture," are not irrelevant to scientific judgment. He was showing that while scientific method brooks no absolutes, it is just this exclusionary rule that implies that a scientific judgment is itself something to be judged. This text makes it clear that if all knowing is criticism, then there is always a need for criticism of criticism, what is sometimes referred to these days as "double hermeneutic":

> If the use made of scientific resources, of technique of observation and experiment, of systems of classification, etc., in directing the act of judging (and thereby fixing the content of judgment) depends upon the interest and disposition of the judger, we have only to make such dependence explicit, and the so-called scientific judgment appears definitely as a moral judgment. If the physician is careless and arbitrary because of over-anxiety to get his work done, or if he lets his pecuniary needs influence his manner of judgment, we may say that he has failed both logically and morally. [*MW*3:19]

With respect to value judgments, then, Dewey makes it plain that it is not merely the character of the *situation* that is under scrutiny in inquiry, but the character of the *individual* conducting the inquiry: "The judger is engaged in judging himself; and thereby in so far is fixing the conditions of all further judgments of any type whatsoever. . . . But from the logical standpoint we say that the judger is consciously engaged in constructing as an object (and thereby giving objective form and reality to) the controlling condition of every exercise of judgment" (*MW*3:23). Dewey was already calling for the criticism of criticism that he was to make the determining characteristic of philosophy in *Experience and Nature*. He was already delineating the territory to be explored in drawing up the "ground-map of the province of criticism."

Because Dewey's theory of moral judgment, his self-reflexive theory of criticism, relies so heavily on the character of both the natural and the social sciences—in particular, social psychology and the sociology of knowledge—it is to be expected that the content of his ethical thought would shift in line with changes taking place in those disciplines. It is also to be expected that changes in the subject-matter of the self and society, of culture and history, would be reflected in the ongoing development of Dewey's work, from his Chicago days to his last publications in the field.

But because these changes have been carefully traced elsewhere, I shall give only a brief sketch of them here.[13]

By 1894, the year of publication of "The Reflex Arc Concept in Psychology," Dewey had already absorbed Peirce's doubt–belief theory of inquiry and applied it to psychology. Moreover, he was already convinced that "The Superstition of Necessity" has no more place in ethics than in science. He had rejected mind–body dualism and was preparing for the reconstruction of values as facts, indeed, he was already launched on a reconstruction of pragmatism in which the theory of inquiry would find the object of knowledge to be both value *and* fact, the object that he would say in 1903 is "constituted in judgment." It is this thesis that dominates the *Ethics* that Dewey and Tufts coauthored in 1908.

In it the central concern is no longer individual self-realization, but social criticism, for both Dewey and Tufts were aware that the problems of individual morality are inseparable from the social context in which the individual finds himself. While the good is still expressed in terms of individual conduct, it is made clear that such conduct is socially contingent. There is a reversion here to the classical model of the *Nichomachean Ethics*. Virtue is seen as a "habit of action" and a consequence of "character," and virtues as socially and politically consequential: "The habits of character whose effect is to sustain and spread the rational or common good are the virtues; the traits of character which have the opposite effects are vices" (*MW*5:359). But it was not to relieve the individual of social responsibility that the virtues were so defined. There is no suggestion of social determinism to lessen the burden, for "it is upon the self, upon the agent, that ultimately falls the burden of maintaining and of extending the values which make life reasonable and good" (*MW*5:359). All the same, a special section is reserved in part 3, "The World of Action," for the discussion of "Social Justice," another for "The Ethics of the Economic Life," and two for the "Unsettled Problems in the Economic Order" (*MW*5:381ff.).

The most marked changes in the "problematic" content of Dewey's ethical theory took place, as might be expected, in the period between the version of 1908 and the extensively revised version of 1932. These changes had already been signaled in *Reconstruction in Philosophy*, in which Dewey had made explicit his rejection of the concepts of both the social and the individual as meaningful moral categories, arguing instead that ethical inquiry should be directed to specific problems, to specific structures and interactions. He was ready to reject the whole idea of moral evolution as aimed, in the fashion of Peirce's doctrine of "Lamarckist" evolution, at the ultimate *telos* of the fulfilled individual. Progress is no longer an assumption but a problem. Dewey had been to Japan and had witnessed a revolution in progress in his two-year sojourn in China; he had visited post-Revolution Russia, Turkey, and Mexico. He had responded to Boas's revolution in anthropology with his own essay on "Anthropology and Ethics" in 1927, to the revolution taking place in social psychology with his *Human Nature and Conduct* of 1922, and to the "new" science of psychology in his *Individualism Old and New* of 1930. His response to the flourishing, but still fledgling, field of political science in *The Public and its Problems* of 1927 initiated a wholesale reconstruction of the social category that had dominated the 1908 *Ethics*. He reconstructed Aristotle's *Politics* as he had reconstructed the *Nichomachean Ethics* and the *Psychology* in *Human Nature and Conduct* and *Individualism Old and New*, with results parallel to those of his reconstruction of the *Metaphysics* in *Experience and Nature* in 1925.

In all these reconstructions the traditional role of reason is gradually assumed by intelligence. Whatever else of Hegel's *Logic* may have remained in Dewey's *Studies* of 1903, the notion that the real is rational and the rational real had been purged. In the 1908 *Ethics* the Stoic and Kantian conception of a transcendental reason autonomously authoritative in moral matters is rejected in favor of an instrumentalist conception of knowing as a way of coping with the problematic situations, but now interpreted in terms of moral conflicts. The vocabulary of reflection had already begun to replace even this instrumentalist view of reason in Dewey's 1910 essay on logical matters for teachers, *How We Think*. In *Reconstruction in Philosophy* the function of intelligence is seen as both analytical and synthetic, as imaginative and creative. It reaches back into past experience, and its consequences extend beyond both habit and social bias; it thus becomes the innovative power requisite for the holistic reconstructions envisaged.

The central role ascribed to "intelligence" in *Human Nature and Conduct* anticipates the role assigned to philosophy as criticism of criticism in *Experience and Nature*, a role identified with the "pedagogy of experience" that Dewey had been tirelessly exploring in his writings on the philosophy of education. In *Democracy and Education* (1916) Dewey had defined *mind* as a "concrete thing," as the power of understanding things in terms of "the use to which they are turned in joint or shared situations." And, he had added, with portentous emphasis, *"mind in this sense is the method of social control."* In *The Quest for Certainty* intelligence has almost entirely replaced both reason and mind as a form of life that contrasts with *"the* philosophic fallacy," already construed as the superstition of necessity and now as the search for an immutable truth and a transcendental authority.

In 1929 Dewey was already anticipating the moral use of intelligence which dominates the revised *Ethics* of 1932. It is the power to reflect on past experience and then use it to reconstruct the present and shape the future; it is the power to analyze ends and means and generic conditions in relation to intentional purposes. In the revised edition the whole emphasis is on ethics as a way of dealing with specific problematic situations, of resolving conflicts of intentional aims by reconstructing the immediately given determinants in order to reach the eventual objects of knowledge that allow control of future action. The shift to the vocabulary of "intelligent behavior" as the character of pragmatic morality is no mere verbal exercise; it is a necessary consequence of Dewey's long trajectory of transformation and reconstruction in philosophy, part of the end product of his reconstruction of pragmatism.

The 1932 version of the *Ethics* contains the final and decisive shift that marks Dewey's mature approach to the whole problem of the relation between science and morality. It takes the form of a radical reconstruction of the role and status of the old idea of the 'good.' In the 1908 version the notion of the 'good' was still tied largely to the holistic notion of self-realization and the development of character in the individual. It was largely a functional concept, serving as a standard measure of character, and was operationally effective through the very concept of judgment that had been outlined in the 1903 essays on logic and morals. By 1932 the 'good' has been largely replaced by the concept of value. It has become more pluralistic, reflecting perhaps Dewey's more extensive experience with both cultural pluralism and the burgeoning conflicts within American culture in the era just past. It certainly reflects advances in psychology and sociology, the greater understanding of the generic conditions of conflicts both within and between cultures that belied the ethics of neutral monism, just as continued developments in the natural sciences and mathematics belied the early hopes of the logical empiricists and positivists.

In the 1932 *Ethics* the focus has shifted once again to the central position of judgment and to the inescapable presence of valuation in all judgments, whether of science or morals, that Dewey had emphasized in his 1903 essay on the "Logical Conditions of a Scientific Treatment of Morality." Far from accepting Perry's reduction of James's pluralism to neutral monism and a theory of value that took "value as any object of any interest," the 1932 *Ethics* accepts that the pluralism of values is a generic condition that means that the *de facto* presence of value disparity—in other words, cultural relativism—is but the problem and not the solution. It recognizes that the theory of value does not end with the discovery of the *de facto* valuations that divide us, but must move to *de jure* values, or valuations that will serve to mediate conflict, not by the holistic reduction of "one-world morality" or through cross-cultural value homogeneity, but by intelligent behavior based on inquiry and the transformational possibilities that result from the repudiation of fixed essences and all ontological logics.

The 1932 *Ethics* views the cultural relativism of values less as what has to be accepted than as a problem to be dealt with, not by a futile search for transcultural similarities, but by social inquiry into the generic conditions of specific situations of conflict. Dewey was already prepared to argue the theme that surfaces in the penultimate chapter of the *Logic*, that of the intellectual poverty of the social sciences consequent on accepting the assumption that value judgments have no place in scientific method. He was already prepared to argue that values are no more "given" than facts, but are instituted in the process of inquiry itself. Values, like facts, are to be accounted for by the genetic method, and just as facts can be analyzed and compared for their extrinsic consequences and traits can be appraised for their eventual meanings, so values can be analyzed and compared and appraised. Just as Dewey had long since rejected the notion that there are facts independent of judgment, so he had long ago rejected the idea of values that are not the products of acts of valuation. Just as there are no facts with intrinsic meaning, so there are no values with intrinsic worth. Indeed, the whole notion of intrinsic values vanishes with the recognition of the superstition of necessity.[14]

There is another important shift between 1908 and 1932, one that is more than merely coincident with the shift from such traditional ethical notions as the 'good' to values. In 1908 the task of philosophy itself was hardly distinguishable from the tradition that Dewey began criticizing in *Reconstruction in Philosophy* and that he was to characterize in *The Quest for Certainty* as having prevailed since the seventeenth century. It is the conception of philosophy that makes it, like religion, a rival of science instead of its complement. At this time, too, criticism of religion as a major source of moral conflict was muted to a point approaching silence. Dewey may have been ready to defend the process of ethical judgment that he had set forth in 1903 and to engage in the critique of the baleful effects of institutionalized religion on the moral life of the community that surfaces in *Reconstruction in Philosophy* and emerges with devastating bluntness in *Quest for Certainty*, but neither intention emerges in the 1908 *Ethics*.

It appears that both Dewey and Tufts were quite willing to leave such criticism to be inferred by the reader. Tufts, after tracing the history of moral theory, makes an indecisive attempt to distinguish between religion and morality in his last few pages; but Dewey, in his section on the "Theory of the Moral Life," singles out neither religion nor science for analysis. In the final section on "The World of Action," the influence of the Church on marriage and the family are distinguished, then dismissed in one paragraph. The word *science* was not deemed important enough to be included in the index, although several chapters were devoted to problems of the civil society, politics, and the economic order.

Although the revisions of 1932 involve little change as far as these issues are concerned, both *The Quest for Certainty* of 1929 and *A Common Faith* of 1934 provide evidence that Dewey's thinking with respect to the relationship of science and morals was changing from the rather theoretical stance of 1903 to a much more practical stance in the 1930s. The shift to a more social perspective in the 1932 *Ethics* is indicative of the devastating effect that the conflict between science and religion was having. The gradual isolation of the churches from other social institutions, which Dewey noted in *The Quest for Certainty* as contributing to the moral irresponsibility of social behavior, becomes a central theme of *A Common Faith*. But while the latter is for the most part critical of institutionalized religion, it is clear that Dewey was increasingly sympathetic to what he distinguishes as the religious qualities of behavior, which he saw as necessary, integral elements in a naturalistic ethics.

This element of sympathy for what he sometimes called a natural piety had influenced Dewey's thinking ever since he had abandoned his own supernaturalism back at Oil City. In an essay on "Religion and Our Schools" in 1909, Dewey had argued that we may not be moving into an increasingly irreligious age at all, that, "for all we know, the integrity of mind which is loosening the hold of (dogmatic beliefs) is potentially much more religious than all that it is displacing" (*MW* 4:176). By 1934, this integrity of mind had become the "development of greater intelligence in relation to social affairs. . . . The method if used would not only accomplish something toward social health but it would accomplish a greater thing; it would forward the development of social intelligence so that it could act with greater hardihood and on a larger scale." He goes on to point out how strongly this development is opposed, not just by the "aristocratic" moral pride of the churches but by all the "vested interests" that are "on the side of the *status quo,* and are therefore especially powerful in hindering the growth and application of the method of natural intelligence." Because these interests are so powerful, he argues, "it is the more necessary to fight for recognition of the method of intelligence in action" (*A Common Faith,* pp. 76–7).[15]

In *A Common Faith* Dewey argues that intelligence as a method is a very different thing from the older conception of reason, for it is inherently involved in action. He argues that there is no opposition between intelligence and emotion. In a passage that reflects his own infusion of intelligence with passion he says:

> There is such a thing as passionate intelligence, as ardor in behalf of light shining into the murky places of social existence, and as zeal for its refreshing and purifying effect. The whole story of man shows that there are no objects that may not deeply stir engrossing emotion. One of the few experiments in the attachment of emotion to ends that mankind has not tried is that of devotion, so intense as to be religious, to intelligence as a force in social action. . . . To say that emotions which are not fused with intelligence are blind is tautology. Intense emotion may utter itself in action that destroys institutions. But the only assurance of birth of better ones is the marriage of emotion with intelligence. [pp. 79–80]

What Dewey has in mind in *A Common Faith* is less the replacement of religion by science, or even raising the level of culture by eliminating the divisive effects of competing cults and sectarian institutions, than to account for those human needs that formerly found fulfillment in traditional faiths and to show that they may be better fulfilled in the secular community. Moreover, even faith is made subordinate to intelligence in the end. For it is intelligence, he says, that has "always been implicitly the common faith of mankind. It remains to make it explicit and militant" (p. 87). An astute and sympathetic critic has remarked of *A Common Faith* that "Dewey had a deep although unorthodox religious sensibility, best expressed perhaps in *Art As Experience*."[16] But it is surely not made explicit in *A Common Faith*.

Both books, in different ways, show how far Dewey had diverged from Peirce and James by 1934. For James, the pragmatist philosophy of religion had become a veritable justification of faith in which intelligence was pushed into the background and science was enlisted in the service of faith in the guise of the psychology of religious experience. Whether due to his family background or to some spiritual crisis in his early life, it was James, rather than Peirce or Dewey, to whom religion was a matter of intense personal concern. Peirce saw the whole matter of the New England religious struggle between orthodoxy and unorthodoxy in terms of a much longer-range perspective than James was ever able to do. For Peirce, who viewed even Christianity as but a phase in a much longer process of evolutionary development—it emerged "out of Buddhism, modified by Jewish belief in a living God"—the strife between sects was of little importance. "The higher a religion, the more catholic," he argued, and he converted from his father's Harvard Unitarianism to the Episcopalianism that he recommended to James. "Why don't you join the Church?" he queried James, invoking the pragmatic maxim to explain that the infighting between Catholics and Protestants over the elements of the sacraments is a bit of foolishness as long as "they agree in regard to their sensible effects." The pragmatic maxim, as "the sole principle of logic which was recommended by Jesus," was not intended to solve any real problems: "It only shows that supposed problems are not real problems," Peirce reminded James, and begged him "to try to think with more exactitude."[17]

But for James, the crux of pragmatism had become what it never was for Peirce, a test of truth in an intensely personal sense. He had understood the thrust of the 1878 articles by Peirce to be an outline of a procedure for making personal decisions, enabling a person to decide between options when the usual modes of inquiry had brought him to an impasse, or when the subject-matter was such that the usual methods were inapplicable. But Peirce had not intended that at all and had tried to clarify his difference with James on this point. But as James's biographer has remarked, this had little effect on James's way of thinking, and "the philosophical movement known as Pragmatism is largely the result of James's misunderstanding of Peirce."[18] In his 1907 lectures on "What Pragmatism Means," James was ready to argue for the pragmatic method in theology: "Interested in no conclusions but those which our minds and our experiences work out together, she has no *a priori* prejudices against theology. If theological ideas prove to have value for concrete life, they will be true, for pragmatism, in the sense of being good for so much. For how much more they are true will depend entirely on their relations to other truths that also have to be acknowledged."[19]

For Dewey, by 1907 if not long before, it was just those other truths that showed that theological ideas have proved to be more of a liability than an asset for concrete life. For whatever value inheres in the religious qualities of a life—and Dewey thought that there was much—has been systematically cut off from the life of the community as such. Transferred to the community, liberated from the fetters of institutionalized religion, from the connection with the supernatural, and enlisted in the service of the shared life of the community, Dewey could commend the value of the religious life. But he could not resist noting the almost universal tendency of theologians to allow themselves to be moved "more by partisan interest in a particular religion than by interest in religious experience."

As I have already suggested, it has seemed to some commentators on Dewey's philosophy that he transferred his religious sensibility to the subject-matter of *Art as Experience*. And there are passages that surely can be invoked to support that view, passages that if we did not know that Dewey was talking about aesthetic experience we would think referred to the religious dimension. In the passage that concludes the book, he writes:

> Shelley said, "The greatest secret of morals is love, or *a going out of our nature* and the identification of ourselves with the beautiful which exists in thought, action, or person, not our own. A man to be greatly good must imagine intensely and comprehensively." What is true of the individual is true of the whole system of morals in thought and action. While perception of the union of the possible with the actual in a work of art is itself a great good, the good does not terminate with the immediate and particular occasion in which it is had. The union that is presented in perception persists in the remaking of impulsion and thought. The first intimations of wide and large redirections of desire and purpose are of necessity imaginative. Art is a mode of prediction not found in charts and statistics, and it insinuates possibilities of human relations not to be found in rule and precept, admonition and administration.
>
> > "But art, wherein man speaks in no wise to man,
> > Only to mankind—art may tell a truth
> > Obliquely, do the deed shall breed the thought.
>
> > [p. 349][20]

Yet the central theme of *Art As Experience* is once again criticism of the philosophic fallacy, the fallacy of apart thought that Dewey had been criticizing all along, but now applied to any aesthetic theory that isolates art from human experience. What Dewey is arguing is not that the aesthetic sensibility be substituted for the religious sensibility, or even that art is just a more sublime form of moral sensitivity. He is arguing that all experience is aesthetic, that art is integral to all human behavior. "The intelligent mechanic engaged in his job, interested in doing well and finding satisfaction in his handiwork, caring for his materials and tools with genuine affection, is artistically engaged" (p. 5). Dewey is again arguing the continuity of experience and the continuity of inquiry. For greatness in art, like greatness in science and political achievement, is imaginative and innovative; it is experimental and pedagogical.

That Dewey saw aesthetic qualities as pervading the logic of experience should have come as no surprise to attentive readers. As Irwin Edman has pointed out: "Those who had read him with care . . . knew from his essay on 'Qualitative Experience,' from more than hints in his early 'How We Think,' from the whole central theme of realized individuality in *Democracy and Education,* that he had been alerted to the aesthetic implications of his leading ideas."[21] All along Dewey had been arguing for the unity of matter and form, for the integrity of experience and inquiry. It was part of the original appeal of Hegel's *Logic* that it held out the promise of such integrity as the social hope of the unity of art and science in a culture transformed, and it was that same promise of a unity of culture that had first drawn Dewey to pragmatism. Moreover, it was the promise that had driven Dewey's own reconstruction of pragmatism, at least since his 1903 essays on logic and the unity of all judgment and action. It had propelled the turn to metaphysics after his move to Columbia in 1904, as well as his linguistic turn, in response to Frege's schismatic distinction between *"Sinn und Bedeutung,"* after his encounter with Russell in 1914. It was a prominent feature of his instrumentalist emphasis on action, on meanings as means of both personal and social fulfillment and freedom.

Dewey's philosophy of art absorbs not only those religious qualities singled out in *A Common Faith,* but all those qualities described as the generic traits of existences of all kinds in *Experience and Nature.* For there is a clear sense in which Dewey had already written the revisions of *Experience and Nature* that he was projecting in the last years of his life in *Art As Experience.* There is a clear sense in which Dewey's philosophy of art projects just that vision of "Experience and Culture" that he wrote to Bentley of wanting to express, the vision of *"knowing* as the way of behaving in which linguistic artifacts transact business with physical artifacts, tools, instruments, apparatus, both kinds being planned for the purpose and rendering *inquiry* of necessity as experimental transaction."[22]

Dewey's philosophy of art as inquiry—for that is the central and pervasive theme of *Art As Experience*—is as insistent as the *Logic* that judgment requires both a strong sense of reference and a keen sense of the meaning of the object of reference. Nowhere is this more prominently displayed than in the chapter on "Criticism and Perception," in the section in which Dewey considers criticism of Impressionist painting. He argues here against what he calls "judicial criticism," the familiar practice of imposing a priori norms of techniques, values, and perspective on what is new in a work of art. He argues against the "influence of custom and inertia" and the self-protective cover erected by the critic against the challenge of the novel, against "openness to life itself." Like the self-critical scientist that Dewey described in his 1903 essays, the self-critical art critic, like the artist himself, must be aware of his intentions and attitudes and bring them under control. He must not react "from the standardized 'objectivity' of ready-made rules and precedents," nor fall into "the chaos of subjectivity that lacks objective control, and would, if logically followed out, result in a medley of irrelevancies—and sometimes does" (p. 304).

He quotes Jules Lemaître, an Impressionist opponent of judicial criticism, to the effect that objective evaluation of a work of art combines acceptance of the artist's own intentions, his "ends-in-view," as the meaning of his work with the immediacy of the response evoked by the work in the critic. He wants to show that such a combination requires analysis both of the work and of the artist, as well as a self-conscious analysis by the critic of his own anticipatory response to the stimulus constituted by the aesthetic transaction.

Lemaître argues that "criticism whatever be its pretensions, can never go beyond defining the impression which, at a given moment, is made on us by a work of art wherein the artist has himself recorded the impression which he received from the world at a certain hour" (p. 304). To which Dewey replies:

> The statement includes an implication which, when it is made explicit, goes far beyond the intention of the impressionist theory. To *define* an impression signifies a good deal more than just to utter it. Impressions, total qualitative unanalyzed effects that things and events make upon us, are the antecedents and beginnings of all judgments. The beginning of a new idea, terminating perhaps in an elaborate judgment following upon extensive inquiry, is an impression, even in the case of a scientific man or philosopher. But to define an impression is to analyze it, and analysis can proceed only by going beyond the impression, by referring it to the grounds on which it rests and the consequences which it entails. And this procedure is judgment. [pp. 304–5]

Dewey points out that the artist who communicates an impression, even if he confines his work within limits that are exclusively subjective and personal, nevertheless gives entrance to something that is objective. He communicates something beyond the bare impression, which gives the critic a ground on which to base his own impression. Dewey adds that "the biography of the one who defines his impression is not located inside his own body and mind." He reminds us that the artist's body and mind are what they are "because of interactions with the world outside," and that the wise critic is similarly aware of his own history and takes into consideration "the objective causes that have entered into that history." And he observes that the sentence quoted from Lemaître "sets forth a proportion that is objective"—as the subject-matter is to the artist, so is the work of art to the critic.

In *Art As Experience* Dewey sums up the task of criticism in words that apply equally to art and science, morals and politics, engineering and education. He expresses the intent of philosophy as criticism of criticism and as the aim of inquiry. It is a text that would be at home if inserted bodily into the central chapters of the *Logic* or the concluding pages of the *Theory of Valuation*. It is possibly the clearest statement we have of Dewey's version of pragmatism and of the character of its method:

> Criticism is judgment. The material out of which judgment grows is the work, the object, but it is this object as it enters into the experience of the critic by interaction with his own sensitivity and his knowledge and funded store from past experiences. As to their content, therefore, judgments will vary with the concrete material that evokes them and that must sustain them if criticism is pertinent and valid. Nevertheless, judgments have a common form because they all have certain functions to perform. These functions are discrimination and unification. Judgment has to evoke a clearer consciousness of constitutent parts and to discover how consistently these parts are related to form a whole. Theory gives the names of analysis and synthesis to the execution of these functions. [pp. 309–10]

This is what inquiry is all about, as described and criticized in the *Logic*. It is the theory of intelligent behavior, the theory of active discrimination and unification, of behavioral analysis and synthesis.

If we had only the text of *Art As Experience* from which to judge Dewey's intentions, it would be easy to conclude that it is art rather than science that provides the paradigmatic cases of judgment and intelligent valuation. It would be easy to conclude that Dewey was trying to raise the epistemological level of science to that of culture, that he saw the achievements of science as lagging seriously behind those of the arts in contributing solutions to the problems of mankind, and that it is the methods of artists and writers, as well as the procedures and operations of artisans and craftsmen, that provide the models on which poets and painters depend, and those that science should emulate. It would be easy to see *Art As Experience* as a first philosophy for science and a background theory for ethics. For in developing a theory of criticism that describes both the material out of which judgment grows and the way in which it enters into the experience of the critic by interacting with his own sensitivity and knowledge, and in emphasizing both the store of past experiences and the aim of discrimination, *Art As Experience* provides a theory of the function of judgment as unification of experience that all inquiry should emulate.

But to draw such conclusions would be to make the same mistake that Rorty makes when he says that "Dewey's insistence that *everything* could be made 'scientific' often seemed to his positivist critics merely to make science itself look unscientific by softening the contrast between it and the rest of culture."[23] It would be to conclude from the fact that Dewey often argues in the *Logic* from examples of legal reasoning to concepts of scientific operations that he regards the adversary procedures of litigation as models for inquiry across the board, or that he sees the judicial process as paradigmatic in the solution of human problems. It would be to make the mistake that specialists in a single aspect of Dewey's thought, say his philosophy of education, have often made, the mistake of understanding him only after they have split him up.

In a paper written toward the end of his life, C. I. Lewis confessed that although he had always been drawn to Dewey's emphasis on the extralogical element involved in every process of reasoning, he could never accept that this element could be what Dewey described as an act of inference. Nor could he ever understand how the implicatory relation could arise from anything like an action at all, since, to his way of thinking, it must arise from an a priori "given," not an a posteriori "taken." In this way he justified his own option for the path of Peirce's conceptual pragmatism, which followed Russell more closely than Dewey and in which it was clear that "all philosophy has for its task such analytic depiction of the *a priori*—to define the good, the right, the true, the valid, and the real."[24] For, "any attempt to identify a universal or a character by reference to the class of individuals of which this character is predicable is doomed to failure . . . [for] there are always, for any given class of existents, at least two predicates (two of which are not equivalent in intension) which are common to all and only those individuals which are members of this class. The predicates 'human,' 'featherless biped,' and 'animal that laughs' constitute a familiar though not too good example."[25] This only goes to show how even such a sympathetic critic of Dewey's *Logic* as Lewis could miss the point of Dewey's reconstruction of the concept of natural kinds and the difference between a priori determinations of class membership and the a posteriori determinations traced in such detail by Dewey as he followed the reasoning procedures of scientists and compared them with those of moralists and theologians, counselors and advocates in courts of law, historians and art critics. Because Lewis could not see how the primitive notion of a commonsense kind could provide for the experience of the projectibility of character across existences that is the ultimate object of formal implication arising from material implication, he continued to claim the hegemony of logic over scientific method to the end. Nor is it surprising that he saw Dewey's account of judgments about values in *The Quest for Certainty* as likely to puzzle his readers. "If only," Lewis complained, Dewey "would not miscall 'logic' what is rightly a much wider thing, the analysis of the constructive thought process!"[26]

Here we come to the crux of the problem of the relation between logic and scientific method. For it was Dewey's contention that until, and unless, logic is seen as a consequence, rather than a critic, of this much wider thing, we will be in the same position as the advocate of judicial criticism faced with an Impressionist painting. If logic is not understood as the product and consequence of "the analysis of the constructive thought process," as opposed to thought's a priori and transcendental *causa essendi,* it will remain apart thought, and the superstition of necessity will not have been eliminated. What Lewis calls the "equivalence of intension," the presupposition that we must have a clear grasp of meaning if we are to understand truth and reach objects of reference, is what Dewey had all along been criticizing as the *the* philosophic fallacy. It is clear that Dewey's project in the *Logic,* his tracing of the path of involvements from the biological matrix of inquiry through the cultural matrix of language to the ordered discourse of logic itself, was designed to show that meanings are not the presuppositions of reference but its consequences. The aim of inquiry is to reach the objects of knowledge and to communicate the significance of those objects in warranted assertions. For it is only through such communication that problematic situations are resolved. It is through knowings and the known that common sense is transformed and the givens of immediate experience are reconstructed, made over into the instruments of language as the means and the meanings that we use in coping with the problems of life, of art, religion, and politics. There is no sense without reference, we might say, reversing Frege, and no reference without inference, for it is only by inference that signs become significant.

The central position of judgment in the *Logic* is emphatic. It is Dewey's effort to show that use is not all there is to meaning, and that if meanings are means and instruments of action, they are effective only insofar as they are expressions of analysis and synthesis, of the strong sense of reference that judgment requires. It is not enough to say that the meaning of words is contextual, that the sense of a proposition is contingent on the system of language in which it is expressed. For while it is a truism that "no sound, mark, product of art, is a word or part of language in isolation" or is "part of an inclusive code," Dewey does not leave the matter there. He goes on to point out that:

> The code may be public or private. A public code is illustrated in any language that is current in a given cultural group. A private code is one agreed upon by members of special groups so as to be unintelligible to those who have not been initiated. Between the two come argots of special groups in the community, and the technical codes invented for a restricted special purpose, like the one used by ships at sea. But in every case, a particular word has its meaning only in relation to the code of which it is one constituent. The distinction just drawn between meanings that are determined respectively in fairly direct connection with action in situations that are near at hand, and meanings determined for possible use in remote and contingent situations, provides the basis upon which language codes as systems may be differentiated into two main kinds. [*Logic,* pp. 49–50]

And it is just this differentiation that "fixes the difference between what is called common sense and what is called science." For:

> In the former cases (ordinary language), the customs, the *ethos* and spirit of a group is the decisive factor in determining the system of meanings in use. The system is one in a practical and institutional sense rather than in an intellectual sense. Meanings that are formed on this basis are sure to contain much that is irrelevant and to exclude much that is required for intelligent control of activity. The meanings are coarse, and many of them are inconsistent with each other from a logical point of view. One meaning is appropriate to action under certain institutional group considerations; another in some other situation, and there is no attempt to relate the different situations to

one another in a coherent scheme. In an intellectual sense, there are many languages though in a social sense there is but one. This multiplicity of language-meaning constellations is also a mark of our existing culture. A word means one thing in relation to a religious institution, still another thing in business, a third thing in law, and so on. This fact is the real Babel of communication. [*Logic*, p. 50]

The ideal of scientific language is different, Dewey says, for it is of a language system wherein "each meaning that enters into the language is expressly determined in its relation to other members of the language system. In all reasoning or ordered discourse this criterion takes precedence over that instituted by connection with cultural habits."

But far from suggesting that ordinary language should be raised to the epistemological level of the scientific language ideal, Dewey points out that this is but one ideal among many, and that "selection of some one of them, even though that one be internally consistent and extensively accepted, is arbitrary," although the very raising of the possibility "reverses the *theoretical* state of the case" (*Logic*, p. 50). For what can solve the problem is not the adoption of some program of "education that indoctrinates individuals into some special tradition," but efforts to "bring about community of activities under existing conditions." For it is only through such community of reference that shared meanings are possible and that something like the meanings of a genuine community of language can be achieved. The shared meanings of the scientific language community are merely examples of how it can be done, in that they illustrate what happens when "meanings are related to one another in inference and discourse and where the symbols are such as to indicate the relation" (*Logic*, p. 51). It was to show that our everyday discourse is capable of achieving genuine community by attending to matters of inference and reference that Dewey put judgment at the center of the *Logic,* thereby demonstrating that intelligent methods of inquiry are everywhere present in intelligent behavior—in art, religion, and politics, as well as science—for meanings without reference are not enough. As he had put it in *Experience and Nature:*

Meaning is objective as well as universal. . . . A meaning may not of course have the particular objectivity which is imputed to it, as whistling does not actually portend wind, nor the sprinkling of water indicate rain. But such magical imputations of external reference testify to the objectivity of meaning as such. Meanings are naturally the meaning of something or other; difficulty lies in discriminating the right thing. . . . Yet the truth of classic philosophy in assigning objectivity to meanings, essences, ideas remains unassailable. [*LW*1:148]

He is not referring to fixed meanings or essences now, of course, but to extensional reference and objectivity in judgment.

Because the *Theory of Valuation* is surely Dewey's strongest and most elaborate defense of the role of knowledge in relation to practice, whether in science or ethics, politics or aesthetics, and because it accurately reflects both the ontological commitments and the metaphysical perspective of the *Logic*, I have characterized it as a sequel to the *Logic*. But it is a sequel also to the theme that Dewey had been pushing all along, that of meliorism and the reconstruction of a culture divided against itself. For, although the immediate target of criticism in the *Theory of Valuation* is the cognitive-versus-noncognitive bifurcation which he saw as arising from logical positivism, his ultimate target is the division between theory and practice that he had been attacking since the 1890s.

The structure of the argument in the *Theory of Valuation* is by now familiar. Dewey begins by showing that the givens of any inquiry into values are no different from the givens of inquiry into anything else; that the purportedly unanalyzable content of interests and likings, desires and prizings, is not fundamentally different from the characteristics and generic traits that furnish the signs leading to the objects of any inquiry. As facts they must be constituted into cognitive objects by means of operations of the sort conducted in any inquiry that seeks to determine what signs indicate. For it is clear, once again, that signification, or meaning, can be determined only by acts of inference that lead to objective reference. Once again Dewey is looking for a causal analysis of the given, for the generic conditions of emotive signs and the involvements they signify. For once these relations have been objectively constituted, they become subject to change and control or, alternatively, to reinforcement and perpetuation. In problematic situations, where conflicting emotions are at work, the resolution is instituted, as in any problematic situation, by action taken to reconstruct the situation. Control of the situation is not assured, of course; however, only a causal knowledge of the situation offers a means of formulating "the aims, purposes, plans, and policies that direct intelligent human activity" (p. 57). We are looking once again at the generic traits of qualitatively individual existences. We are looking at existing valuations to see if "propositions about them are empirically verifiable." Again, knowledge of these valuations, like any factual knowledge, does not of itself resolve any problems. "But such factual knowledge is a *sine qua non* of ability to formulate valuation-propositions" (p. 57).

This summary is given substance by the following text:[27]

> Suppose, for example, that it be ascertained that a particular set of current valuations have, as their antecedent historical conditions, the interest of a small group or special class in maintaining certain exclusive privileges and advantages, and that this maintenance has the effect of limiting both the range of the desires of others and their capacity to realize them. Is it not obvious that this knowledge of conditions and consequences would surely lead to revaluation of the desires and ends that had been assumed to be authoritative sources of valuation? Not that such revaluation would of necessity take effect immediately. But, when valuations that exist at a given time are found to lack the support they have previously been supposed to have, they exist in a context that is highly adverse to their continued maintenance. In the long run the effect is similar to a warier attitude that develops toward certain bodies of water as a result of knowledge that these bodies of water contain disease germs. If, on the other hand, investigation shows that a given set of existing valuations, including the rules of their enforcement, be such as to release individual potentialities of desire and interest, and does so in a way that contributes to mutual reinforcement of the desires and interests of all members of a group, it is impossible for this knowledge not to serve as a bulwark of the particular set of valuations in question, and to induce intensified effort to sustain them in existence. [pp. 59–60]

Dewey was well aware of the difficulties that stand in the way of reaching such improved valuations and value judgments, but he insisted that they are, in the main, practical in nature. They are "supplied by traditions, customs, and institutions which persist without being subjected to systematic empirical investigation and which constitute the most influential source of further desires and ends." He calls for a more effective sociology and cultural anthropology as the needed conditions for a more powerful theory of valuation as an "effective instrumentality, for human organisms live in a cultural environment." He argues that only such a theory of human behavior can break down the "separation alleged to exist between the 'world of facts' and the 'realm of values'," the stock-in-trade of logical positivism.

In the end he argues the melioristic theme that he had been arguing all along, the theme that shows how his whole philosophy hangs together, the transformational theme that shows the character of his reconstruction of pragmatism:

> The chief *practical* problem with which the present *Encyclopedia* is concerned, the unification of science, may just be said to center here, for at the present time the widest gap in knowledge is that which exists between humanistic and non-humanistic subjects. The breach will disappear, the gap be filled, and science be manifest as an operating unity in fact and not merely in idea when the conclusions of impersonal and non-humanistic science are employed in guiding the course of distinctively human behavior, that, namely, which is influenced by emotion and desire in the framing of means and ends; for desire, having ends-in-view, and hence involving valuations, is the characteristic that marks off human from non-human behavior. On the other side, the science that is put to distinctively human use is that in which warranted ideas about the non-human world are integrated with emotions as human traits. In this integration not only is science itself *a* value (since it is the expression and the fulfillment of a special human desire and interest) but it is the supreme means of valid determination of all valuations in all aspects of human and social life. [p. 66]

Although texts like this lend credibility to the notion that Dewey is trying to make everything scientific, what he is arguing for is the meliorism that he has been advocating all along, that would bring about a transformation of the divisive relations between science and culture. It is a thesis directed against the very contentions of the "scientism" that he has been accused of adopting, one designed to show the benefit of placing science in the service of culture and using it as a means to wholly human ends. It is the thesis that had always guided his reconstruction of pragmatism, the transformational thesis that ascribes to philosophy the task of mediating the transactional relations between the world of science and the culture of the live creature. It is the thesis that he had once compressed into a single sentence: "Creative activity is our greatest need; but criticism, self-criticism, is the road to its release."[28] It is what the character of pragmatism as Dewey conceived it is all about; it is the theory of intelligent behavior.

CRITICAL BIBLIOGRAPHY

The critical literature concerning what I have dealt with in this chapter under the rubric of "The Theory of Intelligent Behavior" is vast and various, for it includes an enormous volume of secondary sources on a range of subject-matters treated by Dewey, to which his philosophy of inquiry and action is uniformly central. The range extends from religion to science and includes everything in between—politics, ethics, and education in particular, but also metaphysics and ontology. I shall confine myself to mentioning but a few critical sources that stand out against the generally opaque background. Because the theme of criticism and intelligent behavior is so pervasive in Dewey's philosophy, no general treatment of that philosophy omits it from consideration; yet none does full justice to the methodological and ontological context in which Dewey considers that theme. Even the best of them—Bernstein's *John Dewey* of 1966, for example—leaves us puzzled about the force of continuity in inquiry. George R. Geiger's *John Dewey in Perspective* (cited in the bibliography to Chapter One) is deficient in its neglect of both the metaphysical perspective and the emphasis on inquiry that is central to this work on ethics and culture. Geiger seems to think that Dewey's work should be understood primarily from the perspective of psychology. Robert J. Roth's essay, *John Dewey and Self-Realization* (Englewood Cliffs, N.J.: Prentice-Hall, 1962) is similarly one-sided, although it does bring out the centrality of Dewey's early interest in self-realization: Roth fails to trace the development of that early concern into Dewey's mature social and political philosophy, however. In all likelihood, the best treatment of the development will be the forthcoming book by Abraham Edel and Elizabeth Flower, to be published by Southern Illinois University Press, tracing the changes between the 1908 *Ethics* and the 1932 revisions.

Briefer treatments of more narrowly defined topics present a much more fertile field, however. There is, for example, the essay on Dewey's ethics referred to by Dewey in his letter to Sidney Hook with which my second chapter opens, the essay in which Hook responds to Morton White's misdirected criticism in "Value and Obligation in Dewey and Lewis," *Philosophical Review*, vol. 58, no. 4 (1949): 321–29, and chapter 13 of White's *Social Thought in America* (New York: Viking, 1949). The essay to which Dewey refers is "The Desirable and Emotive in Dewey's Ethics," in *John Dewey: Philosopher of Science and Freedom*, edited by Hook (cited in the bibliography to Chapter One). Curiously, this same volume contains another misdirected essay by White, "The Analytic and the Synthetic: An Untenable Dualism," on Dewey's failure to realize the dualistic implications of the analytic-synthetic distinction. The other essays in this volume, however, combine to give a more accurate perspective. George Boas on "Instrumentalism and the History of Philosophy," Edwin W. Patterson on

"Dewey's Theory of Legal Reasoning and Valuation," Paul D. Wienpahl on "Dewey's Theory of Language and Meaning," and Wilfred Sellars on "Language, Rules and Behavior," should all be considered as *desiderata*. Important sidelights on Dewey's behavior are discoverable in Jim Cork's essay on "John Dewey and Karl Marx" and James T. Farrell on "Dewey in Mexico" and the whole Trotsky affair. Albert Hofstadter's piece "Concerning a Certain Deweyan Conception of Metaphysics" accurately assesses the importance that Dewey places on the ontological centrality of causal involvement, but projects a metaphysics that seems to depart from Dewey's own quite markedly. For Dewey never abandoned the notion of qualitative individuality, which is fundamental to the notion of scientific kinds in the *Logic,* a fact that Hofstadter seems to ignore in working out his own Deweyan conception of metaphysics.

Although I do not fully share either Hook's conception of philosophy or his interpretations of Dewey's conception of philosophy, the connection between Hook and Dewey cannot be ignored. The recent volume of essays in honor of Hook on his eightieth birthday, *Sidney Hook: Philosopher of Democracy and Humanism* (Buffalo: Prometheus, 1983), contains at least two essays that are worth consulting for the light that they shed on Dewey's work. I have quoted from Rorty's essay on "Pragmatism Without Method" in the opening paragraph of this chapter; although I disagree with the theme of his essay, I do think it useful to compare Dewey's work with that of Heidegger with reference to their respective treatments of science and culture. Jack Kaminsky's essay "Ontology, Formalism, and Pragmatism" makes equally useful comparisons of Dewey and Quine, although I believe that Kaminsky, in his enthusiastic defense of Dewey's ontology against Quine's and his neglect of Quine's extensional realism, makes them out to be further apart than may actually be the case. Kaminsky ·thinks, rightly in my view, that Dewey would be appalled at Chomsky's late rationalism and Kripke's curious defense of rigid designators, but fails to mention the great similarity between Putnam's and Quine's approach to the rehabilitation of natural kinds and that essayed by Dewey in the *Logic*. It may be that Kaminsky's emphasis on the Deweyan thesis that all existences are individuals has misled him into presupposing that kinds cannot also exist. At any rate, Kaminsky quite properly draws attention to the difficulty that "formal logicians" have always had in dealing with "objects that are in the process of being made or which one is planning to make or which it is possible to make" (pp. 280–1). It is, of course, just these objects as kinds that concern Dewey and toward which his characterization of all knowing as doing and making is directed. And Kaminsky's point that Dewey's ontology is a full realization of what James had suggested early on is well taken. For Dewey indeed, in what I have called his "strong sense of reference," worked out the implications of James's statement: "On the pragmatist side we have only one edition of the universe, unfinished, growing in all sorts of places, especially in the places where thinking beings are at work." Kaminsky is also on the right track, it seems to me, when he points to the similarity of the ontological presuppositions of Wittgenstein's notion of language games and family resemblances to the pragmatic conception of what I would refer to as "provisional ontologies." This essay by Kaminsky is an excellent counter to the formalist view represented by C. I. Lewis in the texts cited in this chapter.

Kaminsky is not, of course, the only critic of Dewey's conception of philosophy to note the connection with Wittgenstein. The introduction to the Carbondale edition of *The Quest for Certainty,* by Toulmin, makes much the same connection. Indeed, it is Toulmin's view that it is precisely this that shows us "just how different John Dewey's philosophical methods and arguments were from those of William James or Charles Sanders Peirce, and so how misleading it can be to lump them all together, as the single school of 'pragmatists'," and he goes on to comment on Dewey's "delicate feeling for the intellectual relations between philosophy and the natural sciences" (*LW*4:ix). It is just this delicate feeling that I have wanted to bring out in this chapter, and which is the very point that is missing in Rorty's "Pragmatism Without Method" and *Philosophy and the Mirror of Nature,* and which belies his heavy-handed criticism of the resurgence of interest in realism in recent philosophy of science and of any attempt to view Dewey as making his own connection between scientific methods and criticism. Thus Toulmin's perspective is a needed counterbalance to Rorty's. "By putting John Dewey's arguments alongside those of his younger contemporaries, Ludwig Wittgenstein and Martin Heidegger," Toulmin says, "we can see just how deeply his critique of traditional epistemology was capable of cutting." But he goes on to emphasize the positive aspect in Dewey, an aspect that is not as prominent a feature in Wittgenstein or Heidegger—the constructive element signaled by the subtitle that Dewey gave to *The Quest for Certainty,* "The Relation of Knowledge and Action."

One of the more fascinating episodes in the history of Dewey criticism is afforded by the use made of certain of Dewey's ideas in Charles L. Stevenson's influential treatise *Ethics and Language* (cited and discussed in the bibliography for Chapter Six). Stevenson had tried to approach Dewey's theory of the sign–signification relation through Charles Mor-

ris's version of it in *Foundations of the Theory of Signs* of 1938, a work
which Dewey repudiated as inaccurate as regards both Peirce's views and
his own on the relation between language and action in his essay "Peirce's
Theory of Linguistic Signs, Thought, and Meaning," *Journal of Philoso-*
phy, 43 (1946): 85–95. What distressed Dewey was Stevenson's contention that his own treatment of the analysis of how ends and means are
related "is not dissimilar, in its broad outlines, to that found in the ethical
writings of John Dewey" (*Ethics and Language*, p. 12). For the analysis
that Stevenson proceeded to give conflated logic and psychology while
disastrously—from Dewey's point of view, that is—isolating the cognitive and emotive uses of language. In his response to Stevenson, in
"Ethical Subject-Matter and Language," *Journal of Philosophy*, 42 (1945):
701–12, Dewey protested as vigorously at the conflation of the logical
and the psychological as he did at the treatment of the cognitive and
emotive as mutually exclusive uses of language.

In the end, perhaps, the main point of Dewey's protestations against
both Morris and Stevenson was that they had failed to accord to his own
sign–signification theory the clear explication that he thought he had given
in both the *Logic* and the *Theory of Valuation*. For what he calls attention to
is the failure of both Morris and Stevenson to recognize the strong sense of
reference requisite to judgment that is the central point of the sign–
signified relation. Against Stevenson's assumption that there are signs
without signification, Dewey insists that something becomes a sign only
when its significance has been reached in judgment—a problem "not even
raised in Mr. Stevenson's treatment." And Dewey goes on to say: "If it
were discussed, I think it would be clear that the conditions in question are
those of a behavioral transaction in which *other* events (those called 'referents' or, more commonly, 'objects') are joint partners along with the event
which as bare event is *not* a sign." And he winds up his discussion of
Stevenson's interpretation of his use of predictive terms as *hortatory* by
saying that predictions are only as good as the conditions on which they are
based, a fact that pertains equally to predictions of facts and to the anticipated consequences of value choices as ends-in-view. It is morally necessary
that matter-of-fact estimates of consequences based on "what has been and
now is, as conditions," be given. "For in my opinion sentences about what
should be done, chosen, etc., are sentences, propositions, judgments, *in the*
logical sense of those words only as matter-of-fact grounds are presented in
support of what is advised, urged, recommended to be done—that is,
worthy of being done on the basis of actual evidence." Far from arguing
that moral choices can be evaluated by means of their consequences alone,

as James had sometimes implied, Dewey is arguing here that the act of moral judgment is, like all judgment, based on causal conditions, past histories, and present involvements and must have objective referents as the objects of its claims. Actual consequences may show that judgment has been in error when moral choices have been made, of course, but they may also serve to confirm those choices. But neither subsequent confirmation or disconfirmation is proof positive of the truth or falsity of the original judgment. The warrants for moral claims, like those for all hypotheses, increase and decrease in force according to the pedagogy of experience. (See my essay on Stevenson's view: "Noncognitivist Ethics May Not Be What It Seems," *Studies in Philosophy and Education*, vol. 3, no. 3 (1964), pp. 200–14.) In an essay on "Pragmatism, Religion, and Experienceable Difference," in *American Philosophy and the Future*, edited by M. Novak (New York: Scribner's, 1968), pp. 270–323, I have tried to work out the different criteria used by Peirce, James, and Dewey.

8: *Meliorism as Transformational*

*I*t has been the burden of this essay to present the character of pragmatism as Dewey conceived it. It was a conception that began with the critical rejection of the idealism of Morris and Green, that moved rapidly to the reconstruction of the pragmatism that he learned from Peirce and James, and that subsequently issued in a reconstruction of the received traditions of philosophy so thorough that, before he was finished, even Dewey himself could see it as a system. It is not that he had set out to build such a system from the start; it is just that the intention of meliorism with which he began worked out that way. As a system, Dewey's philosophy of pragmatism is as much a protest against the pretensions of the great system-builders of the past as it is a successor to them. It belongs as much to that genre of philosophical literature made famous by Kierkegaard's *Concluding Unscientific Postscript* and Nietzsche's *Twilight of the Gods* as it does to the genre of the system-builders, from Plato and Aristotle to Kant and Hegel. It is only when we view it as a system that we begin to grasp its power as a protest, as well as its transformational consequences for philosophy.

Seen as a system in which the divergent elements all hang together, the character of Dewey's transformational conception of philosophy stands in sharp contrast to the system that Peirce spent most of his life trying to put together, as well as to the loosely concatenated pragmatism of James. Dewey's conception of the role to be assigned to metaphysics was in no way comparable to the foundational role envisaged by Peirce in his cate-gorial scheme; the metaphysical background worked out by Dewey trans-forms the function of metaphysical theory altogether. Nor was Dewey's conception of logic at all like that of Peirce. Whereas Peirce's conception took him in the direction of Frege and Russell, Dewey's conception took him in a different direction altogether. Whereas Frege was committed to a conception of logic as "the laws of the laws of nature," in which it is the meaning of a sentence that determines its reference, Dewey was committed to a logic of experience in which it is the reference of a sentence that determines its meaning. In Dewey's theory of language in *Experience and Nature,* it is not form that determines matter, but matter that determines form. Already in his work with Mead and Angell at the University of Michigan, Dewey was tracing the emergence of logical forms from the practice of inquiry. He was already prepared to argue against Peirce that logical necessity emerges only as needed in the practice of science, that it has no a priori hegemony. While Peirce remained loyal to a transcendental form of Scotistic realism and was somehow able to reconcile this essentialist commitment with objective idealism, Dewey was ready to abandon all forms of transcendentalist logic and the doctrines of transcendental metaphysics and fixed essences that encumber them.

The contrast between Dewey's conception of philosophic method and that of James is no less sharply defined. Where James persisted in the belief that somehow *pragmatism* is just a new name for an old way of thinking—and gave his *Pragmatism* that subtitle in the 1907 edition—Dewey in his 1903 *Studies* was showing it to be a radically new way of thinking. Whereas James was unwilling to let go of the idea that somehow mental structure can be invoked as responsible for the necessary truths of logic and metaphysics, that it is mental structure which expresses itself in aesthetic and moral principles, Dewey was prepared to relinquish psychologism altogether, though not, of course, psychology. Dewey was open to behaviorism in ways that James was not, and also to the promise of a social psychology that he had begun to explore with Mead and Angell at Michigan. Whereas James remained, as even a sympathetic critic has remarked, "self-centered and abysmally ignorant of massive social inequities,"[1] Dewey's melioristic conception of philosophy drove him to unrelenting criticism of those inequities. In its very character as a system, Dewey's pragmatism possessed a ground-map whereby those inequities could be identified and diagnosed, as well as a method for resolving them. It possessed a spirit of selfless urgency, an awareness of the pressing need for social change, that was strangely lacking in the genial character of pragmatism as expressed by James, and that was entirely foreign to the tone of optimistic fatalism that sometimes seems close to the heart of Peirce's philosophy. Whereas both Peirce and James were able to contemplate the unfinished character of the universe with equanimity, Dewey saw it as a challenge, fraught with peril, that tests our powers of intelligent behavior. Existence, he tells us, is perennially problematic, "perilous beyond peradventure."

Like both Peirce and James, Dewey saw how important it was to integrate into philosophy the new perspectives arising from the successes of science, the transformational consequences of the Copernican revolution and of human evolution. Like Peirce he saw the need for a wholly new approach to the philosophy of science, one that would integrate the methods of logic with the procedures of the laboratory. That his way of tackling the problem brought him to repudiate Peirce's formalist conviction as to the supremacy of logic and closer to the pluralism and informalism of James does not diminish Dewey's debt to Peirce. His experimental logic of inquiry merely expands on Peirce's doubt–belief theory to include a reconstruction of the realism on which that theory is grounded. Dewey's realism of the eventual object is a signal reminder of Peirce's influence, as is the stress on the continuity of inquiry. Dewey's transformation of Peirce's doctrine of synechism, expressed in the *Logic* as the principle of the continuity of inquiry and the category of transformatìon, shows both how different Dewey's conception of philosophic method was from Peirce's and how much Dewey's theory of inquiry owes to him. It is this aspect of Dewey's conception that differs most sharply from James's nativist approach to the understanding of the role of the mind, the remnant of idealism that James retained to the end. But this opposition to James's recalcitrant psychologism does not lessen Dewey's debt to the James of the *Essays in Radical Empiricism* and *A Pluralistic Universe*. If Dewey was to embrace a form of methodological monism as a result of Peirce's arguments, he was to make James's metaphysical pluralism a central feature of his completed system. Dewey's eventual realism resonates with Peirce's conception of "the *real*, in the sense of being as it is regardless of what you or I may think of it." But it also resonates with James's conception of the essence of a thing as "that one of its properties which is so important for my interests that in comparison with it I neglect the rest."

In his valuable introduction to *The Writings of William James*, McDermott states that "the central problem of pragmatism is to account for mediation between an interest-oriented self and a processive pluralistic world."[2] Dewey's attack on this problem is wholly his own. The interest-oriented self is transformed into the social self and is linked by the language that he uses with the processive pluralistic world. Events are transformed into artifacts of language and become instruments for redirecting the course of subsequent events; they thus become the eventual as well as the eventful objects of knowledge. In his metaphysics Dewey wanted to portray the generic traits of the existential world as capable of both sustaining our interests and frustrating them. He conceived of the logic of experience as a method of disciplining the interest-oriented self through the chastening effect of the process of problem solving and the objective requirements of warrantable assertions. He imposed the empirical stringency of experimental science on the subject-matter of metaphysics and applied the breadth of his metaphysical perspective to his conception of the reach of science. And he worked the whole thing out in the everyday language that knows no final separation of matter and form, the natural language that grounds our lives with each other and that makes those lives possible.

Peirce was of the opinion that he could not express his philosophy in the vocabulary of the everyday world; he was forever coining new terms for the categories that constituted the character of his thought. He managed to articulate the architecture of his system only by a battery of neologisms especially constructed for the purpose, a move that is oddly prescient of the turn to the construction of "metalanguages" and the ideal language systems of Frege and his successors. For it is just such a turn that resulted in Carnap's *Der Logische Aufbau der Welt* and the subsequently abandoned structure of phenomenological language that was the foundational system of Wittgenstein's *Tractatus Logico-Philosophicus*.[3] Peirce's neologisms, his semiotic conception of logic, like the artificial language systems of logical positivism and the early Wittgenstein, are attempts to avoid the intractable ambiguities and intolerable vaguenesses of ordinary discourse. They were Peirce's way of building a foundational language on which the architecture of theories could rest secure.

By contrast, James was forever reducing the technical vocabulary of the tradition to the homely jargon of the marketplace. He was the master of a style of philosophical discourse that is uniquely adapted to the public lecture hall, one that he himself recognized as racy and journalistic. It is a style that is not readily redacted to the demands of professional journals, one that leaves critics without restraint as to the rich variety of interpretations that can be offered. This may have been a calculated intent of James, for there is evidence that this unrestrained variety of interpretation did not bother him at all. Charged by Lovejoy with having sired a family of thirteen pragmatisms, James, according to C. I. Lewis, was pleased that his pragmatism had such wealth of meaning and embraced them all. But, Lewis quickly adds, "such variety merely marks the fact that pragmatism is a movement, not a system."[4] James had little interest of the kind that motivated Peirce's pursuit of the architecture of theory and the *elenchus* involved in his semiotic system of the logic of relatives. Nor was James capable of Dewey's patience in his prodigious effort at reconstruction, the project of transforming the role of experience in philosophy that James's *Principles of Psychology* had suggested. Although James sometimes speculated on the importance of discourse and on the particles of grammar that hold it together, he preferred to *use* everyday language, rather than spend time working out a theory of it.[5]

In Dewey's view, our everyday language is an emergent feature of our biological and social evolution. It is every bit as much a consequence of our natural history as the emergence of the human hand or brain; like them its forms arise as progressive adaptations of the organism to its environment. Dewey was delighted with Malinowski's observation of the anthropological linkage between the hand, the tool, and language and concurred with his conclusion that "language is little influenced by thought, but thought on the contrary having to borrow from action its tools—that is, language—is largely influenced thereby" (*LW*1:160, n.4). It is practice that gives rise to theory, as matter gives rise to form. It is the primacy of inference from *praxis* to *theoria* and the consistency with which Dewey maintained it that distinguish his philosophy from the philosophies of his contemporaries, from the positivists and the phenomenologists, as well as from Peirce and James. It is the consistency with which Dewey opposed what he called the procedure of all ontological logics that distinguishes his path from the mainstream developments leading from Frege to the Vienna Circle to the linguistic turn in the aftermath of the Second World War.

Dewey recognized all along how much his conception of the origins of formal logic differed from mainstream conceptions and how differently he conceived its application. In a letter published both in the *Journal of Philosophy* and as an appendix to *Knowing and the Known*, his joint publication with Bentley in 1949, Dewey acknowledged that the title of *Logic: The Theory of Inquiry* had led to some misapprehension on the part of its readers as to what the book was trying to do. He says: "I tried the experiment of transferring the old well known figures from the stage of ontology to the stage of inquiry," but he confesses that "the force of the word 'Logic,' in all probability, has overshadowed for the reader the import of what in my intention was the significant expression, *The Theory of Inquiry*."[6] Dewey was not trying to block the development of formal logic, but he *was* trying to block the road to its application in the ontological reductions of logical positivism. He had already rejected the atomic facts and atomic propositions that Otto Neurath foreswore as a condition of Dewey's participation in the *Encyclopedia of Unified Science* project. Dewey wanted us to see even formal logic and mathematics as instruments of science, as experimental tools *for* inquiry as well as objects *of* inquiry. He wanted us to see the norms and forms of logic as experimental hypotheses rather than as a priori rigid rules to which experience must conform through logical necessity.

Toulmin has commented on our habitual failure to see "just how different John Dewey's philosophical methods were from those of William James or Charles Sanders Peirce, and so how misleading it can be to lump them all together, as the single school of 'pragmatists'."[7] In asking us to compare Dewey's philosophy with the philosophies of Wittgenstein and Heidegger, Toulmin is wanting us to see the extent of Dewey's criticism of traditional epistemology. He wants us to see how thoroughly Dewey's positive theory of the relation of knowledge and action is worked out in *The Quest for Certainty*. "Some readers are still misled by the apparently homespun instrumentalism of Dewey's work on *experimental logic* and the unduly 'scientistic' language that he sometimes used in writing about it." The result, Toulmin says, is "that the force of his argument is needlessly blunted, and it is harder to recognize just how central a position he occupies in one of the classical traditions of philosophy." It is a tradition that Toulmin traces back to Aristotle's *Topics*, and that is ranged in opposition to the Platonism of Frege's successors; it is the tradition of logic as an organon of inquiry rather than a foundation of science and mathematics.

Perhaps Toulmin's way of expressing Dewey's relation to his predecessors in pragmatism and his legacy to his successors is as good a way as any of bringing this section to a close:

> The skeptic in Dewey rejects any *a priori* model of knowledge . . . in favor of an account of perception and discovery which respects the most reflective and up-to-date results of scientific analysis; which the pragmatist in him finds the primary subject matter for a theory of knowledge . . . in the actual reasoning practices of human thinkers. So, between them, the two halves of Dewey's philosophy dovetail to provide a complete system, on which the functional analysis of cognition, reasoning and knowledge can safely build. [*LW* 4:xxii]

Toulmin leaves unmentioned a third feature of Dewey's philosophy, a feature that, in my view, plays a major role in binding the rest together. It is the "intention of meliorism," the aspect of Dewey's conception of philosophy that stands in sharpest contrast to the work of his younger contemporaries. For, although Wittgenstein and Heidegger share something of Dewey's concern for the release of philosophy from the constraints of tradition, they share little or nothing of Dewey's concern with the application of philosophy once released. They have none of Dewey's concern regarding the practice of philosophy in social and political criticism or the relation of knowledge and action in social and political practice. It is that concern that has led Dewey's admirers to call him a "philosopher of freedom and democracy," and his detractors to think of him as subversively undermining the very foundations of the freedoms that he extolls.

In the midst of the Great Depression, Robert M. Hutchins, then chancellor of the University of Chicago, sought to cast a large part of the blame for what he saw as the failure of the American educational system on the turn to practical subjects pushed by the progressive education movement that Dewey's work had done so much to set in motion.[8] Hutchins proposed a return to the intellectual authority of the classics, to those subject-matters that would restore the preeminence of *theoria* over *praxis*. He couched the whole proposal in terms strongly suggesting that a return to first principles and to the authority of fundamentals was a matter of national survival. It was a bitter attack on the very theory of inquiry that Dewey was then trying to work out, on the theory of intelligent behavior that he had been seeking to articulate for most of his life. Dewey's response was characteristically measured, but it was designed to show how Hutchins's proposal would once again plunge education back into a position of irrelevance and aloofness from contemporary social and economic life. The authoritarianism implicit in the proposal, Dewey pointed out, is "akin to the distrust of freedom and consequent appeal to some *fixed* authority that is now overcoming the world."[9]

Only a few weeks after his response to Hutchins was published in *Social Frontier*, Dewey prepared to leave for Mexico, where he was to conduct the hearings that would exonerate Trotsky from the charges that had been brought against him by Stalin in the Moscow Trials. In the aftermath of those hearings, at Trotsky's request, Dewey was invited to respond to an article in *The New International* entitled "Their Morals and Ours" in which Trotsky attacked the moral posture of American liberalism. Trotsky tried to show that the moralism of the response of American liberals to the Moscow Trials was nothing more than a "bridge from revolution to reaction."[10] He argued that, although he agreed with Dewey's proclaimed view of the relation of ends and means, Dewey had failed to see how that relation morally justified the Marxist commitment to the means of revolution. He wrote:

> A means can be justified only by its end. But the end in its turn needs to be justified. From the Marxist point of view, which expresses the historical interests of the proletariat, the end is justified if it leads to increasing the power of humanity over nature and to the abolition of

the power of one person over another. . . . Since this end can be achieved only through revolution, the liberating morality of the proletariat of necessity is endowed with a revolutionary character. . . . It deduces a rule for conduct from the laws of the development of society, thus primarily from the class struggle, this law of laws.[11]

Trotsky's use of the terms "of necessity" and "deduces a rule of conduct" could not have been more clearly designed to contrast with the conception on which Dewey had been working ever since his attack on Peirce in "The Superstition of Necessity."

Under the title "Means and Ends," Dewey pointed out that insofar as Trotsky had proposed as an end a moral purpose like the liberation of mankind, he could take no exception to it, for it would be a goal that others could accept. But he went on to say that what has given the maxim that "the end justifies the means" a bad name is that it is put into practice without regard to "the objective grounds upon which it is held: namely, the consequences that will actually be produced . . . (and) the use of means that can be shown by their nature to lead to the liberation of mankind as an objective consequence."[12] One would expect, Dewey went on, that Trotsky would want to examine all the possible means that are available and likely to attain the given end, that "every suggested means would be weighed and judged on the express ground of the consequences it is likely to produce." But this, manifestly, is not what Trotsky has done at all: "The principle of interdependence of means and an end has thus disappeared or at least been submerged. For choice of means is not decided upon the ground of an independent examination of measures and policies with respect to their actual consequences. On the contrary, means are 'deduced' from an independent source, an alleged law of history which is *the* law of all laws of social development."[13] And, to drive his point home, Dewey goes on to say that the case is no different if the word *alleged* is eliminated, for then it would be even more obvious that it is not the end that determines the means but, rather, an independent law that has been construed as the "*fixed law* of social development."

Alluding to his own long-standing commitment to democratic socialism, to the liberation of mankind from the oppression of a system that is sometimes justified in the name of freedom from economic regulation, Dewey reiterates that he certainly does not base his rejection of Marxism on a denial of the class struggle as such. It is based, rather, on the fact that there are "presumably several, perhaps many, different ways by means of which the class struggle may be carried on." And he concludes:

There appears to be a curious transfer among orthodox Marxists of allegiance from the ideals of socialism and scientific *methods* of attaining them (scientific in the sense of being based on the objective relations of means and consequences) to the class struggle as the law of historical change. Deduction of ends set up, of means and attitudes, from this law as the primary thing makes all moral questions, that is all questions of the end to be finally attained, meaningless. To be scientific about ends does not mean to read them out of laws, whether the laws are natural or social. Orthodox Marxism shares with orthodox religionism and with traditional idealism the belief that human ends are interwoven into the very texture and structure of existence—a conception inherited presumably from its Hegelian origin.[14]

As for Trotsky, Dewey remarks that "in avoiding one kind of absolutism Mr. Trotsky has plunged into another kind of absolutism."[15] This statement was scarcely designed to appeal to the critics of pragmatism from either the conservative right or the radical left. During the Second World War Dewey found himself under severe attack from both directions. Responding in a prescient statement of the consequences of the war and in defense of his intention of meliorism, Dewey wrote:

As the war is a global war, so the peace must be a peace that has respect for all the peoples and "races" of the world. I mentioned earlier the provincialism which leaves non-Christians of the world, especially of Asia (later Africa will come into the scene) outside the fold, which philosophical nonsupernaturalism admits within the fold only upon conditions dictated by its own metaphysics. A philosophical naturalist cannot approve or go along with those whose beliefs and whose actions (if the latter cohere with their theories) weaken dependence upon the natural agencies, cultural, economic, scientific, political, by which a more humane and friendly world can alone be built. On the contrary, to him the present tragic scene is a challenge to employ courageously, patiently, and with wholehearted devotion all the natural resources that are now potentially at command. He cannot conceal, no matter how charitable his disposition, what antinaturalism does to check and hamper the use of means that are admitted to be the only ones actually within the power of human beings in their natural environment.[16]

It is difficult indeed to see how this vocabulary leaves room for anything like "*ungrounded* social hope" (my emphasis).[17] But it is not at all difficult to see it as an expression of the character of pragmatism as Dewey conceived it, and of the intention of meliorism.

CRITICAL BIBLIOGRAPHY

The bibliography for Chapter One above includes the most significant sources for the problems that are addressed in the first part of this chapter. The best attempts to present Dewey's philosophy as a system are the earlier ones, such as Hook's *John Dewey: An Intellectual Portrait* and the essays contributed by Dewey's colleagues and admirers in the three *Festschriften*. Arthur E. Murphy's essay on "Dewey's Theory of the Nature and Function of Philosophy" in the 1940 collection *The Philosopher of the Common Man,* ed. S. Ratner (New York: Putnam's), is an example. But what these studies gain in a sense of immediacy is offset by the absence of the perspective that only time provides. Bernstein's introductory essay to his anthology of Dewey's writings, *On Experience, Nature, and Freedom,* gains from the perspective of time and represents the high point of Bernstein's appreciation of the coherence of Dewey's philosophy. Bernstein's 1966 *John Dewey* is flawed by his misreading of what Dewey was trying to do in his metaphysics and logic; it presents a Dewey already split up again. The best study, then, remains Thayer's contextual study, *Meaning and Action,* of 1968. It is the only study that anticipates the perspective on Dewey's work that I share with Toulmin—that is, that we can best grasp the depth of Dewey's criticism of the tradition when we compare him with his younger contemporaries Wittgenstein and Heidegger.

If I depart from either Thayer's or Toulmin's perspective on the holistic character of Dewey's conception of philosophy, it is in the direction of a greater emphasis on the centrality of Dewey's transformational theory of language and logic and the link provided by the theory of language between his theory of inquiry and his metaphysics. I have stressed Dewey's emphasis on the need for a theory of language that does not separate matter and form, not because I wish to construe Dewey as a linguistic philosopher, but because I think that we should compare Dewey's approach to language, meaning, and truth with the tradition initiated by Frege. Thayer, like Toulmin, suggests that Dewey should be compared with Wittgenstein, but neither suggests that their point of convergence is their common rejection of Frege's conceptions of language, meaning, and truth.

As I indicated in the bibliography for Chapter Four, Dummett appears to be the reigning authority on Frege, and so it is appropriate that two of his books be added to the bibliography here: *Frege: Philosophy of Language* (London: Duckworth, 1973), and *Truth and Other Enigmas* (London: Duckworth, 1978). The most accessible of Frege's own writings is his essay "On Sense and Reference," in his *Philosophical Writings: Translations,* edited by Max Black and Peter T. Geach (Oxford: Basil Blackwell, 1960). Dummett's reading of Frege is challenged by H. Sluga in his *Frege* (London: Routledge and Kegan Paul, 1980), but perhaps the most relevant criticism of Dummett is found in Barry Stroud's essay on Dummett's Fregean reading of Wittgenstein, "Wittgenstein and Logical Necessity," *Philosophical Review,* 74 (1965): 504–18; reprinted in *Essays on Wittgenstein,* edited by E. D. Klemke (Urbana: University of Illinois Press, 1971). I take this to be relevant to the view of Dewey's conception of logical necessity that I have tried to develop, on account of the passage that concludes Stroud's essay:

> At the end of his paper Dummett recommends interposing between the Platonist and constructivist pictures of thought and reality an intermediate picture "of objects springing into being in response to our probing. We do not *make* the objects but must accept them as we find them (this corresponds to the proof imposing itself on us); but they were not already there for our statements to be true or false or before we carried out the investigations which brought them into being" (p. 348). As far as I understand this, it seems to be just the picture to be derived from Wittgenstein if my interpretation is in general correct. Logical necessity, he says, is not like rails that stretch to infinity and compel us always to go in one and only one way; but neither is it the case that we are not compelled at all. Rather, there are the rails we have already traveled, and we can extend them beyond the present point only by depending on those that already exist. In order for the rails to be navigable they must be extended in smooth and natural ways; how they are to be continued is to that extent determined by the rails which are already there. I have been primarily concerned to explain the sense in which we are "responsible" for the ways in which the rails are extended, without destroying anything that could properly be called their objectivity. [p. 463]

The reader who has paid close attention to my discussion of Dewey's difficulty in making his sense of objectivity clear, his insistence that the object of knowledge is the *eventual* object of inquiry that results from the operations of inquiry, will have little difficulty in seeing the relevance of this passage to Dewey's struggle. Dewey was trying to work out a conception of objects somewhere between the Platonism of Peirce's ontology and the constructivism that he saw as a possible flaw in James's denkmittel. Dewey's view corresponds to the proof imposing itself on us in a way that James's does not. But this view, as both Dummett and Stroud recognize, is not at all the view that Frege held.

In my view, Frege's contention that sense determines reference dominates logical positivism; it is responsible for Ayer's *Language, Truth and Logic* and for Carnap all the way to the enlarged edition of *Meaning and Necessity* (Chicago: University of Chicago Press, 1956) and continues to be reflected in the work of Donald Davidson (see Davidson, *Essays on Action and Events* [Oxford: Clarendon Press, 1980]; *Inquiries into Truth and Interpretation* [Oxford: Clarendon Press, 1984]). It is this progression that I have referred to as the path followed by Frege's successors. It is the path that Dewey was trying to block from the time of his first contact with Russell in 1914, the path that Wittgenstein abandoned in 1929 and that Otto Neurath forswore in Dewey's living room in the presence of Nagel and Hook in 1938. (Dewey, it should be added, contributed not only the essay *Theory of Valuation* to the *Encyclopedia of Unified Science,* but also a brief essay on "Unity of Science as a Social Problem," to vol. 1, no. 1 [1938], pp. 29–38.) It is the path that Dewey was still describing in 1949 as the path followed by all ontological logics. (See Dewey's reply to Albert Balz.) Davidson thinks that it is this path that Quine was still following in his 1960 *Word and Object,* despite his express disclaimer in the chapter called "Entia non grata." (See Quine, *Word and Object* [Cambridge, Mass.: MIT Press, 1960], section 50; Davidson, "Reality Without Reference," in *Inquiries into Truth and Interpretation,* pp. 215–25.) But in my view it is clear that Quine had abandoned that path by 1951, when his "Two Dogmas of Empiricism" appeared, and that he had already veered therefrom in his 1948 essay "On What There Is." (Both essays are reprinted in *From a Logical Point of View* [Cambridge, Mass.: Harvard University Press, 1953].) In any case it seems clear that if we are to regard Quine as in any sense a successor to Dewey, as I think we should, it can only be due to his having given up Frege's notion that logic can somehow provide us with the laws of the laws of nature.

Not only was Dewey's conception of logic adamantly opposed to this Fregean idea, but his conception of society, the state, and the law was adamantly opposed to the traditional theory that there is a natural law basis for the laws that we adopt for governing ourselves. Once again it must be said that the early literature on Dewey's political and social philosophy is far superior to what has come later. One has only to compare Hu Shih's

1940 essay on "The Political Philosophy of Instrumentalism" and Edwin W. Patterson's on "Pragmatism as a Philosophy of Law"—both written for the 1940 Festschrift, *The Philosopher of the Common Man* (New York: Greenwood, 1940)—with A. H. Somjee's *The Political Theory of John Dewey* (New York: Teachers College Press, 1968) or A. J. Damico's *Individuality and Community: The Social and Political Thought of John Dewey* (Gainesville: University Presses of Florida, 1978) to grasp the point. Somjee tries to interpret Dewey's political views in terms of his theory of knowledge, but since he does not understand that theory he has a hard time of it. Damico does better, but not much; he comes to the remarkable conclusion that "Dewey's preoccupation with scientific method is a central weakness in his entire political theory" (p. 95). A few more recent essays, however, are worth consulting. Charles Frankel's contribution to *New Studies in the Philosophy of John Dewey,* "Dewey's Social Philosophy," is worthwhile, despite Frankel's evident neoconservative bias. In contradistinction to Frankel, Peter T. Manicas, in "John Dewey and the Problem of Social Justice," *Journal of Value Inquiry,* 15 (1981), complains that "Dewey was insufficiently radical regarding the difficulties standing in the way of transforming 'The Great Society' into 'The Great Community'," although he hastens to add that "he never fell victim to pat solutions" (p. 290). As both Frankel and Manicas suggest, Dewey's political theory is not the strongest part of his system, even though it stands up well against the competition. (See especially Manicas's comparison of Dewey with Nozick and Rawls, and Damico's defense of Dewey against Hartz's defamatory identification of pragmatism with a kind of Whiggish absolutism in politics; Louis Hartz, *The Liberal Tradition in America* [New York: Harcourt Brace, 1955], pp. 58–9.) On the whole, McDermott's *The Culture of Experience: Philosophical Essays in the American Grain* (New York: New York University Press, 1976), though written from an angle rather different from my own, expresses the spirit and temper of Dewey's social thought about as well as anything yet available. Rather than comparing Dewey's theories with those of Rawls and Nozick, as Manicas does, McDermott compares Dewey's approach to experience and culture with the approaches of Norman Brown and Herbert Marcuse, in a valuable antidote to the arid treatment of pragmatism by political science.

Although, as mentioned, Toulmin has suggested that Dewey's work be compared with that of Heidegger, he has not carried through on the suggestion to any great extent. However, Michael Sukale has done so in an extremely useful essay: "Heidegger and Dewey," *Comparative Studies in Phenomenology* (The Hague: Nijhoff, 1976). (In the same volume Sukale brings together Husserl and Frege in his discussion of "The Problem of Psychologism." This is a more extensive discussion of Frege's relation to Husserl than was given by Dagfinn Føllesdal in his *Husserl and Frege* of 1958.) I have found Sukale's approach to phenomenology and its relation to Dewey's thought more valuable than the better-known work of V. Kestenbaum, *The Phenomenological Sense of John Dewey* (Atlantic Highlands, N.J.: Humanities Press, 1977), or that of R. B. Webb, *The Presence of the Past* (Gainesville: University of Florida Presses, 1976).

There is almost no literature on Dewey's philosophy of language worthy of consideration except James Campbell's essay on "Politics and Conceptual Reconstruction," *Philosophy and Rhetoric,* vol. 17, no. 3 (1984), and Edith Wyschogrod's "The Logic of Artifactual Existents: John Dewey and Claude Levi-Strauss," *Man and World,* 14 (1981): 235–50. Max Black's earlier essay "Dewey's Philosophy of Language," *Journal of Philosophy,* 49 (1962): 505–23, promises much by comparing Dewey and Wittgenstein but in fact delivers little. Black thinks that Dewey's approach to language suffers from being metaphysical, in contrast to Wittgenstein's; but his claim that Wittgenstein's approach is not metaphysical does not accord with most current Wittgenstein scholarship. The accepted view is that the language of the *Tractatus* was phenomenological, but that this was rejected in favor of natural, or physicalistic, language in Wittgenstein's later work. (See David Pears, "The Relation Between Wittgenstein's Picture Theory of Propositions and Russell's Theories of Judgment," *Philosophical Review,* 86 [1977]: 177–96, and Jaakko Hintikka and Merrill B. Hintikka, "The Development of Wittgenstein's Philosophy," in *Epistemology and the Philosophy of Science: Proceedings of the 7th International Wittgenstein Symposium* [Vienna: Holder-Pichler-Tempsky, 1983], pp. 425–37.)

On Dewey's conduct of the Trotsky hearing, see Dykhuizen and *Guide to the Works* for a full bibliography. There are indeed events in which actions speak louder than words, and when Dewey's political theories come under attack for being either too conservative or too radical, it is well to recall Dewey's own *apologia:* "I reached fairly early in the growth of my ideas a belief in the intimate and indissoluble connection of means and ends reached. I doubt if the force of the idea in the theory of social action would have come home to me without my experience in social and political movements, culminating in events associated with my membership in the Trotsky Inquiry Commission. . . . My belief in the office of intelligence as a continuously reconstructive agency is at least a faithful report of my own life and experience" (quoted by Jane Dewey in Schilpp, p. 44).

Notes

Chapter 1: On Interpreting Dewey

1. This is an adaptation of a point made by Frank Kermode in *The Classic: Literary Images of Permanence and Change* (New York: Viking, 1975).
2. Richard Rorty, "Comments on Sleeper and Edel," *Transactions of the Charles S. Peirce Society*, vol. 21, no. 1 (1985), p. 39.
3. I take this to be the gist of Rorty's *Philosophy and the Mirror of Nature* and *Consequences of Pragmatism*.
4. *Mirror*, p. 360, is a good source text for what Rorty means by *edification*. The idea of "coping" with culture is explained in the essay "Method, Social Science, and Social Hope," in *Consequences*, pp. 191–210. Rorty makes the connection between Dewey's "vocabulary" and "unjustifiable hope" on p. 208.
5. My own diagnosis is tentatively given in "Rorty's Pragmatism: Afloat in Neurath's Boat, But Why Adrift?" *Transactions of the Charles S. Peirce Society*, vol. 21, no. 1 (1985): 9–20. It was first presented as a contribution to the "Symposium on Rorty's *Consequences of Pragmatism*" which took place at the 1983 meeting of the Eastern Division of the American Philosophical Association. Compare also the contribution of Abraham Edel to this symposium and Rorty's reply, published in the same issue of *Transactions*, and the critical bibliography above.
6. Dewey's prose is said to be clumsy and difficult to read. The point I am making here is very different. From the prodigiousness of his output, it is obvious that Dewey had no difficulty writing philosophy. (See *EW*5:151 for Dewey's comment on writing philosophy as "hard work." With regard to citations from the writings of Dewey, see the Critical Bibliography to Chapter One.)
7. Abraham Edel, "A Missing Dimension in Rorty's Use of Pragmatism," in the symposium cited in n. 5 above, p. 21.
8. By 1903 James may already have abandoned the concept of necessary truths that he had given in the *Principles* of 1890. Peirce, however, stuck to his account of logical necessity to the end, a matter that I will discuss more fully in Chapter Three.
9. Sidney Hook, "The Metaphysics of the Instrument, Part I," *Monist* 37 (1927): 335–56. See also Hook's *The Metaphysics of Pragmatism*.
10. Rorty, *Consequences*, p. xviii. Compare also Rorty's contribution, "Pragmatism Without Method," to the Festschrift edited by Paul Kurtz, *Sidney Hook: Philosopher of Democracy and Humanism* (Buffalo: Prometheus, 1983), pp. 259–73. We will look further at Dewey's attempt to block the road to logical positivism in Chapter Four.

11. W. V. Quine, *Ontological Relativity and Other Essays* (New York: Columbia University Press, 1969), p. 27. See also, in the same volume, Quine's essay "Natural Kinds," pp. 114–38. The line taken by Quine in "Epistemology Naturalized," pp. 69–90, is that taken by Dewey in his 1938 *Logic*, as we will see in Chapter Five.

12. The phrase "general theory of language" is Dewey's, from the preface to *Logic: The General Theory of Inquiry* (New York: Holt, Rinehart and Winston, 1938), p. iv. I regard this preface as a *desideratum* for the understanding of how logic and metaphysics are linked by language in Dewey's theory, albeit one that is universally neglected by his critics.

13. Dewey, *Logic*, "Part Three: Propositions and Terms," pp. 281–367, passim.

14. Rorty, "Pragmatism Without Method," p. 259.

15. This is the accusation that Morton White levels against Dewey. It nicely parallels Rorty's and may be Rorty's (unacknowledged) source. Compare White's essay "Experiment and Necessity in Dewey's Philosophy," in his *Pragmatism and the American Mind*, pp. 138–54.

16. John McDermott, "Symposium," p. 1. McDermott quotes Dewey from *Characters and Events*, edited by Joseph Ratner (New York: Henry Holt, 1929), vol. 1, p. 129.

17. It would be hard to find another philosopher who could, for example, be the subject of a book such as *Dewey and His Critics*, consisting of some seven hundred pages drawn from a single periodical.

18. Wherever possible I have tried to cite criticism on both sides of an issue of conflicting interpretation. Where countervailing criticism was not available, I have discussed the issue in the main body of the text.

19. Rorty, *Consequences*, p. 87.

20. Lewis Mumford, *The Golden Day: A Study in American Experience and Culture* (New York: Boni and Liveright, 1926), pp. 157ff.

21. John Dewey, "The Pragmatic Acquiescence," *The New Republic*, 5 January 1927; reprinted in *Characters and Events*, vol. 2; the quote is found on pp. 441–42.

22. John Dewey, *Philosophy and Civilization* (New York: Capricorn, 1963), p. 7. An earlier edition was published by Minton Balch in 1931.

Chapter 2: The Conception of a Philosophy

1. The original is in the Sidney Hook Collection of John Dewey, Collection 143, Special Collections, Morris Library, Southern Illinois University at Carbondale. It is quoted with the permission of the Center for Dewey Studies, Southern Illinois University at Carbondale, and of Sidney Hook.

2. Quoted from the last letter from Dewey to Bentley published in: *John Dewey and Arthur F. Bentley, A Philosophical Correspondence, 1932–1951*, p. 646.

3. The phrase "drifted away" is from Dewey's own account of his philosophical development, "From Absolutism to Experimentalism," first published in 1930; quoted from *LW*5:154.

4. "The Pantheism of Spinoza," quoted from *EW*1:9.

5. "Kant and Philosophic Method," published in 1884, the year in which he received his Ph.D.; quoted from *EW*1:35.

6. Dewey, "From Absolutism to Experimentalism," *LW*2:153. The quotations immediately following are from the same source.

7. "Psychology as Philosophic Method," published in 1886; quoted from *EW*1:164. But see this whole series beginning in January of 1886 with "The Psychological Standpoint" (*EW*1:122–43) and concluding in July of 1887 with "Knowledge as Idealization" (*EW*1:176–93). He responds to criticism by Shadworth Hodgson in a

polemical "Illusory Psychology," published in January 1887 (*EW*1:168–75). He attacks Hodgson's metaphysical approach to experience, insisting on the scientific approach of psychology instead. Five years later Dewey had abandoned the psychological standpoint in favor of a straightforward scientific approach (see *EW*3:211). As this scientific approach to experience develops, it becomes the *logic* of experience.

8. The key text showing the influence of James on Dewey's developing conception of logic is "The Present Position of Logical Theory," published in October 1891 (*EW*3:125–41), though Dewey does not mention James at all. Dewey takes direct aim at the disjunction between the a priori and the a posteriori, arguing that this disjunction can no longer be maintained. The essay concludes by pushing beyond the hesitations of James in the concluding chapter of the *Principles,* both as to the scientific character of logic and the future role of metaphysics (see *EW*3:140–1). This whole matter is discussed more fully in Chapter Three.

9. Several accounts of Mead's arrival at Michigan are given in the critical bibliography for this chapter, of which the most useful is probably Coughlan's *The Young John Dewey.*

10. Coughlan, p. 148.

11. John Venn's book was actually called *The Principles of Empirical or Inductive Logic* (London: Macmillan, 1889), and the diagrams he invented still appear in logic textbooks.

12. Dewey's logic of experience is based on the insight that experience possesses certain formal qualities. The norms of purely formal logic are abstractions from these qualities, and so are not, strictly speaking, a priori or self-evident. The rules of implication are strictly a posteriori, therefore, and in practice depend on inference (see *EW*3:81).

13. Dewey continued to protest against those ontological logics that import their ontology *from* logic, of course, for he thought the procedure should be reversed. His kind of realism would always take scientific objects as the source from which to abstract the principles of logic; logic should, in a sense, recapitulate the ontology of science.

14. This way of putting the transformational effect of ideas on facts is, of course, congenial to idealism. Dewey's turn to realism is the result of the constraints that facts put on ideas, something he does not emphasize until somewhat later. At this point he is just trying to get away from the idea that facts contain fixed essences.

15. According to James, the term *pragmatism* did not come into general use until 1898, as a result of his California lecture in which he revived the term from Peirce's 1878 *Popular Science Monthly* articles (James, "What Pragmatism Means," in *Pragmatism: A New Name for Some Old Ways of Thinking* [New York: Longmans, Green, 1907]).

16. "The Reflex Arc Concept in Psychology" (*EW*5:96–109). The metaphors of skeleton and framework are echoed in his 1903 *Studies in Logical Theory,* where that of scaffolding also appears.

17. It was Dewey's insistence on this point that would later distinguish his view of logic from that of James. James was still ready to "flourish" Locke in the *Principles,* and he dedicated *Pragmatism* to Mill. Dewey anticipates Quine's attack on this dogma of empiricism; see W. V. Quine, "Two Dogmas of Empiricism," *Philosophical Review,* 1951; reprinted in Quine's *From a Logical Point of View* (Cambridge, Mass.: Harvard University Press, 1953), pp. 1–46.

18. The ground-map metaphor is found in *Experience and Nature* (*LW*1:309). The characterization of experience as pedagogical is due to McDermott; see his *The Philosophy of John Dewey,* vol. 2, p. 421.

19. Max Eastman, "John Dewey," *The Atlantic Monthly*, 167 (1941): 673. But see also Dewey's account in "From Absolutism to Experimentalism" (*LW*5:153–4), where he speaks of a "trying personal crisis," while denying that it ever constituted a "leading philosophical problem."

20. Lewis S. Feuer, "John Dewey and the Back to the People Movement in American Thought," *Journal of the History of Ideas*, vol. 20, no 4 (1958): 545–68. Dykhuizen gives details of Dewey's church membership both before and after the year spent at Minnesota. See the critical bibliography for other sources.

21. Jane M. Dewey, ed., "Biography of John Dewey," in Schilpp, pp. 3–45.

22. Wayne A. R. Leys, in his introduction to volume 4 of the *Early Works*, points to this talk and the address "Christianity and Democracy" (*EW*4:3–43) as showing "tactful respect for religious sensitivities" (*EW*4:ix). The introduction to philosophy course introduced a year earlier shows no such tactful respect; Christianity is there described as responsible for perpetuating the "fixed and rigid separation" of theory from practice (*EW*3:227).

23. Josiah Royce, *International Journal of Ethics*, vol. 6 (1895): 113; cited by Leys (*EW*4:xiii).

24. In "From Absolutism to Experimentalism" Dewey suggests that in order to "make straight and open the paths that lead to the future," a chief task of "those who call themselves philosophers is to help get rid of the useless lumber that blocks our highways of thought" (*LW*5:160). The metaphor of *antifoundationalism* refers to this latter function.

25. The term *necessity* when applied to pragmatism reflects Dewey's reference to the path that he was "forced to travel" in "From Absolutism to Experimentalism" (*LW*5:155–6).

Chapter 3: The Logic of Experience

1. Peirce's letter to Dewey is quoted from *CSP*, 8.243–4.

2. Peirce's essay on "What Pragmatism Is" was published in the *Monist*, 15 (April 1905): 161–81, and is here quoted from *CSP*, 5.416–34.

3. Peirce here refers to the sequel to "What Pragmatism Is," which appeared in the *Monist* of October 1905 under the title "Issues of Pragmaticism" (15: 481–99). In it Peirce concludes of himself that "he is therefore obliged to subscribe to the doctrine of a real Modality, including real Necessity and real Possibility." The contrast between him and Dewey with regard to necessity and its place in inquiry is total.

4. The essay on "The Law of the Mind" appeared in the *Monist* as the third in a series of five essays, which had begun in January of 1891 with "The Architecture of Theories." It is clear from both the first and third essays that Peirce has undertaken the formulation of synechism in order to reconcile his doctrine of absolute chance with the "real Necessity" that is the backbone of his logical realism. Peirce is quoted here from *CSP*, 6.163. (For various other attempts to explain synechism, see also 6.163–213, especially 6.185 on "The Logic of Continuity.")

5. *CSP*, 5.433–4.

6. Ibid., 8.244.

7. Quoted from Ralph Barton Perry's *The Thought and Character of William James*, vol. 2, p. 375.

8. Ibid., p. 501.

9. James, *Pragmatism*, p. ix.

10. A similar comparison with Peirce's other essays in the *Monist* series of 1891 rein-

forces the conclusion that Peirce retains in his realist logic an ontological sense of necessity that Dewey explicitly rejects (see n. 4 above).

11. The series was intended as "Illustrations of the Logic of Science." "The Fixation of Belief" appeared in the issue of November 1877 (12: 1–15), "How to Make Our Ideas Clear" in that of January 1878 (12: 286–302). The latter was originally written in French, for the *Revue Philosophique* (vol. 6, December 1878), and the former was translated for that journal (vol. 7, January 1879). See *CSP*, vol. 5.

12. Although Dewey's use of the term *teleological* here is clearly that of James, he does not refer to its source, James's *Principles of Psychology*, until a few months later, in "Self-Realization as the Moral Ideal" (*Philosophical Review*, 2: [November 1893]; *EW*4:47). Dewey quotes the first edition, vol. 2, p. 235, whereas I quote the collected works version, in which the pagination is consecutive over the two volumes, and the text quoted by Dewey is on p. 961. James, of course, uses *teleological* in reference to the "only meaning of *essence*," whereas Dewey applies it to "*logical* necessity" (my emphases). (Quotations of the *Principles* are from the 1981 edition, unless specified otherwise.)

13. I have borrowed the term *nativist* from Gerald E. Myers's introduction to the 1981 edition of *Principles*. The term speaks to James's unique conviction that there is something about the evolved structure of the human brain that is capable of accounting for the a priori character of necessary truths. Only C. I. Lewis's "pragmatic *a priori*" seems to account for logical necessity in anything like James's sense (see C. I. Lewis, "A Pragmatic Conception of the *A Priori*," *Journal of Philosophy*, 20 [1923]: 169–77).

14. I do not mean to suggest that the logic of experience somehow neglects what is cause for despair in human experience. Dewey's philosophical logic is almost unique in its capacity to deal even-handedly with the positive and negative elements that are the necessary ingredients of pragmatic social hope as he conceived it.

15. Dewey's admission that he had a system came in "Nature in Experience," *Philosophical Review*, vol. 49, no. 2 (1940): 244–58, in response to some criticisms brought by Morris Raphael Cohen and William Ernest Hocking: "I find that with respect to the hanging together of various problems and various hypotheses in a perspective determined by a definite point of view, I have a system. In so far I have to retract disparaging remarks made in the past about the need for system in philosophy."

16. William Robert McKenzie, in his Introduction to volume 5 of the *Early Works*, p. xiv. See also Gordon W. Allport's assessment in his contribution to the Schilpp volume. Elizabeth Flower has provided a brilliant exposition of this paper in her treatment of Dewey in *A History of Philosophy in America*, pp. 829–46. She correctly links it to Dewey's developing theory of valuation and to the social psychology that emerges in *Human Nature and Conduct* of 1922.

17. This unification is clearly Dewey's response to Peirce's synechism. It is central to his theory of communication in both *Experience and Nature* and the 1938 *Logic*, in which he credits his conception of the continuity of inquiry to Peirce's influence (pp. 468–70) but makes it plain that his own conception of the continuity of inquiry is a "free rendering of Peirce" (p. 14).

18. *The Significance of the Problem of Knowledge* (Chicago: University of Chicago Press, 1897) is hardly more than a pamphlet (*EW*5:4–24). "Some Remarks on the Psychology of Number" was first published in *Pedagogical Seminary*, vol. 5, of 1898 (*EW*5:177–91). It is a polemical response to a review of the book that Dewey produced with James Alexander McLellan, *The Psychology of Number and Its Application to Methods of Teaching Arithmetic*, International Education Series, vol. 33, edited by William Torrey Harris (New York: D. Appleton, 1895).

19. Dewey develops the link between the logic of experience and abstract number concepts in the 1938 *Logic,* pp. 200–19 and ch. 20, "Mathematical Discourse." Dewey's naturalization of numbers should be compared with the conception of "Mathematical Reality" in Philip Kitcher's *The Nature of Mathematical Knowledge* (Oxford: Oxford University Press, 1984).
20. The metaphors of foreground and background are Dewey's. In this connection, see his response to Santayana's review of *Experience and Nature* entitled "Half-Hearted Naturalism" (*LW*3:73–81); Santayana's review is included as an appendix to the same volume (*LW*3:367–84).
21. I discuss this attack at some length in Chapter Four. But see Russell's essay on Dewey's philosophy of logic in Schilpp.
22. See Hook's treatment of this in his *Metaphysics of Pragmatism.*
23. James, in *A Pluralistic Universe* (1909), moves toward a conventionalist position in which almost anything goes. While it may be consistent with his "The Will to Believe," this extreme pluralism does not square with Dewey's strong sense of the real as a limiting condition.
24. The full text of Putnam's remark is even more instructive: "Like Wittgenstein, Goodman doesn't believe in looking for guarantees, foundations, or the 'furniture of the universe'. (He goes even farther than Wittgenstein in his rejection of traditional philosophy, describing himself in his most recent writing as a 'relativist' and an 'irrealist'.) What we have in Goodman's view, as, perhaps, in Wittgenstein's, are practices, which are right or wrong depending on how they square with our standards. And our standards are right or wrong depending on how they square with our practices. This is a circle, or better a spiral, but one that Goodman, like John Dewey, regards as virtuous" (Hilary Putnam, foreword to Nelson Goodman's *Fact, Fiction, and Forecast,* 4th ed. [Cambridge, Mass.: Harvard University Press, 1983], p. ix).
25. See Joseph Ratner's introduction to the collection of Dewey's writings that he edited: *Intelligence in the Modern World: John Dewey's Philosophy* (New York: Modern Library, 1939). Ratner also edited *Characters and Events;* see ch. 1, n. 19.

Chapter 4: Dewey's Aristotelian Turn

1. Early on Royce had taken an interest in mathematical logic and had described the work of Frege and Russell with enthusiasm. (See Josiah Royce, "Recent Logical Inquiries and Their Psychological Beginnings," *Psychological Review* 9 (1902): 105–33, and "The Principles of Logic," in *The Encyclopedia of the Philosophical Sciences,* Volume 1: *Logic* (London: Macmillan, 1913), pp. 67–135.)
2. See Hook's introduction to volume 8 of the *Middle Works,* p. xx.
3. Ibid.
4. It is alleged that Dewey introduced his course in modern philosophy with the outrageous pun that he would be putting "Descartes before the course," although there is no reliable source for this allegation.
5. In his 1912 *Problems of Philosophy,* Russell had contrasted being and existence as follows: *being* is said to be exact, rigid, "delightful to the mathematician, the logician, the builder of metaphysical systems," and so on, and *existence* to be fleeting, vague, and without sharp boundaries. See Ronald Jager, *The Development of Bertrand Russell's Philosophy* (London: George Allen and Unwin, 1972), ch. 2, for an excellent discussion of Russell's thought in this period.
6. Bertrand Russell, "Professor Dewey's 'Essays in Experimental Logic'," *Journal of Philosophy,* vol. 16, no. 1 (2 Jan. 1919): 5ff.

7. Ibid., p. 5.
8. See Jager, p. 318.
9. Ibid.
10. Ibid.
11. Some idea of the historical context in which what I have referred to as "mainstream logic" developed can be gleaned from the fact that a standard history of logic from Plato to the 1980s—William Kneale and Martha Kneale, *The Development of Logic* (Oxford: Clarendon Press, paperback edition, 1981)—devotes six of twelve chapters to Frege's logic and post-Fregean developments.
12. See Russell's preface to *The Principles of Mathematics* (Cambridge: Cambridge University Press, 1903).
13. It should not be discounted that Dewey's 1939 *Theory of Valuation* was both a sequel to his 1938 *Logic* and a valedictory to noncognitivism in ethics, written at the express request of a former member of the Vienna Circle, a request that I discuss more fully in Chapter Seven.
14. Quoted from Jean van Heijenoort, ed., *From Frege to Gödel: A Source Book in Mathematical Logic, 1879–1931* (Cambridge, Mass.: Harvard University Press, 1967), pp. 124–5.
15. Quoted from W. V. Quine, *The Ways of Paradox* (Cambridge, Mass.: Harvard University Press, 1966), p. 11. The Kneales refer to this as a postscript dated October 1902 and give a slightly different translation (p. 652).
16. A large part of Dewey's attack on Lotze's *Logik* could be applied, *mutatis mutandis*, to Russell's, the similar treatment of logical entities being a case in point. As Quine says of the *Principles of Mathematics*, "Russell's ontology was unrestrained" ("Russell's Ontological Development," in *Theories and Things* [Cambridge, Mass.: Harvard University Press, 1981] p. 74). It seems clear that Frege's ontology and Lotze's were similarly unrestrained. At least Frege's epigram to the effect that the laws of logic are not laws of nature, but laws of the laws of nature, would indicate that logic has a superior ontology to that which might be derived from natural science. And it is the presupposition of just such a superior ontology that is common to Lotze, Frege, and Russell. (See Kneale and Kneale, pp. 739–42.)
17. It is this stress on the real as encountered *within* the process of inquiry that marks off Dewey's realism from that of James, while helping to explain why Dewey calls himself an empirical pluralist (see Dewey's 1917 essay on "Duality and Dualism," *MW*10:64). The realism of classes that Dewey is struggling to express is pluralistic because the real is encountered only in process. It would be tempting to call this view of Dewey's "processive realism," albeit with the caveat that the word *processive* be understood as referring to controlled inquiry. For Dewey's struggle to find a form of realism that he could accept, see the essay on "The Need for A Recovery of Philosophy" (*MW*10:3ff., esp. pp. 39ff).
18. Dewey's conclusion should be compared to Quine's similar conclusion in "Natural Kinds," in *Ontological Relativity*, pp. 114–38. Quine concludes that the similarity notion underlying all class and common property distinctions becomes superfluous when not in use in the context of inquiry.
19. The conclusion here should be compared with Frege's claim that words have meaning only in the context of sentences. Dewey expands the context to that of the use of the sentences in inquiry in ways that suggest Wittgenstein's point about language games, a matter to be discussed further in Chapter Six.
20. Russell had tried to convince Wittgenstein that "irreducible and independent simples" could be made the foundational elements of philosophy (see David Pears, "The Relation Between Wittgenstein's Picture Theory of Propositions and Russell's Theories of Judgment," *Philosophical Review* 86 (1977): 177–96). Russell's view

was expressed in his paper "Knowledge by Acquaintance and Knowledge by Description" of 1910, which was reprinted in *Mysticism and Logic, and Other Essays.* Much of the explanation for Russell's enthusiasm for logical atomism lies in this drive to find logical simples. Wittgenstein also tried to work it out, but ended up, in the *Tractatus,* with the conclusion that it wouldn't work (see Kneale and Kneale, pp. 628–34). In the posthumous *Remarks on the Foundations of Mathematics,* Wittgenstein came to the conclusion that no such foundations as simples are necessary, even for mathematics. Moreover, he concludes: "The rules of logical inference are rules of the *language game*" (ibid., G. H. von Wright, R. Rhees, and G. E. M. Anscombe [Cambridge, Mass.: MIT Press, 1983], p. 401).

21. See Dewey's 1916 essay on "The Pragmatism of Peirce" (*MW*10:71ff.). In this essay Dewey explicitly construes Peirce's conception of the real in a way that conforms to his own (*MW*10:75). He compares Peirce and James, concluding that Peirce is more of a pragmatist than James (p. 76). He does not mention Peirce's doctrine of synechism at all; his reading of Peirce's pragmatism is based entirely on the doubt–belief theory, and the later Peirce might just as well not have existed!

22. Joseph Ratner, "Dewey's Conception of Philosophy," in Schilpp, p. 66.

23. The term *denkmittel,* with a lower-case *d,* is repeatedly used by James in *Pragmatism;* and the "seven league boots" are also James's.

24. Nagel implied as much in his first review of the *Logic* published in the *Journal of Philosophy,* vol. 36, no. 21 (1939), and reprinted in *Dewey and His Critics,* pp. 560–65.

25. See the appendixes to volume 1 of the *Later Works* for Dewey's belated attempt to substitute the word *Culture* for *Experience* in the title of *Experience and Nature.*

26. Morris Raphael Cohen makes this bestowal in his *American Thought* (New York: Collier, 1962), p. 364.

27. Henry Steele Commager, *The American Mind: An Interpretation of American Thought and Character since the 1880's* (New Haven: Yale University Press, 1950), p. 100. For a somewhat divergent appraisal, see Bruce Kuklick's evaluation in *Churchmen and Philosophers: From Jonathan Edwards to John Dewey* (New Haven: Yale University Press, 1985), pp. 191–261. Kuklick makes much of the "neo-orthodox" theological opposition to Dewey's influence on the part of such popular religious spokesmen as Reinhold and Richard Niebuhr.

Chapter 5: Existence as Problematic

1. See Joseph Ratner's "Editor's Note" to the "Re-Introduction," in *LW*1:329.

2. A new preface and an extensively revised first chapter were supplied for the 1929 edition. That these failed to avert misunderstanding is shown by an address entitled "In Reply to Some Criticisms" that Dewey read to the American Philosophical Association in December 1929 (reprinted in *LW*5:210–17). It is a response to essentially the same issues as Santayana had raised in his review of the 1925 edition (*LW*3:367–84), issues to which Dewey had responded in "Half-Hearted Naturalism" (*LW*3:73–81).

3. See Ratner's note in *LW*1:361 and Dewey's edited typescript, ibid.

4. This brief manuscript, which Ratner dates to January 1951, is clear evidence of Dewey's continuing concern with what is now called the sociology of knowledge. It appears to have been stimulated by his reading of Malinowski's article on culture in the *Encyclopaedia of the Social Sciences,* edited by Alvin Johnson (see *LW*1:363n3).

5. It is clear that Dewey thought that the term *culture* would emphasize the importance he ascribed to the artifactual character of language, a character that had

largely been overlooked. Even in the 1925 edition it had been a central theme, and it became the major contention of the 1938 *Logic*. It is the instrumentality of linguistic artifacts that drives the whole transformational thrust of Dewey's philosophy in both books and that distinguishes his philosophy of language from those of both the ideal language theorists and the ordinary language analysts.

6. Rorty, "Dewey's Metaphysics," in *Consequences*, p. 72.

7. Ibid.

8. Dewey, "Experience and Existence: A Comment," *Philosophy and Phenomenological Research*, vol. 9, no. 4 (1949): 709–13.

9. Rorty appears also to have missed the point that Dewey's reconstruction of the task of metaphysics is accompanied by a reconstruction of the task of epistemology. In the latter, too, the generic traits of existences that Rorty dismisses as pointless are crucially important. Rorty's use of the phrase "metaphysics of experience," apparently borrowed from Bernstein, may account for these lapses. See Rorty's "Dewey's Metaphysics," *passim*, but esp. p. 77 in the *Consequences* reprinting.

10. As already indicated, I see Bernstein as mainly responsible for the currency of the phrase "metaphysics of experience," but his use of it, as well as Rorty's, seems to have been anticipated by Santayana. See n. 1 above, for Dewey's efforts to counter such a use, which, though largely unsuccessful, at least indicate how Dewey wished to be understood.

11. "Dewey's Metaphysics," in *Consequences*, pp. 72 and 77.

12. That it *was* an offense is particularly apparent both in Santayana's review (see n. 2 above) and in Woodbridge's critical essay "Experience and Dialectic" (*LW*5:487–95). Dewey was simply not playing their game, and they were offended by his disloyalty.

13. See Hook's introduction to *Experience and Nature* (*LW*1:xvi) and Rorty, *Consequences*, p. 73.

14. The passages in the 1929 revision of chapter 1 (*LW*1:18–9) recall Dewey's argument against taking the part for the whole in "The Superstition of Necessity."

15. Woodbridge, "Experience and Dialectic" (*LW*5:487–95).

16. As in his response to Russell, Dewey does not see that there is any problem in accepting that there is knowledge of the existence of the external world. Dewey's point is just that our commonsense knowledge of existent objects is very different from scientific knowledge of the same objects, a difference that arises from the different operations involved in the different kinds of knowing. Woodbridge apparently sided with G. E. Moore in thinking that the existence of the external world constitutes a genuine problem.

17. Dewey, *Logic*, pp. 371–93.

18. In his responses to Woodbridge, Dewey adamantly refuses to equate having an experience of something with knowing it. It seems that he wants to reserve the term *knowing* for the results of inquiry, in loyalty to the doubt–belief theory that had started him on this path. He could satisfy Woodbridge only by admitting that we can know an object to exist without first doubting its existence, an admission he refuses to make. He insists that having an experience of an object in the external world is not the same thing as doubting its existence, that it is, in fact, accepting it as existing, at least provisionally. It is subject to correction by inquiry; like any immediate inference, its genesis in immediate experience is insufficient certification of its validity.

19. See Peirce, "The Reality of God," *Hibbert Journal* 7 (1908): 96–112 (also in *CSP* 6.452–93). Dewey, writing on "The Pragmatism of Peirce" in Morris Cohen's

collection of Peirce's writings *Chance, Love and Logic* (New York: Harcourt Brace, 1923), is careful not to mention this side of Peirce's philosophy. Cohen omits it from his collection as well.

20. The quote comes from the chapter entitled "Escape from Peril" (*LW*4:3).

21. Compare Wittgenstein's remark that "essence is expressed by grammar," in *Philosophical Investigations*, trans. G. E. M. Anscombe (New York: Macmillan, 1968), no. 371 in Wittgenstein's system. It is not clear that Wittgenstein's meaning here is not ironic. If Wittgenstein is mocking the fallacy of essentialism, as I suspect he is, his view corresponds very closely to Dewey's. And he continues, in no. 372, to say: "Consider: 'The only correlate in language to an intrinsic necessity is an arbitrary rule. It is the only thing which one can milk out of this intrinsic necessity into a proposition.'" Dewey considered this sort of thing in "The Superstition of Necessity" and confirmed it, but perhaps Wittgenstein hesitated, for in the next remark he says: "Grammar tells us what kind of object anything is. (Theology as grammar)."

22. Dewey's procedure is not to be confused with that of the ontological logics that Dewey so frequently criticizes for deriving their ontologies from a priori logical principles, as Russell's did in 1914. The passage that follows should be read in the light of his dispute with Nagel concerning the link between logic and ontology. (Nagel's article "Can Logic be Divorced from Ontology?" is reprinted in *LW*5:453ff., and Dewey's response, "The Applicability of Logic to Existence," is given in *LW*5:203ff.) In this exchange, it should be recalled, Nagel had not yet decided that logic should be divorced from ontology. He was still under the influence of Morris Cohen, apparently, and had not yet adopted his later positivist view. See "Logic Without Ontology," in *Naturalism and the Human Spirit*, pp. 210–41, for his later view.

23. The idea of newly emergent properties is in direct contrast to the essentialist view of fixed properties. See Dewey's *Logic*, p. 260, for his use of the word *character* for what changes, *identity* for that which endures.

24. I refer here to Dewey's *strict* use of the term *intrinsic*, but he used it casually as well.

25. This is from the 1929 preface, which, in some ways, is clearer than the revised first chapter. It emphasizes the social character of language and thus suggests more strongly the link between the metaphysics and the logic.

26. This ontological commitment is explicitly shared and is evidence of Dewey's continuing allegiance to at least one of Peirce's major points, but modified in the direction of Mead's work in social theory. It should be compared to the "strong programme" in the sociology of science mounted by Barry Barnes and David Bloor, among others (see the articles in *Rationality and Relativism*, edited by M. Hollis and S. Lukes [Cambridge, Mass.: MIT Press, 1982]).

27. In this matter Dewey seems clearer than Wittgenstein, although there is plainly a family resemblance.

28. McDermott, *The Philosophy of John Dewey*, p. xxv.

29. Dewey is quite definite about this by comparison, for example, with Barry Barnes in *Scientific Knowledge and Sociological Theory* (Boston: Routledge and Kegan Paul, 1974), pp. 153–7, and Saul Kripke in *Naming and Necessity* (Cambridge, Mass.: Harvard University Press, 1980), pp. 156–64, esp. 163, both of whom dodge the question for different reasons and stop short with the social character of language, as if that were enough. (See also Nelson Goodman, *Fact, Fiction, and Forecast* [cited in the bibliography to Chapter Three].)

30. Mead, "The Genesis of the Self and Social Control," quoted from Charles W. Morris, *Six Theories of Mind* (Chicago: University of Chicago Press, 1932), p. 322.

31. Mead, "A Behavioristic Account of the Significant Symbol," quoted from Morris, p. 323.
32. James Campbell has indicated that I may not be entirely correct concerning the mutual influence between Mead and Dewey. But see David L. Miller, *George H. Mead,* p. xxvi, and Dewey's own memorial to Mead: "George Herbert Mead as I Knew Him," reprinted in *LW*6:22ff.
33. In this last sentence I mean to recall Dewey's repeated reference to taking the part for the whole in "The Superstition of Necessity." For a similar emphasis, see D. J. B. Hawkins, "Towards the Restoration of Metaphysics," in *Prospect for Metaphysics,* edited by Ian Ramsey (London: Allen and Unwin, 1961), p. 119.

Chapter 6: *The Language of Logic and Truth*

1. See Nagel, "Dewey's Reconstruction of Logical Theory," originally in *The Philosophy of the Common Man;* reprinted in *Sovereign Reason,* pp. 119–40. *Sovereign Reason* also contains two essays on Peirce in which Nagel states that Peirce's proto-positivism was more pronounced than his penchant for idealism (p. 86). He also suggests that the task initiated by Peirce in the logic of relations was all of a piece with his pragmatic maxim, and that the maxim was brought to a degree of superior precision by Carnap and others (p. 93). Nagel makes no similar effort to relate Dewey's *Logic* to the contemporary positivism of the Vienna Circle. Nagel's work on Peirce originally appeared in a series of papers in the *Journal of Philosophy* (vols. 30, 31, and 33), beginning in 1933 and concluding in 1936. Another more general piece, "Charles S. Peirce, Pioneer of Modern Empiricism," appeared in *Philosophy of Science* 7 (1940) and was first read at the Fifth International Congress for the Unity of Science at Harvard University in 1939.
2. I base my causal account of Dewey's theory on the meaning of the word *involvement* given on p. 278 of the *Logic.* Dewey's index cross-references *involvement* with *connections* and *inference,* all terms that are used to refer to existential relations, which Dewey holds distinct from relations of discourse or logic, which are symbolic rather than existential. The implicatory relation is strictly symbolic, although it is the abstract counterpart of existential inference. See Gail Kennedy, "Dewey's Logic and Theory of Knowledge," in *Guide to the Works,* pp. 61–98.
3. Dewey anticipates Quine's use of kinds to resolve Goodman's problem with "grue emeralds" and Hempel's problem with "non-black ravens" (see W. V. Quine, "Natural Kinds," in *Ontological Relativity,* pp. 114–38; also Rom Harré's use of kinds for similar projects in *The Principles of Scientific Thinking* [Chicago: University of Chicago Press, 1970], pp. 154ff.; and Hilary Putnam, *Mind, Language and Reality* [Cambridge: Cambridge University Press, 1975] and *Philosophical Papers,* vol. 2 [Cambridge: Cambridge University Press, 1984], pp. 215–71).
4. Cf. Morris, *Six Theories of Mind,* pp. 325–7. Dewey contributed a gloss on Morris's interpretation that is included in the footnotes.
5. Compare the use of *causa essendi* in *Logic,* p. 4. The "conjugate relation of facts and conceptions" is indexed in the *Logic,* p. 538, where a dozen specific references are given. The "conjugate relation of generic-universal," of "singular-generic," of "form–matter," and of "induction–deduction" are also given specific citations.
6. All categories in Dewey's use are logical. There is room for confusion here, since I have taken his existential relations as causal relations of involvement. He makes a clear distinction between causation as a logical category and existential relations, only the latter being directly ontological. That he avoids calling causation an

existential relation may be because he insists on involvement as an interactional or transactional relation. The ordinary meaning of *causal* misses this connotation of reciprocity that is an important and distinctive feature of Dewey's theory.

7. Wittgenstein, *Remarks*, p. 413. See also pp. 99, 237, 284, and 431. The paragraph numbered 16 on page 378 gives a view of the role of analysis almost identical with that of Dewey. The paragraph numbered 18 on pages 381 to 382 gives an approximation to Dewey's view of the pattern of inquiry linking mathematics and empirical experiment.

8. *Dewey and His Critics* (cited in the bibliography to Chapter One), p. 546.

9. The example is that given by Kennedy, in *Guide to the Works*, p. 74.

Chapter 7: The Theory of Intelligent Behavior

1. The history of the Vienna Circle is given in Victor Kraft, *The Vienna Circle: The Origin of Neo-Positivism* (New York: Philosophical Library, 1953), in a translation by Arthur Pap, from the German *Der Wiener Kreis*.

2. Nagel, in *Dialogue on John Dewey*, ed. C. Lamont (New York: Horizon Press, 1959), pp. 11–3.

3. Ayer had attended gatherings of the Vienna Circle and, according to Kraft (p. 9), perpetuated the movement—along with L. Susan Stebbing—at the University of London. Stebbing, but not Ayer, is acknowledged in Dewey's *Logic* in a critical footnote (p. 20).

4. The suggestion that Dewey was "trying to make everything scientific" is Rorty's, in "Pragmatism Without Method," in *Sidney Hook: Philosopher of Democracy and Humanism*, p. 259.

5. Carnap and Morris were listed in the volumes of the *Encyclopedia* as associate editors. Russell, Nagel, Hans Reichenbach, Alfred Tarski, and L. Susan Stebbing, among others, were listed as members of the advisory committee, along with Dewey himself.

6. I have resisted using Dewey's own title, "Creative Intelligence," out of fear that it might suggest that Dewey was more interested in creativity than criticism. The two go hand in hand in the theory of intelligent behavior.

7. This phrase is the title of section 73, part V, A, of Carnap's *The Logical Syntax of Language* (London: Routledge and Kegan Paul, 1937), p. 281.

8. "Two Dogmas of Empiricism" first appeared in the *Philosophical Review* in 1951 and was reprinted in W. V. Quine, *From a Logical Point of View*. The quoted phrases appear on p. 20 of the second edition (Harper Torchbooks, 1961).

9. Stevenson's *Ethics and Language* (New Haven: Yale University Press, 1944) alleged a similarity in viewpoint between the noncognitivist position in ethics and Dewey's view. Dewey repudiated it in "Ethical Subject-Matter and Language," *Journal of Philosophy* 42 (1945): 701–12. See the critical bibliography to this chapter for details.

10. Quine, *From a Logical Point of View*, p. 20. The references to Carnap and Lewis that follow are found on p. 46.

11. The intuitive approach to values had been suggested by G. E. Moore and others, of course, and Dewey attacks it again in chapter 10 of *The Quest for Certainty*. See Toulmin's introduction to the Carbondale edition (*LW* 4:vi–xxii), where he shows how Dewey's relation to the epistemological tradition in ethics reaches back to Pyrrho and Sextus Empiricus, to Aristotle's *Nichomachean Ethics, Topics, Politics*, and *Rhetoric*, as well as forward to Wittgenstein, Heidegger, and Quine. This is an excellent antidote to the contention that Dewey was merely responding to logical positivism in his later work on ethics and language.

12. In his emphasis on the identification and reidentification of particulars, Dewey

anticipates the thesis of P. F. Strawson's *Individuals* (London: Methuen, 1959). See also the thesis presented by Rom Harré in his treatise on *The Principles of Scientific Thinking*. Harré argues that Strawson has demonstrated that "the material things of the world as manifested are reidentifiable individuals" (p. 298). This, of course, was Dewey's claim in 1903 and is a central thesis of *Experience and Nature*. Unlike Dewey, neither Strawson nor Harré emphasize that inference is action. The latter emphasis, however, is an important theme in Stuart Hampshire's *Freedom of the Individual* (London: Chatto and Windus, 1965), in which he applies to ethics the theory of action that he worked out earlier in *Thought and Action*. See especially chapter 3: "Two Kinds of Knowledge," also "Public and Private Morality" in a volume of essays of the same name that Hampshire edited (Cambridge: Cambridge University Press, 1978).

13. See the extensively researched introduction to the Carbondale edition of the 1932 revision of the *Ethics* of Dewey and Tufts by Elizabeth Flower and Abraham Edel, *Later Works*, volume 7 (1985).

14. Kaminsky, in his essay on "Ontology, Formalism, and Pragmatism," in *Sidney Hook: Philosopher of Democracy and Humanism*, p. 275, points out that this elimination of the intrinsic meaning of the "value of a variable" is the connecting link between the ontology of pragmatism and that of Quine. See my discussion of Kaminsky's essay in the critical bibliography to this chapter.

15. The references to *A Common Faith* that follow are taken from the paperback edition (New Haven: Yale University Press, 1960).

16. That the critic here expresses a different angle of vision on *Art as Experience* from mine seems clear, though I do not challenge the assertion here, which is from McDermott's headnote to his selection from *A Common Faith* in his collection *The Philosophy of John Dewey*, p. 696.

17. The quotations from Peirce in this paragraph, in the order that they appear, are from *CSP*, 6.441, 6.442, and 5.401. The letter from Peirce to James is given by Perry, *Thought and Character*, vol. 2, p. 437. On real problems, see *CSP*, 8.259.

18. Perry, *Thought and Character*, vol. 2, p. 438.

19. James, *Pragmatism*; I am quoting from Joseph L. Blau's edition, published by Washington Square in 1963, p. 35.

20. All quotations from *Art as Experience* are from the original edition (New York: Minton Balch, 1934).

21. Irwin Edman, "Dewey and Art," in *John Dewey: Philosopher of Science and Freedom*, p. 47.

22. *John Dewey and Arthur F. Bentley*, p. 646.

23. Rorty, "Pragmatism Without Method," p. 259.

24. *The Collected Papers of Clarence Irving Lewis*, edited by J. D. Goheen and J. L. Mothershead, Jr. (Stanford, Calif.: Stanford University Press, 1970), p. 17.

25. Ibid., p. 440.

26. Ibid., p. 12.

27. John Dewey, *Theory of Valuation* (Chicago: University of Chicago Press, 1939), and still in print.

28. From Dewey's lecture on "Construction and Criticism," delivered as the first Milton Judson Davies Memorial Lecture to the Institute of Arts and Sciences at Columbia University, 25 February 1930 (*LW*5:143).

Chapter 8: Meliorism as Transformational

1. McDermott, review of Barzun's *A Stroll With William James*, in *The New England Quarterly*, vol. 57, no. 1 (1984): 127. McDermott's estimate of James on this score is

elaborated by reference to James's "cavalier approach to the Civil War, the Irish Question, suffragettes (and) his romanticization of the San Francisco earthquake."

2. McDermott, *The Writings of William James*, p. xxxv.

3. See F. Waismann, *Ludwig Wittgenstein and the Vienna Circle*, edited by Brian F. McGuiness (New York: Harper and Row, 1979), p. 45; also Wittgenstein, *Philosophical Remarks* (Chicago: University of Chicago Press, 1984), p. 51. In the latter, Wittgenstein says: "I do not now have phenomenological language, or 'primary language' as I used to call it, in mind as my goal. I no longer hold it to be necessary."

4. C. I. Lewis, "Pragmatism and Current Thought," an address to the American Philosophical Association, 30 December 1929, quoted from *LW* 5:477.

5. It may be disputed that James did not give us a theory of language. McDermott, in the introduction to his volume of *The Writings of William James*, suggests that it is a theory that moves in the direction of phenomenological analysis. But he also cites a remark of Dewey's to the effect that "long ago I learned from William James that there are immediate experiences of the connections linguistically expressed by conjunctions and propositions." Dewey, at least, suggests that this does not imply a phenomenological analysis, for he goes on to say: "My doctrinal position is but a generalization of what is involved in this fact" (Schilpp, p. 533, n. 16).

6. Albert G. Balz and John Dewey, "A Letter to Mr. Dewey concerning John Dewey's Doctrine of Possibility, published together with his Reply," *Journal of Philosophy* 46 (1949): 313–42; and Appendix in John Dewey and Arthur F. Bentley, *Knowing and the Known* (Boston: Beacon Press, 1949), pp. 313–29.

7. Toulmin, introduction to the Carbondale edition of *The Quest for Certainty* (*LW* 4:ix).

8. Robert M. Hutchins, *The Higher Learning in America* (New Haven: Yale University Press, 1936).

9. Dewey, "President Hutchins' Proposals to Remake Higher Education," *Social Frontier* (January 1937), pp. 103–4.

10. Quoted from Trotsky by David Salner in the preface to *Their Morals and Ours, Marxist vs. Liberal Views on Morality*, containing essays by Leon Trotsky, John Dewey, and George Novack (New York: Pathfinder Press, 3rd printing, 1979), p. 10.

11. Ibid., p. 48.

12. Dewey, "Means and Ends," reprinted in *Their Morals and Ours*, p. 70.

13. Ibid.

14. Ibid., p. 73.

15. Ibid.

16. John Dewey, "Antinaturalism in Extremis," in *Naturalism and the Human Spirit*, p. 16. The essays in this volume provide an excellent overview of the naturalistic implications of Dewey's conception of philosophy. Edel's "Naturalism and Ethical Theory" and Thelma Z. Lavine's "Naturalism and the Sociological Analysis of Knowledge" are undisputed classics that show the direction in which naturalistic accounts of knowledge should proceed. (See also C. Wright Mills's posthumously published *Sociology and Pragmatism: The Higher Learning in America*, edited by Irving Louis Horowitz [New York: Oxford University Press, 1969].)

17. The phrase "ungrounded social hope" is Rorty's in "Method, Social Science, and Social Hope," in *Consequences*, p. 210. I am indebted to James Campbell for references to two articles that Dewey contributed to *Commentary* in the years after the Second World War that correct the mistaken impression that Dewey had nothing to say about the crisis situation created by the holocaust and the implications of nuclear war: "The Crisis in Human History: The Danger of Retreat to Individualism," in the March issue, 1946, and "Philosophy's Future in Our Scien-

tific Age," in the October 1949 issue. These show that Dewey, along with Hannah Arendt, was one of the few philosophers in America to relate the current condition of philosophy to these issues. In the first of these articles Dewey points out that "there is no guarantee for optimism," although he goes on to say that "there are resources within our grasp which, if used, will tend toward a favorable outcome" (p. 9). Rorty's claim that Dewey wanted to make everything scientific is offset by Dewey's remark in the later article that "there is probably no case in which the good achieved by the intervention of science has not been offset by some evil" (p. 390). I am further indebted to Alan Rosenberg for pointing out that these remarks are consistent with Dewey's earlier statement that "there are issues in the conduct of human affairs in their production of good and evil which, at a given time and place are so central, so strategic in position that their urgency deserves, with respect to practice, the names ultimate and comprehensive." Rosenberg further relates these remarks to Dewey's conception of the transformational role of philosophy, citing Dewey's text to the effect that "philosophy marks a change in culture. In forming patterns to be conformed to in future thought and action, it is additive and transforming in its role in the history of civilization." For these texts and others, see Rosenberg's valuable article on the Holocaust and philosophy, "An Assault on Western Values," in *Dimensions: A Journal of Holocaust Studies*, vol. 1, no. 1 (1985): 5–11.

Index

John Dewey's books and essays are not included in this index but are discussed in the bibliographical essays following each chapter. Information on the collected works (published by Southern Illinois University Press and complete to 1938) can be found in the essay following Chapter 1.

University of Illinois Press
1325 South Oak Street
Champaign, IL 61820-6903
www.press.uillinois.edu

Printed by Printforce, United Kingdom